Human Life: The First Ten Years

John J. Mitchell

Holt, Rinehart and Winston of Canada, Limited
Toronto   Montreal

Printed in Canada
1 2 3 4 5   77 76 75 74 73

This book is dedicated to my mother and father,
who nurtured seven children to health and strength
through "the first ten years".

Acknowledgements

Several people were especially helpful to me in the writing of this book. Mary Hendricks, my research assistant, assisted tremendously in the compilation of information and also diligently gleaned the relevant literature. Joan Andrishak dutifully typed each and every draft of the manuscript; Alanne Kee and Edie Franks served as editors of the final manuscript. The photographs were handled by C. Nickerson and R. Pape, courtesy of the A.V.M.C., University of Alberta. The most crucial assistance, however, came from my father, Robert Vincent Mitchell, who proofed and edited the original manuscript with his customary professional excellence. To each of these individuals I am especially grateful, and to each of them I say "thank you".

J. J. Mitchell
Edmonton, Alberta
March, 1973

Contents

Human Life: The First Ten Years

Chapter One
Some Developmental Guidelines

This book is about children, their growth, their feelings, and their impact on the world in which they live. We shall probe the significant trends and traits of the first ten years of life starting with the protoplasmic globule of fertilized egg which eventually becomes a fetus, an infant, and then a child. Our study of this part of the human saga ends just before the pre-adolescent years, but encompasses the foundation upon which virtually all human growth and development is established.

The first ten years of life are in some respects too monumental to encapsulate, too complex to describe, and too diverse to be summarized. Hundreds of volumes have been written on the first week of life, thousands more on the first year, and no one knows how many have been written about the first decade. From this voluminous writing new knowledge continues to surface; old data is buttressed by the new; and theoretical insight crops up from unexpected corners. There will be no end to our expanding knowledge of childhood. Although this book will add precious little *new* information, it does present fresh perspective to established theory and fact, and explores some partially charted waters which require, and fully merit, greater exploration. All explorers, however, must have compasses, landmarks, and guidelines, and as a rule their success is contingent upon them. To this generalization we do not bear exception, and in order that we may share in the understanding of how this exploration of the first ten years of life is to be conducted we must examine first our *general* guidelines, and second the *specific* concepts upon which we most critically rely.

The purpose of this book, quite obviously, is to understand the nature of children. The approach is distinctly inter-disciplinary with developmental psychology being the discipline most heavily relied upon. Our objectives are to more fully understand the forces which mould the child and to more humanely appreciate how the child moulds his world into greater harmony with himself. There is always a certain tension between child and environment as well as between child

1

and parent, but this is one of the few books currently available which credits the child with his share of "victories" in his perpetual confrontation with "helper-tyrants". As we shall continuously observe, most differences between parent and child centre around the self-evident circumstance of different developmental levels but, as if to keep anything from being too simple, some developmental stages during the first ten years of life predispose the child to seeing eye to eye with parents.

The child, especially after his first year, is not a determined creature, and should not be perceived as such. He has both freedom and choice and craves their exercise. Internal growth mechanisms *influence* him, external environmental demands *restrict* him, parental and social reinforcers *guide* him, biological limitations *establish upper limits* for him, and a host of other historical factors partially determine his behaviour. However, the moment one believes the child acts as he does because of extraneous determinants one has lost the sensitivity required for understanding the subjective dimension of childhood. The child is free, but not totally free; the child is determined, but not totally determined. It is our task to recognize and understand when the child's total action patterns are being influenced by forces beyond his control and when his behaviour can be more honestly understood as self-determined. This dilemma of ascertaining when the child is merely a pawn of fate and when he is the master of his own fate will be our philosophical albatross throughout the balance of this book.

It is paramount that the concerned student of human growth not fall prey to the lure of various determinisms. A deterministic viewpoint is simply one which asserts that human behaviour is determined: *environmental determinists* claim human behaviour is determined by the environment; *biological determinists* reduce human behaviour to biologically-based factors; *social determinists* view human behaviour as a product of the particular social structure in which the child is socialized. It is likewise paramount that we avoid the habit of explaining all human behaviour in terms of "free will". There is no accepted formula for balancing the outside forces which act upon the child with the internal forces which oppose them. For this we have only theories. For the most part we shall omit theoretical excursions in this book, concentrating instead on the behaviour of the child and how this behaviour affects himself and his immediate world. Upon this knowledge of child behaviour, however, future theory can be constructed with full confidence that the foundation will not collapse.

Let us now look into some *general* guidelines as well as some *specific* developmental concepts which will serve as our navigational aids in this investigation of the first ten years of life.

General Guidelines for The Study of Human Growth and Development

1.   *Children are unique and individual yet at the same time are influenced by traits characteristic of our entire species.* All people are unique. They have private lives and hidden experiences and in no way is it possible to consider two different people to be exactly the same. Even identical twins, which are the most biologically similar forms of human life, are unique and quite different from one another. It is likewise true that all people are, to a certain degree, similar. In many respects their lives are alike and their experiences common; in this regard it is impossible to consider them totally different. Quite obviously each person has elements which he shares with other men and elements which are unique to only him.

Two extremes must be avoided in our study of the first ten years of life: (1) we must not succumb to the temptation to conclude that because each child is unique unto himself, which obviously is true, that his behaviour, inclinations, and needs are *completely* unique; and, (2) we must avoid the antithesis of this statement which claims that the child is best understood by studying only those behaviours, needs, and inclinations which he shares with others. Balance as well as compromise is called for because there is a tendency for students of childhood to think *either* in terms of shared traits, *or* in terms of unique traits. In this book we shall primarily study *normal* childhood patterns because they are based upon the commonalities of childhood existence. However, we shall temper this tendency and keep it in check by reminding ourselves that some of the most important factors in all human behaviour (including childhood) are the unique elements of individuality which are to be found in one person and one person only.

As investigators of the first ten years of life it will be our responsibility to keep an attentive eye fixed upon those *species traits* which characterize all humans, without losing sight of the unique *personal traits* which also influence human behaviour.

2.   *Children are social animals.* Like all animals, man must gratify the biological requirements of survival: nutrition, elimination, sexuality, oxygen, shelter from the environment, and safety from harmful adversaries. For man, however, all needs are met within a social framework and therefore have social implications and connotations. During the first ten years of life the rewards which assume greatest priority, the goals which are most earnestly sought after, and the experiences which register the deepest emotional response are inextricably interwoven with social life. The punishments which are most avoided, the reprimands which inflict the deepest hurt, and the acts which are most

feared are likewise social in context. No human need, no matter how significant, can be completely understood unless considered *also* from the social pains and pleasures associated with it. To become exclusively preoccupied with man's social nature is not our intent, rather what is hoped for is a balanced insight into human development which comes about only when we view human behaviour with an eye for the social realities intermeshed with it.

Social needs and requirements have many developmental components which must be considered in our investigation of childhood. The social needs of the four-month-old infant are radically different from those of the sixteen-month-old child; most social needs experience transformation throughout the childhood years — social needs do not remain constant. Parental approval is the key to the preschool child's social life; however, for the pre-adolescent, parental approval becomes subservient to peer group approval. Social realities influence all human conduct, and developmental changes influence most social realities.

3. *Children have biological as well as psychological needs.* It is generally understood that biological needs are those needs required for proper functioning of the body and if they are not taken care of the organism will become ill or die. For the most part, there is little controversy about biological needs in the field of child psychology. It is agreed that children must have certain levels of nutrition, that they must be immunized against diseases, and they must be sheltered from those elements which cause biological malfunction. On the other hand, psychological needs are not precisely understood; there is no consensus concerning their origins or even exactly what they are. Psychological needs are similar to biological needs in that when the child is deprived of them there is an experience of incompleteness or that something is missing, but they differ from biological needs in that the consequences of deprivation are subtle and often not observable. Despite the complexities associated with understanding psychological needs it is impossible to avoid their crucial influence during childhood.

It goes without saying that if biological needs are not taken care of the child is in serious trouble. However, for most North American children, biological needs *are* well taken care of and, consequently, in terms of influence on day-to-day living, psychological needs exert tremendous influence. *When biological needs are consistently gratified the child spends the vast majority of his time attempting to satisfy his psychological and social needs.*

Because there is lively disagreement among experts as to which psychological needs are *learned* and which are part of man's *natural*

4

makeup, we shall primarily attend to the *behavioural and personal consequences* of needs rather than concentrating on their origin. It is here assumed that all children have in addition to basic biological needs the following psychological needs:

1. the need for affection,
2. the need for security,
3. the need for acceptance,
4. the need for self-respect,
5. the need for achievement,
6. the need for recognition,
7. the need for independence,
8. the need for order,
9. the need to actualize potentialities.

These needs manifest themselves differently at different stages of growth and we shall time and again observe their central role in childhood growth and development.

4. *Human growth can be properly understood only from an interdisciplinary framework.* It is impossible to understand changes in the human growth cycle without taking into consideration information and theory which derives from such varied disciplines as medicine (especially pediatrics), sociology (especially socialization theory), anthropology (especially cross-cultural family studies), psychology (especially perception and motivation), genetics, physiology, nutrition, and a variety of others. Studies of childhood which overly concentrate on one given aspect of the global growth process fail to take into account those factors which may ultimately prove most essential to its understanding. Also, there seems to be a general principle which operates on students of the childhood years and causes them to acquire rigidity of thought in direct proportion to their narrowness of inquiry. By keeping our investigation open, by considering evidence and information from all disciplines, hopefully we will avoid the pitfalls of rigidity and the dehumanization of thought which invariably accompanies it.

5. *Reasons for studying human growth and development are both academic and humanistic.* The proper study of human growth requires a subtle blending of scientific rigour, humanistic appreciation, artistic creativity, and philosophical dedication — the extent to which any one of these is dominant is the extent to which the study's scope is distorted and made less than it should be. An honest synthesis of these four dimensions must always be pursued if one is to confront human life with integrity and humility.

No legitimate scientific discipline. (as psychology purports to be), can effectively meet its objectives unless it is rigorous in method and thorough in academic content; and for this reason the scientific spirit must always permeate the study of psychology.

However, method, no matter how rigorous, and academic content, no matter how pure, are not themselves sufficient to understand human behaviour. Each must be blended with a humanistic appreciation for the *people* to whom psychological information relates. Knowledge does not exist in a vacuum; it exists in relation to man, and the function of knowledge is to serve man, allow him to blossom and mature, to become better than he presently is, and to grow.

Concern for human welfare is not sufficient by itself; it must be acted upon before it is useful or relevant. Human interaction requires artistic flair, so to speak, an ability to learn, to grow, to cultivate new realities. In child psychology, the scientist without the artist is as incomplete as the artist without the scientist.

Fruitful study of child growth is no easy task, to be sure. It requires a sense of dedication as well as a fairly crystallized sense of purpose and identity. Many of today's rigorously trained university graduates flounder in the quagmire of the real world precisely because they do not have either the sense or purpose or the fundamental courage required to carry out their work. This is why each person requires philosophical purpose to buttress his dedication as well as his sense of right-doing. The study of human development is as much concerned with what should be as with what is. There is no way we can know what a child should not be until we know what he should be.

For each of the above reasons the study of human development can be neither completely detached nor completely personalized. There must be a synthesizing of the disparate elements which relate to the developing child. It is my personal conviction, however, that without a genuine humanistic appreciation for the child and the *experiences* of childhood most developmental information falls upon deaf ears and, therefore, is only neutral data and will remain such until given life by a concerned person.

6.   *Child behaviour becomes progressively more influenced by environment as age increases.* It is fictional to arbitrarily separate the respective roles of heredity and environment in children's behaviour; however, considerable benefit derives from observing a few key variables in this relationship. It is imperative to recognize that all human behaviour takes place in some kind of environment and this environment always imposes restrictions and limitations on behaviour. Thus, it is impossible to talk about hereditary influence except within an environmental context. A second consideration is that if the environment

does not provide the requirements essential for growth, the organism will not realize its hereditary potential — this generalization applies to all animal life. There are numerous examples of societies where nutrition, medication, or even parental attention is insufficiently available and therefore many individuals never reach their intellectual or physical growth potential. A third consideration reminds us that when the environment adequately provides for basic needs, both biological and psychological, then hereditary forces are freed to exert their *normal species influence*. Therefore, when the environment adequately provides for all human needs, we are able to witness normal hereditary influence at work.

In this text, information concerning the role of maturation and heredity is founded on two general assumptions (1) the environment in which the child lives is adequate to provide the basic requirements of survival; and (2) the environment does not *teach* the child to act in a manner contrary to what would normally evolve if the teaching were absent.

In conditions where environment provides the basic biological requirements we observe a completely predictable phenomenon: the first year of human life is dominated by universal species-wide traits and, after the first year, behaviour becomes progressively more influenced by societal and environmental factors. Thus, even though a four-month-old Ugandese infant is virtually indistinguishable from a black New York born infant, before their second birthday they will manifest marked differences in perceptual abilities, speech intonation and mannerism, dietary preference, ability to cope with environmental obstacles, gestures of affection and, perhaps, even physical strength — all because of environmental differences. Despite the importance of environment there are striking *similarities* in childhood development among all cultures and they also shall be of special concern to us.

In the next section we shall define ten *specific* concepts of human growth which also influence normal childhood patterns during the first ten years of life. These specific principles differ from the general principles in that they relate much more directly to the field of developmental psychology and are concerned more with the specific rules of childhood growth than with general principles of human behaviour.

Some Specific Principles of Developmental Psychology

1.   *Growth proceeds in a head-to-foot direction.* This fundamental principle of growth reflects the *directionality* of human unfolding: areas near the head develop first and with greater priority than areas in

lower parts of the body. This principle is perhaps most graphically observed in the earliest stages of fetal development where the head constitutes almost one-half of the total body volume and, as the rest of the body matures, it assumes progressively less prominence. At birth the head is the most developed part of the body and both eye and mouth behaviours are more developmentally advanced than those of the fingers or toes. The infant requires months of practice and maturation before he can coordinate his extremities. The principle of head-to-foot growth is referred to as *cephalocaudal* development and mentions of its influence are found throughout Chapters 3 and 4.

2.   *Growth proceeds outward from the centre axis to the body extremities.* The central parts and organs of the body mature earlier and begin working efficiently before those parts away from the centre. That this is a maxim of human growth as well as biological survival is almost self-evident. The vital organs such as the heart, liver, and kidneys must promptly function with precision and predictability not required of the hands, feet, or shoulders; in fact, it is possible for the child to survive with the latter parts of his anatomy deformed or even absent, but this cannot be the case with the vital organs. *Proximodistal* (the technical term for centre-to-extremity growth) development functions in conjunction with cephalocaudal directionality to insure that any part of the body essential to survival will receive developmental priority. The reader will do well to keep these basic principles of developmental directionality in mind when reading the chapters on fetal development and the first year of life; these age spans are dominated by head-to-toe and centre-to-extremity growth gradients. Eventually these patterns of growth lose their dynastic control over the child but only after they have served their evolutional and developmental purpose, and only after they have exerted a dominant effect on the physical appearance of the young child.

3.   *The body is dominated by accelerated development of different body systems at different ages.* The principle of *asynchronous growth* reflects the fact that the body does not grow in a uniformly consistent way, but rather experiences periods in which one part of the body grows more rapidly than others, only to settle back to a normal growth pace after going through a sudden burst. It is quite obvious the human body does not mature at a uniform rate, otherwise the legs would always have the insignificant size they have at birth and the head would be hideously enlarged by adulthood. The principle of asynchronous growth serves to remind us of the temperamental inconsistency of the human body. Some examples of this phenomenon will help to further clarify its meaning. During the first year after birth there is little devel-

opment of higher brain centres; they seem content to bide their time until more fundamental development has occurred; during the *pre-school* years, however, there is a blossoming of activity triggered by higher brain centres which are now undergoing rapid growth. Puberty is one of the more striking examples of asynchronous growth. Genital development, which during the first twelve years or so assumes little developmental priority, now becomes a dominant part of development. Puberty commonly takes place so abruptly that the person is almost taken by surprise. During a twelve-month period (usually around the age of 13) genitals, body contours, facial features, voice, interests, even fantasies undergo radical transfiguration. For a brief span in the total life cycle (but a significant part of the adolescent period) body growth is dominated by sexual priorities in Nature's frenzied attempt to assure that her children will be able to reproduce themselves. Specific *parts* of the body are also subject to asynchronous groundplans. During the first two months after conception the heart grows so rapidly and with such furor that by forty-five days it may be as much as nine times larger in proportion to its body than it will be fifteen years later. The social life of the child manifests several parallels to asynchronous growth: there are time periods when the child has an excessive preoccupation with one small part of the environment. The three-year-old's mania for demanding "why?" compensates for his ignorance of casuality; the ten-year-old's obsession with sport heroes and movie celebrities passes predictably with time, but only after it has been a major force affecting his life. Asynchronous growth assures that children will never be completely preditable or static and will always have a touch of excess to spice their lives and the lives of those who share with them.

4. *Human growth proceeds from general to specific action.* Early infant attempts to cope with the environment are crude, awkward, and conspicuously lacking in precision and consistency. However, when compared with the even less precise, even more awkward behaviour of the six-month *fetus* they are almost ballet-like in refinement. All body parts and organs initially are *general* rather than specific in their functioning. Some parts of the body, such as the feet of the newborn, are so general in *initial* function that they serve almost no useful purpose at all. The two principles of developmental directionality (cephalocaudal and proximodistal) allow us to accurately predict which parts of the body will be the first to assume specific function and which will be the last to continue with general function. Whether development begins early or late in life, it invariably begins with rough, general execution and then progressively becomes more refined and specialized.

A close inspection of prehensile (grasping) development reveals not only the principle of general-to-specific growth but also demonstrates how physical growth exerts influence on the social behaviour of the developing child. In our society it is traditional for the child to begin making letters with a pencil at about age five, to begin playing ball sports at about age eight, and to begin playing cards with peers (rather than parents) at about age nine or ten. This social sequence is influenced by the physiological fact that the wrist and fingers become sufficiently mature to properly manipulate a pencil somewhere near the fifth year; it is not until about the eighth year, however, that the wrist can coordinate itself with prehensile grasping with enough precision to grasp a ball propelled through the air; and it is rarely before the tenth birthday that manual dexterity or wrist flexibility are refined to the degree required to shuffle a deck of cards without forcing an impromptu game of 52 pick-up. Thus we observe that the developmental guidelines imposed by nature indirectly manifest themselves in the social games of children who have never heard of the concept of maturational readiness.

The general-to-specific growth tendency (some scholars refer to this phenomenon as *differentiation*) is also dramatized by the progressive specificity with which the body reacts to pain. If the chubby rear end of a six-month infant is accidentally pricked by a safety pin, he will cry, squirm, and flail his *entire* body; at six years the same inconvenience will cause him to cry, flail parts of his body, and rub the spot which has been pained; at ten years he may or may not cry, may or may not flail, but definitely will rub; at twelve he probably will rub and might possibly even administer salve where it will do the most good. This sequence demonstrates how the infant body reacts with global and undifferentiated action to the experience of pain; however, as the child matures there is a progressive reduction in the amount of *general* reaction and an increase in the *specific* reactions which allow the individual to deal directly with his source of pain.

The learning of social and physical skills likewise follows a general-through-specific sequence, as we will have ample opportunity to observe in our study of the preschool and early childhood years.

5. *There are time periods when the child is highly susceptible to positive growth and other time periods when he is highly susceptible to negative growth.* Most frequently these periods of growth sensitivity are referred to as *critical periods* even though the historical derivation of the term applies only to specific kinds of animal behaviour. There are not many precisely datable critical periods in human development, but a number of trends in human growth reflect the principle of critical period and therefore the concept should not be ignored. Again, a few

examples are in order. As we shall shortly discover in the ensuing chapter, there are several critical periods during fetal development most of which are of the *negative growth* variety. Between the fourth and sixth week after conception the embryo is extremely susceptible to disfiguration by the drug thalidomide. However, after the seventh week and before the third week this drug seems to have little influence on the developing fetus. During the critical period of twenty-eight to forty-two days after conception, however, thalidomide has the capacity to destroy and deform the embryo's barely visible stubs which normally mature into sturdy arms and legs. Another critical period occurs during the third month of pregnancy when German measles in the mother frequently proves fatal to the fetus; however, if the mother contracts German measles during the eight month, there is no such consequence. As the person gets older, critical periods become less definable and have less predictable results, creating disagreement among experts as to the known consequences of critical periods. Some developmental psychologists and pediatricians assert that the last six months of the first year of life is a critical period in the child's emotional development, and if given insufficient love and contact comfort during this period he will suffer in later emotional development. Some educational psychologists maintain that between the sixth and ninth year perceptual and attitudinal changes are such that if the child does not learn certain school-related skills during these years he will experience considerable difficulty acquiring them at a later age. It is believed by some psychologists that children are developmentally predisposed to learn to speak between eighteen and twenty-four months and to walk between twelve and eighteen months. *If trained and encouraged during these ages they will learn more rapidly and with greater efficiency than at earlier or later ages.* Generally understood, a critical period is a time when the growing child is maximally susceptible to positive or negative growth. Throughout this book we shall refer to this concept, but it will be understood in a general sense rather than as a specific formula to be applied to particular ages.

6. *Certain kinds of behaviour emerge only when the child is maturationally "ready".* The *law of readiness* (so named during psychology's adolescent period when it tried furiously to imitate natural and physical sciences even to the extent of calling general principles "laws") states that any organism will participate in a given behaviour only when it has matured sufficiently to be ready for that behaviour. For the most part, practice, training, or will power have only marginal impact on accelerating the onset of behaviour which is governed by the principle of readiness. All forms of behaviour, however, are not affected by maturational

readiness. Whether a person decides to join a particular church is determined no more by maturation than if he cheers for the Boston Bruins in the Stanley Cup. Readiness refers to those behaviours *specifically related to maturation of physical, mental, or social skills.* One cannot teach a child to accelerate the rate at which he will cut his permanent teeth any more than teach his parents to do the same with their wisdom teeth; these phenomena, regulated by maturation, proceed at their own pace. Assuming the environment normal in its offerings, each child will learn to crawl or walk only when maturationally ready. Providing him with extra practice or coaching exerts only minimal and short-term influence. For most children speech begins sometime around the fifteenth month, but the onset of speech cannot be brought about at an earlier age than it otherwise would. Refinements of speech, such as word combinations, phrases, and sentences likewise have a maturational component which cannot be *significantly* modified. Certain infant, childhood, and adolescent behaviours simply do not occur until the organism is biologically ready for them to happen.

The seeming rigidity of the principle of readiness is loosened by an elementary, yet critical fact: no one knows *for certain* when a particular child is maturationally ready for a particular behaviour. Essentially we must rely upon our knowledge of norms and averages, a practice which proves precise to the exact degree that norms are precise. Some children are ready to walk at nine months and chatter like magpies fifteen months later; others don't locomote until halfway through their second year and use words only in emergencies. *The precision with which we can predict maturational readiness for any given behaviour is reduced as the child gets older.* We can predict accurately (often within a matter of hours) when the fetus will be born; we can predict within a few days when the infant will first lift his head or reach with precision for a distant object; we can predict with marginal accuracy (within a month or so) when he will begin to crawl; but when it comes to walking we find that the child may be maturationally ready to walk anytime between nine and eighteen months — an error factor almost equal to his entire life span. The degree of imprecision continues as the child gets older; this is one basic reason why child psychology is a more precise discipline than is adolescent psychology.

Despite limitations regarding its specific application, readiness is essential to understanding the growth of the child, as well as for adapting ourselves to the limitations, inclinations, and interests he displays at different ages. It does not require a sophisticated knowledge of human development to appreciate that a ten-year-old boy stays away from twelve-year-old girls for the same reason that he stayed away from steep stairwells when he was two years old — in each case they represent obstacles beyond his level of maturational readiness!

The concept of readiness and various implications which spring from it permeate this book, and we shall constantly be reminded of its importance in the social, intellectual, and motor abilities of the growing child.

7. *Egocentrism interferes with the child's ability to understand or perceive the world from vantage points other than his own.* It is natural for the young child to assume that his perception, or his experience, of a given situation is the only possible perception or experience associated with the situation. He does not comprehend that people view things differently than he, or that they do not know exactly what he himself is feeling. Time and experience free the child from this propensity to equate the *perceived* world with the *real* world. As the child grows older he becomes progressively less egocentric and more capable of viewing the world from perspectives other than his own. This phenomenon of *egocentrism* is imperative to the proper understanding of childhood. More than any other principle, it accounts for the child's narrowness of cognition and resistance to innovation. During the first weeks of life the newborn responds only to physical stimuli which directly impinge upon his body — nothing else registers. During the last months of his first year the infant learns about other people and is capable of distinguishing self from non-self; during toddlerhood the child learns that what "I want to do" does not always jibe with what others expect of him; during the preschool years he learns there are reasons why rules are imposed; during middle childhood he understands that rules which govern social life exist not only because parents and authorities say so, but because they possess some defensibility unto themselves; by late childhood a genuine concern emerges for *understanding* the principles which govern not only the physical world but also the social world. Thus egocentrism, though a dominant factor in the child's thinking, becomes progressively less dominant as time passes.

The greater the child's egocentrism the more difficult to modify a viewpoint or behaviour which serves his personal purposes (this reaches its apex during the "terrible-twos"). The term "egocentrism" is commonly associated with Jean Piaget; in this book it is used in a style more accordant with its historical and philosophical usage and implies centredness about the self or ego.

8. *Children tend to engage in those activities which are rewarded, other things being equal.* This principle is referred to as the *law of effect* and, though carried to excess among some schools of psychology, should remain in the front of our minds when attempting to understand

human development during the first ten years of life. All children have fundamental requirements for achievement, recognition, praise, acknowledgement, and love and, as a general rule, they will engage in any behaviour which they have reason to believe will lead to gratification of these requirements. A great deal of otherwise nonunderstandable behaviour makes sense once one discovers the rewards offered for this behaviour. Sometimes rewarded behaviour becomes so thoroughly ingrained that it turns into habit and endures without further reward. The law of effect helps to temper the enthusiasm of overly zealous developmental psychologists who now and again lapse into the practice of explaining all child behaviour in terms of developmental levels, critical periods, readiness, maturation, and other principles indigenous to our discipline. If anyone cannot afford to become overly parochial or provincial in his thinking it is the student who desires to learn about the diverse factors which mould the developing human being.

9.   *The body is able to regulate itself and displays a certain "wisdom" in doing that which is in its long-range best interests.* This concept had been bandied about academic circles long before developmental psychology came onto the scene, and is still far from resolved. When employed with reasonable perspective, however, there is ample scientific evidence in its support. First, a word as to what *wisdom of the body* is not. The body does not have any kind of omniscient mechanism insuring that it will always make correct decisions in its own regard; anyone who has observed the excesses of unrestrained or undisciplined children will attest to this. Nor does the body have wisdom with regard to maintaining itself during abnormal circumstances (one of the body's most ancient emergency reactions, shock, is frequently more harmful to the body than the crisis which causes it). Wisdom of the body does not mean that each person has within him the capacity to automatically take care of himself in all situations. Wisdom of the body essentially means that each person will acquire habits of sleep, diet, exercise, play, and work which are suited to his particular disposition and needs if given freedom of choice and opportunity. This concept is especially crucial to understanding individual differences, idiosyncratic behaviour, and irregularities of ordinary patterns. Some children function optimally only when they get eleven hours of sleep each night, whereas others get along quite well with seven or eight; some children require 800 calories per day more than others; some fragile children always seem to need an extra sweater on chilly days. To these requirements each child eventually will adjust if opportunity is present and if he has not been taught to avoid what he lacks. It always is valid to *listen* to the solutions which a child generates in response to his own unique needs;

however, the listener must be critical as well as knowledgeable lest the child be credited with wisdom beyond his years. Despite the body wisdom he may possess, no child is above pulling the wool over the adult's naive eye in order to get something otherwise unattainable!

10. *The child craves practice of all newly emerging skills.* Whenever the child is on the verge of adding a new behaviour to his repertoire of skills, he will practice this behaviour as much as possible. This tendency affects not only gross motor skills such as crawling, walking, and running, but also verbal and intellectual skills. Practice may surround the onset of a new skill in two general ways: (1) practice may come before the skill, partially accounting for its existence; and (2) practice may begin after the skill has been acquired. The former is most commonly associated with physical skills and the latter with mental and verbal skills. An example of each will help clarify the relationship of practice to the formation of new skills. As a generalization (to which there are always exceptions especially when humans are involved) children do not learn to stand upright in a short span of time. A good deal of practice is required before upright posture is achieved; even when the child is sufficiently mature to stand, he must practice to become proficient. In learning to stand the child first pulls himself upward, he clings to supports; he teeters, loses balance; he falls. He goes through the same pattern again and again, each time with slightly greater precision. Eventually, standing is mastered. The child does not rest on his laurels upon reaching this achievement; rather, he practices more than ever because standing upright hastens the onset of walking, which now becomes the newly emerging skill he craves to practice. Standing upright can only be achieved with *beforehand* practice. On the other hand, some skills emerge without benefit of practice, and are *refined* by practice after their emergence. A child "discovers" (recognizes) that one block placed upon another results in a building of sorts. This discovery is not taken casually: immediately the child builds, tears down, and rebuilds his two-story highrise. He may entertain himself for an hour or more with this kind of block building until proficiency is acquired. He quits when he is bored with the project, but this rarely occurs before competence in the particular skill is achieved. The child is especially prone toward after-the-fact practice during his peak months of speech development. Upon learning the name for an object he will repeat it over and over, proudly (this word should not be taken lightly because mastery of words *is* a source of pride for the toddler) displaying his new found knowledge. When he learns that by saying "Whazzat?" he can elicit from the adult the name for almost any environmental object, he exercises this discovery to exasperating extremes.

The major effect this principle holds for the growing child is that his life is always dominated to a certain degree by newly emerging skills; tolerance must be accorded the child in these days of preoccupation with one small aspect of growing. The tendency to practice newly emerging skills persists through adolescence and adulthood (remember when you first learned to play checkers or bridge?) and only man's habit of learning quickly, and just as quickly getting bored with what he masters, prevents this tendency from dominating life even more than it does.

The foregoing concepts of human growth and development are not the only significant concepts employed in the study of childhood, but owing to their wide application they assume special prominence. In the following chapters we shall refer back to these general and specific guidelines in order to more clearly define the nature of the first ten years of life.

Summary

In this chapter we have overviewed the general guidelines, the specific developmental concepts, and some philosophical issues which directly relate to understanding the first ten years of life. The reader is encouraged to familiarize himself with these in order to accommodate more readily to the remainder of the book.
The general guidelines include:
1. Children are unique (idiosyncratic) as well as normative.
2. Children satisfy all needs within a social context and therefore cannot be completely understood without appreciation of their social dimension.
3. Children have biological as well as psychological needs.
4. Children can be globally understood only from an interdisciplinary perspective.
5. Children are studied for academic as well as humanistic reasons.
6. Children become progressively more influenced by environment as they age.
The specific developmental concepts include:
1. Growth is cephalocaudal.
2. Growth is proximodistal.
3. Growth is asynchronous.
4. Growth proceeds from general to specific.
5. Growth is characterized by critical periods.
6. Growth is significantly influenced by maturational readiness.

7. Life during the childhood years is dominated by egocentrism.
8. Behaviour during childhood is significantly influenced by the law of effect.
9. The child craves practice of newly emerging skills.
10. The body has some wisdom with regard to its self-regulation.

We are now ready to commence our investigation of the first ten years of life, and it shall begin precisely where it should — within the mother.

Chapter Two

Fetal Development

The great American man of letters, Mark Twain, once suggested that the biography of every man should begin with an analysis of the quality of wine shared by his mother and father on the evening of conception. It is uncertain just what information would accrue from such an investigation, and though offering some interesting possibilities, it is beyond the limited scope of this text. We shall, conventional as it may seem, restrict ourselves in this chapter to describing growth patterns which occur in the human organism from conception till birth. Special attention will be paid to those growth patterns which reflect general development principles as established in Chapter 1, as well as to those which manifest unusual influence on the first months of life after birth. We shall catalogue prenatal growth by means of a month-to-month description of the 270-day gestation period.

Most of us lapse into the habit of thinking of life as beginning at birth rather than thinking of birth as only one event in the total growth style. This habit leads us to overlook the critical events which have taken place during the nine months prior to birth when the unborn human grows from a fertilized egg (called a *zygote*) to a multibillion-celled newborn infant. The journey is one of the most miraculous in nature and fully worthy of our attention not only because of the instruction it provides concerning human development but also for the sense of appreciation, even awe, it interjects into our knowledge of man.

The systematic study of human fetal development is not an easy undertaking. The fetus is not readily accessible for us to observe, and direct investigation of his intra-uterine world may lead to its destruction. In disappointing fact, much of our knowledge about the first week of life is inferred from our knowledge of other animals which have been more rigorously studied in the surgical laboratory.

The prenatal life of all animals is divided into three stages by embryologists: (1) the germinal period, (2) the embryonic period, and (3) the fetal period. We shall adhere to this general classification scheme even though general headings are of considerably less consequence than the particular events of prenatal life. It is the latter to which we shall most fully attend.

The germinal period:

The male sperm displays unusual determination in its struggle against gravity, time, and fellow sperm to fertilize the female egg. The microscopic spermatozoon, meager in size though it may be, when coupled with the ovum, itself only about 1/175 of an inch in diameter, does form the humble beginning of all human life. The egg is fertilized in the Fallopian tube and then journeys to the uterus, a three-day sojourn if nothing interferes. Sometimes, however, the fertilized egg becomes lodged within the Fallopian tube, resulting in a tubal pregnancy which may prove harmful to the mother and therefore must be surgically terminated. Upon reaching the uterus the fertilized egg eventually attaches itself to the uterine wall, marking the end of the germinal period. In the entire process which takes from seven to fourteen days, the mother usually has no experiential awareness whatsoever of what is taking place. Only women who are extremely sensitive to internal body changes are able to detect the hormonal and chemical changes which have been occurring daily since conception.

The embryonic and fetal periods:

Between the second and eighth week of development the human organism is referred to as an *embryo,* from the Greek "to swell", but after the eighth week is known by its most common name, *fetus,* a Latin word meaning "young one". Because of complex developments during the embryonic and fetal stages it is necessary to devise more precise time spans for describing the growth trends which take place before birth. Therefore, we shall take a month by month overview of the nine months of life preceding birth. In preface, however, it must again be stressed that our knowledge of human embryology is comparatively imprecise; even in those rare circumstances when our knowledge is precise, we constantly are foiled by the fact that the fetus is a highly individualized and unique form of life which, if capable of such behaviour, would take delight in doing exactly the contrary of what is expected. For this reason we must guard against thinking that generalizations are always true, that norms are always representative of particular individuals, that sequences are always perfectly sequential, or that observations made in one setting will be perfectly replicated in another. As is the case in all psychology, respect for the person forms the guideline by which we conduct our study. Now, on to the matter at hand — the first nine months of life.

The first month:

Unlike the first month after *birth* when growth is slow and rather uneventful, the first month of life following conception is a spectacular growth period unequalled in the remainder of the human growth cycle. At thirty days the embryo is ten thousand times larger than the fertilized egg, but despite this Malthusian growth, it is still no more than one-quarter of an inch from head to heel. The tiny embryo bears some resemblance to the form he will later evolve but could easily be mistaken for a fish or monkey embryo. The body is formed of a gelatin-like substance and affords little indication of the skeletal sturdiness shortly to come.

Despite the embryo's unseemly appearance, the groundwork for humanness is well underway. Tiny bulges, barely observable, are the first indications of four emerging limbs; the head has begun to form and the two halves of the forebrain can be distinguished; the kidneys, liver, digestive tract, blood stream, and heart are partially formed and in some instances functioning; body tissue has begun to trifurcate into *ectoderm* which will become skin and nerve tissue, *mesoderm* from which the heart, blood vessels, muscle and bone tissue emerge, and *endoderm* which gives rise to the digestive and alimentary tracts as well as the respiratory organs.

Growth during the first thirty days is remarkably coordinated; cells develop in relation to each other, and all organs function in such a manner as to complement one another. No part of the organism, when functioning properly, negatively interferes with the growth of any other part of the organism. Organismic unity is the keyword for understanding embryonic development and will continue to be a guiding principle throughout life. It is definitely in the interest of survival that the body unfolds in such a coherent and systematic manner. Sufficient hazards operate outside the embryo that, if it did not operate well unto itself, it surely would perish during the first month of life. Corner (1944) has estimated that one-third of all ova fertilized do not live until birth, and though it cannot be known for certain, most attrition probably occurs during the first month.

During the first month we observe the rudimentary beginnings of human life, and although appearance is not yet *distinctly human* the internal workings are, and in only a few weeks — even before it assumes the status of fetus — we will be able to recognize the embryo as being human. This first chapter in the biography of the embryo to a significant measure determines how the rest of his story will unfold.

The second month:

Significant growth changes during this thirty-day period cause the embryo to take on conspicuously human features. The head, which now constitutes about one-third of the body volume, has definite features including the dark circular beginnings of eyes and a mouth with lips. The entire facial area assumes a distinctly human contour and the eyes move closer together, which causes the embryo to lose some of its reptile-like appearance. Early development of the cerebullum and cerebral hemisphere is now taking place, and the internal ear has already undergone considerable development. At this stage of its career the embryo is about one-third of an inch in length and weighs but a fraction of an ounce — an incredibly small organism for such complex and intricate growth. The limbs continue to mature and are much more plainly visible; a slight elbow bend appears in the arm, and even though the legs are less developed than the arms (as they will be throughout prenatal life and the first several years of postnatal life), knee, ankle, and toe differentiations are noticeable. During the second month, sexual differentiation of the gonads becomes clear, and on very close inspection it is possible to recognize the sex of the embryo. The prominent tail which extends from the tip of the spine is at its maximum length and in time will disappear altogether, stripping the embryo of one observable reminder of man's evolutionary heritage.

By the eighth week virtually all major structures and organ systems are differentiated and functioning. During the next four months they will undergo such radical acceleration in growth that the infant will be capable of extra-uterine survival before age twenty-eight weeks. The most fascinating discovery which investigation of uterine darkness reveals is a giant heart, seven times larger in proportion to its body than the adult heart, whose rhythmic beat is already serving a definite role in the survival of the embryo. Though not structurally equivalent to the neonatal heart, significant partitioning has already begun and will be completed shortly after the newborn infant takes his first gasp of air. The principle of asynchronous growth leads us to conclude that the heart is disproportionately large because of its central role in embryonic survival.

It is during the second month (approximately twenty-eight to forty-two days) that the embryo is vulnerable to the drug *thalidomide;* during this *critical period* arm and leg buds are highly susceptible to disfiguration and aberration. Newborn babies disfigured by thalidomide usually have stump-like limbs highly similar to those of this embryonic period which serve as permanent reminders of the delicate balance upon which human normality rests.

The third month:

After the eighth week the growing human is technically referred to as a

21

fetus. The maturational signal for this name change is the formation of the first real bone cells which replace the cartilage. Between the eighth and twelfth weeks the fetus assumes undeniable infant features. When shown photographs of a twelve-week fetus, first grade children invariably report that they are looking at a human baby; facial features become so refined that even university undergraduates seem not to mind looking at the three-month fetus. The head is not yet childlike but is rapidly approaching that distinction. The eyelids are sealed tightly shut, as the amniotic fluid would aberrate retinal development; the lips exhibit the first sucking motions and several parts of the body respond reflexively if stroked or stimulated. The kidneys begin to secrete urine although most waste material is removed through the *placenta.* The fetus develops while enveloped in a warm, salty, pellucid liquid called *amniotic fluid,* which is confined by the transparent *amnion sac.* At ten weeks the sac measures about two inches and houses an organism one-half as long; however, by fourteen weeks the fetus may be three inches long. The liquid environment provides room for the fetus to move and stretch; fetal movements have been taking place for several weeks but they now become more global, involving arm waving, neck flexing, and trunk rotating. Also present is a crude tonic-neck-reflex which causes one side of the body to flex when the opposite side extends. The fetus is now architectually sound and will increase proportionately in strength and durability as time progresses.

The mother does not yet feel the growing fetus, the womb has not begun to stretch, and there is no way an untrained bystander could determine that the woman is pregnant. Women who do not experience morning sickness, or who have irregular menstrual periods, may be quite shocked when informed by a doctor that they are pregnant and serving as the life-line for a fetus sufficiently mature to have its own individuality, habits, sleeping positions, facial features, and perhaps even a loose resemblance to one or both parents.

The fourth month:

For the normal fetus the first trimester of development is complete. The second trimester, starting with the fourth lunar month, is characterized by sensational growth. In one month the fetus increases his weight sixfold, and his length by five inches so that he is a full eight inches long; despite this prodigious growth, however, he still weighs less than half a pound. The mother is noticeably with child; the womb expands to accommodate the burgeoning baby, the breasts begin to enlarge, and the pelvic girdle also must adjust. The tremendous supply line of nutrients required for the growth spurt of the four-month-old fetus saps the mother's reserves, making it incumbent upon her to take in surplus vitamins and calcium to keep up with the demands of her unborn child. It is a fair, though loose, generalization that as goes the mother's health so goes the health of the baby.

The *placenta,* the organ through which all essentials are supplied to the fetus, is connected to the fetus by the *umbilical cord.* At birth the placenta is detached (actually it is expelled in the final stage of labour) and the umbilical cord is severed — their function has been outlived. Although the mother and baby have completely separate blood streams, the placenta is not able to filter out *all* undesirable substances which may enter the fetus from the mother's blood stream. Anesthetics and drugs in the mother's blood stream make their way to the fetus. Perhaps one of the most tragic manifestations of this occurs when a heroin-addicted mother gives birth to a child who contracted her addiction in *utero.* Instances have been reported where the newborn is so completely addicted to heroin that when separated from his source at birth the withdrawal pains cause death.

The fourth fetal month is the last month during which medical abortions are performed under normal circumstances. Although possible to perform at a later date, owing to the danger late abortion holds for the mother, as well as the reluctance of some doctors to surgically abort after the twelfth week, termination of the fetus is rare beyond this month. It is also during the fourth month of pregnancy that medical doctors can most meaningfully conduct tests on the fetus to determine the probability that he will be born with abnormalities. This is determined by inserting a probe (a very narrow needle) into the womb and extracting samples of amniotic fluid. This procedure is referred to as *amniocentesis.* The test is primarily useful for determining if there is a medical basis for terminating the life of the fetus because of the probability that he will be born with inherited deformity, or deformity from infection such as rubella. It is difficult to conduct amniocentesis before the tenth week because cell change may not be apparent before then. It is recommended that this test be conducted when there is a family history of mental deficiency or inborn errors of metabolism. As the reader will observe in the last section of this chapter, however, the decision to medically abort a child is not based solely upon medical information. The ethical beliefs of the mother, the father, as well as the doctor are highly critical factors in deciding upon abortion as a course of action.

Most bones are now formed but ossification will continue for several years. Connections between neurons and between neurons and muscle fibres are processing and one visible consequence of this is the increased smoothness of motion displayed by the four-month fetus. The legs are still scrawny and under-developed compared to the upper body; the hands, designed by nature to manipulate, are flexing, bending, and pincing in preparation for their future tasks. The fetus is becoming infantlike with alarming swiftness and, though less than half of his uteral life is complete, he is now much more adapted to intra-uterine life than he will be to extra-uterine life at four months after birth.

The fifth month:

The fetus is preparing systematically and with stoic discipline for birth. The essential requirements for post-uterine existence, sucking and breathing, are now observable. The swallowing reflex is well developed, the lips participate in definite feeding behaviour, and the fetus may occasionally even suck his thumb; breathing has begun although it is liquid, not air, which is passed in and out of the lungs. The digestive tract is mechanically as well as chemically functional, as is the liver. (It is thought by some that the enlarged liver partially accounts for the potbelly of the newborn.) The heart is strong and regular, pulsing away at about 160 beats per minute, twice the adult pace, and can be heard by a stethoscope placed on the mother's stomach. Just before birth the heartbeat will reduce to about 140 beats per minute.

The fetus is now a foot long, weighs one pound, and is beginning to find for the first time that living quarters are getting cramped. His flexing and stretching are getting more gymnastic and the mother may now experience the sensation of fetal movement. The fetus sleeps and wakes much like a newborn and can be incited to movement by sudden sounds from the extra-uterine environment. The mother, usually over morning sickness by now (some mothers never experience it), is rapidly learning that pregnancy restricts her mobility, reduces her stamina, and shortens her temper. Her discomfort is mild compared to the final weeks of pregnancy however, when heavy work such as mopping the floor, and unnecesssary social engagements are dropped altogether. The fetus gives fair warning that soon he will be a dominant factor in the lives of all those who share his world.

The fetus is not yet *viable,* meaning he will not survive if born. For this he requires the further growth and maturity which accrues during the sixth and seventh fetal months.

The sixth month:

The fetus becomes progressively more viable during the sixth month although the chances of surviving birth are still remote. His total action system shows refinement and the organ system is well coordinated. If

24

born, the fetus has a slight chance for survival if medical attention is good, an incubator is available, and he is of unusual respiratory precociousness. The youngest known human to survive was born between twenty-three to twenty-five weeks and weighed about one pound. At this stage the birth process is rather easy, requiring no labour, and sometimes the baby is born still encased in the amnion sac (in full-term babies it ruptures shortly before birth). The baby is characterized by extreme fragility and almost invariably the lungs and respiratory tract are too immature to sustain life. At six months the skin is so transparent that veins, arteries, and some of their tributaries are clearly visible, leading an observer to marvel at the intricate complexity of the human circulatory system.

Near the end of the second trimester of intra-uterine life the eyelids open and the eye demonstrates some response to light. Buds for permanent teeth appear; a fine woolly substance covers part of the arms, legs, and back, but it usually disappears before birth; blood cells are being formed in the marrow cavities of fetal bones; and the grasping reflex is of sufficient strength that the baby can grasp and hold tightly to a rod placed in its palm. Crying and hiccuping may occur. One unusual case has been reported where a fetus cried so loudly he could be heard by doctors and nurses tending to the expectant mother. Anticipating an incredulous response to this phenomenon, one alert doctor recorded the sounds made by the crying fetus in order to confirm that it actually happened (Merry and Merry, p. 72).

Three major events take place during the sixth month which are essential for development of air-breathing capacities: (1) the nostrils reopen, (2) the pulmonary alveoli develop, and (3) the medulla respiratory centre undergoes prefunctional organization. In the absence of these events the fetus has no chance for extra-uterine survival. The human cell has no capacity to store oxygen and therefore requires a smoothly operating and efficient respiratory network to provide this life-giving element.

The fetus now awaits the last third of his uterine stay. During the next three months he will put on additional weight, gain in length, increase in strength, and receive many finishing touches before being forcefully expelled into the world of the nonfetal. These last three months of uterine life witness the refinement of the developing organism; the fetus is similar to the toddler or the preschooler in that he will rarely attempt something for which he is not biologically capable. Therefore he must await additional growth and maturity before he is ready for his first major life-shock: birth. As we shall observe in the next chapter, birth is indeed a shocking experience to the strong but totally sheltered fetus, and his ability to survive it is completely dependent upon the final growth refinements he undergoes during the last twelve weeks of intra-uterine life.

The seventh month:

Approaching the twenty-eighth week of life the fetus may weigh up to two and a half pounds, a one pound increase over the past month. His overall body strength and advanced organ development now make him ready for birth if for some reason he is born prematurely. Although the mortality rate is high for infants born only twenty-eight weeks after conception, this is the age at which survival can first be hoped for with some medical justification. Because the layer of fat which insulates the baby has not yet developed he is extremely sensitive to temperature change; premature babies lose body heat so rapidly some doctors wrap them in cotton blankets even before the umbilical cord has been severed. A heated incubator is required to prevent the infant from literally freezing to death.

During this four-week period (twenty-four to twenty-eight weeks) the baby begins to receive from his mother the special disease-combating proteins called *antibodies* (Flanagan, 1962, p. 78). The mother carries in her blood antibodies against those diseases which she has had and against which she has a certain degree of immunity. These usually include, among others, measles, mumps, the common cold, and if she has received vaccine, polio. Since these immunities wear off by the time the child is six months old, he then must rely upon the strength of his own system to cope with infectious adversaries. Because he cannot do this completely, he must go through sickness in order to acquire some immunity. However, the critical survival function has been served by granting the newborn amnesty from illness during the first few months after birth when he is recuperating from birth-shock and building his strength. By toddlerhood he will be so strong and resilient that he can take most illness as well as injury in stride with only a minimal recuperation period before he is back about the business of being a child.

As far as survival is concerned, perhaps the most significant development during the seventh month is maturation of the lung tissue so that it becomes capable of absorbing inhaled oxygen.

The eighth month:

The eighth-month fetus is somewhat akin to the thirteen-year-old pre-adolescent in that he has outgrown comfortable living in one environment but is of insufficient skill and maturity to live well in another. There is nothing to do except wait for time to bestow growth and strength. The thirty-week fetus can cope with birth but it will tax to the very limit his entire system. During the eighth month protective fat

26

emerges and with it comes about two additional pounds. Housing becomes even more crowded and somersaults and other such activities which have been going on for the past few months are now greatly restricted for the simple reason there is no place to exercise. The fetus is now biding time until he has sufficient stamina and organ efficiency to make the great transition to extra-uterine life, which will occur sometime during the next thirty days.

The eighth month of fetal development shares several parallels with toddlerhood as well as the preschool years because it is the time for finishing touches. The child does not walk nor does he climb stairs before he is maturationally ready. Readiness, however, includes the incidental refinements which assure that *attempting* to walk will not injure or excessively strain other parts of the body not directly related to walking. Before the child is able to walk he must have more than mature legs. He must possess balance, arm coordination, depth perception, and he must be able to fall without injury to wrists, face, or spinal cord. Before the child walks *other body developments must be sufficiently mature to cope with walking behaviour.* Here we see the parallel with the eight-month fetus: although he can survive birth, it would put tremendous strain on those body parts (and processes) not yet completely ready for the birth process. Therefore, the eighth month of fetal life is the preparation period when the organism finalizes the subtle, inconspicious requirements of birth readiness.

The ninth month:

When the uterus cannot expand any further, the infant will be born. For about 75 percent of all babies this occurs within eleven days of the 266th day after conception. The baby now weighs between five and seven pounds, has a substantial layer of fat to assist the maintenance of thermal constancy and, if development has been normal, will possess every biological mechanism required for survival outside the womb. During the last week of uterine life the placenta loses most of its nutritional efficiency, presumably because of old age, triggering a chemical reaction which facilitates the onset of labour. There are three stages of labour. The first stage, which requires the greatest time, is the period when the cervix is dilated to allow passage of the infant head; the second stage involves passage of the baby through the vagina or birth canal into the extra-uterine world; the final stage involves the expulsion of *afterbirth: placenta,* the *amniotic and chorionic membranes* and the remainder of the umbilical cord (Stone, 1968, p. 46). Occasionally the labour process is severely strained when the fetus attempts to exit buttocks first in what is known as a *breech birth.* In some circumstances the doctor will remedy this dangerous blunder by realigning the fetus so that a more normal delivery is possible; however, often the most feasible solution is to remove the child surgically by caesarian section.

The activity which characterized the *thirty-six-week fetus* also characterizes the *thirty-six-hour infant* with a few minor exceptions: breathing involves oxygen not liquid; food enters the body by way of the mouth not the umbilical cord; crying is vocal now that air can vibrate the vocal cords; and the infant becomes but one speck in his environment instead of the dominant factor within it. Perhaps most significantly, from a humanistic perspective, at birth the mother ceases to be only a carrier and impersonal provider and begins to assume her maternal role as the child's first source of love and contact, a role which in a few years will become more important and certainly more complex than providing nutrition.

Summary

During the past nine months the fetus has proceeded in lawful and systematic fashion from a circular speck smaller than the period at the end of this sentence to a seven pound, multibillion-celled, organismically sound human infant. His growth is *cephalocaudal,* unfolding in a head to toe direction, and *proximodistal* in its growth from centre to the periphery. The fetal journey began with gross, global, and undifferentiated behaviour and concluded with refined, specific, almost "purposive" activity. All body members and organs became progressively differentiated; the hand converts from a shovel-like stub to a five-digit instrument capable of prehension; and the frog-like bulbous head acquires childlike facial contours, functional brain hemispheres, and the cortical foundations for higher thought processes. All body parts do not mature at the same rate and/or in the same sequence; thus the underdeveloped legs of the fetus remain so for the infant and the toddler, but by middle adolescence they will take up one-half the body length; conversely the disproportionately large fetal head gradually loses prominence until by adulthood it constitutes only one-tenth of the body length.

We have observed the fetus prepare for neonatal existence by practising sucking, breathing, swallowing, digesting, crying, and eliminating, all of which are required for neonatal survival. We now know that the parasite fetus depends completely on the mother for nourishment, disease immunity, and shelter and thereby establishes his life trademark as a socially dependent creature.

The remarkable fetus staggers us with his perplexing mixture of complexity and simplicity; durability and fragility; predictability and individuality; inability and potentiality. The infant he will soon become provides us no relief from these polarities of human existence, in many respects they become magnified.

We now find ourselves ready to make the great transition to the first twelve months of life after birth in our study of human growth and development. But first some *brief* comments on the metaphysics of prenatal existence.

The Fetus as Sacred

The degree to which we understand a given phenomenon does not determine the degree to which we value it. Sometimes one causes the other but not always. Tolstoy bemoaned the fact that Russian peasants loved and valued the Church more intensely than the bishops who served in its hierarchy. The richness of our knowledge of fetal life, for example, will not determine how we value fetal existence. For the great majority of us, however, the degree to which we value fetal life will determine how we *apply* what we know about it. The purpose here is not to persuade the reader that one value approach is better than another, but rather to present two prevailing viewpoints for consideration and analysis.

Part of the value structure of certain religious and ethical viewpoints asserts that any form of human life is sacred and under *no* circumstances may it be justifiably taken. This includes acts of war, self-defence, or other forms of taking human life. This is a rather "extremist" posture. A more widely accepted viewpoint asserts that human life is sacred and cannot be taken except in the defence of human life. This allows defensive warfare, for example, but does not condone the taking of fetal life unless it directly threatens the life of the mother. This latter viewpoint has been part of Western morality and legal structure since before Christ, but it became an official part of doctrinal Christianity only after the great Carthage debates of the fourth century in which St. Augustine established the concept of "natural law" with regard to fetal life. His belief, which in large part is held today by the Catholic Church although it has been relaxed by most Protestant denominations, is that fetal life assumes sacredness at the moment of conception and its willful termination is contrary to natural law and is therefore an act of murder. This belief is maintained even when pregnancy will directly harm the life of the mother. The same principle which denies *euthanasia* (mercy killing) among the elderly prevents the taking of human life before birth. The viewpoint of those who consider the fetus a sacred form of life is therefore contrary to the viewpoint which holds that the human fetus is not really "human" in the complete sense of the word before it is *viable* and therefore the termination of its life is not inhumane.

The Fetus as Disposable

An alternate viewpoint asserts that as the fundamental rights of pregnancy belong to the expectant mother, the termination of fetal life is essentially a medical issue which mother and doctor must decide upon. Advocates of this persuasion argue that it is unethical to bring a child into the world who is not wanted or who might have deformity. In defence of this they claim that during the germinal and embryonic stages of development such little resemblance to the newborn infant is seen that one is not taking the life of a human being, but merely life which has the potential to become human. It also is believed by those who claim the mother has a right to rid herself of unwanted pregnancy that human life is made "sacred" not by divine action, but rather by the love and respect of fellow humans; in other words, the fetus (or embryo) is not *unto itself sacred*. Additional support for the right to terminate fetal life comes from the conviction that the expectant mother has moral responsibility to *society* as well as to the developing fetus, and that by bringing new children into the world she might be inadvertently contributing to a host of societal ills such as overpopulation or famine.

In some parts of North America the viewpoint just presented has been made part of the legal code, whereas in others the former viewpoints dominate the legal code. The general mood of the times suggests that the viewpoint which stresses the rights of the mother is increasing in popularity whereas that which stresses the rights, or sacredness, of the fetus is losing acceptance. Whatever the case may be, the ethical belief each person adheres to will significantly determine how he implements his knowledge of fetal life.

Many individuals are today finding that rapid changes in medical technology as well as the widespread changes in what is considered socially acceptable behaviour are forcing them to reconsider their own ideas about fetal life. In the 1960s few authorities could foresee the extent to which abortion laws would change during the coming decade. In the 1970s there are few authorities who will predict with complete confidence what new legal legislation will be enacted with regard to unborn humans. It cannot be denied that overpopulation is one of the major crises of the twentieth century. It also is obvious that the earth cannot continue to provide indefinitely for man at his present rate of growth. In medicine there is a growing demand to use aborted fetuses for medical research and indications are that this demand will grow stronger rather than weaker in the coming years. The following news item taken from the Associated Press, July 8, 1972 relates to this trend:

British medical and legal experts have called on the government to allow scientists to use human fetuses obtained in abortions for such projects as the search for a cancer cure.

But the experts stressed that such use of unborn babies should be strictly controlled and there should be no monetary trade in fetuses.

The recommendation came from a team of doctors and lawyers headed by Sir John Peel, former president of the Royal College of Obstetricians and Gynecologists.

The government set up the panel two years ago to consider the ethical, medical, social and legal implications after there had been reports of abortion clinics selling fetuses for research.

The experts reported that the contribution to the health and welfare of the entire population from the research use of fetuses and fetal material was so important that the development of such research should continue, subject to safeguards.

Chapter Three

The First Year of Life

The first year of life begins with a reflex-induced gasp of air caused by a doctor's smart swat to a bare behind and ends with a misdirected burst of air caused by an excited mother's coaxing to blow out a birthday candle. Between these two events incredible growth takes place. The newborn infant has no voluntary control over his limbs and no ability to move himself; he cannot perceive the world except by means of underdeveloped eyes, insensitive ears and a sense of touch so imprecise that it often cannot respond to pain. The newborn does not recognize his own mother, and does almost nothing on his own volition, relying instead on primitive reflexes. He has no emotions as adults experience them, instead, he experiences only various states of excitement. Except for a piercing and persistent cry, he is incapable of oral communication. Not one of the abilities which distinguish man from other animals is his. The newborn, proficient at nothing, would die within hours if left unattended. From this meagerly equipped seven-pound package of incomplete humanity will develop the most complex, intelligent, and creative animal on earth. How does it happen? The foundations are established during the first year of life, and as every wise man concedes, a structure is only as strong as its foundations.

Developmental psychology is only one of the disciplines which attempt to understand the beginnings of human life and, as we outlined in the first chapter, it operates from its own biases, procedures, and conceptual starting points. In this chapter we shall venture through the first year of life by analysing three distinct age spans, *each* of which has its own unique though interrelated events. The age spans have been selected to correspond with significant growth patterns during the first year of life, and include: (1) *birth to six weeks* — when life is dominated by reflexes, recuperation from birth, and the pooling of strength which will allow the infant to become increasingly involved in learning about the outside environment; (2) *six to sixteen weeks* — when the infant greatly expands his levels of awareness and comes to *interact* in a limited fashion with his physical and social environment; and (3) *four through twelve months* — when social, intellectual, and motor skills are actively focused on mastering different aspects of the physical environment and the anatomical self.

During each of these age spans we will closely attend to those events which are of greatest import to the infant, his parents, and his future development, with little note of behaviour which does not so relate. Although it is difficult to arbitrarily make distinctions between "important" and "nonimportant" developments during the first year of life, we cannot escape the conclusion that some are more important than others. As a matter of humanistic concern, however, those developments which directly relate to the child's interaction with other humans are of major importance. The classic issues of humanism, as they are reflected in the study of childhood, will provide many of our guidelines in this chapter.

Our primary concerns in the first section of this chapter will focus on the birth of the infant, his appearance at birth, the reflexes he is born with, the behaviour he is capable of, and his experiencing of the world. We will view these events within a time perspective of six weeks, bearing in mind that the infant is making the transition from a fetus to a newborn. It is the most strenuous transition in the human growth cycle.

The Great Transition: The First Six Weeks After Birth

Birth shock
Birth shock is the biological stress experienced by the infant during the transition from intra-uterine to extra-uterine life. It affects the total organism. Though the newborn shortly is engaged in meeting the requirements of his new environment, some parts of his system will require several days to recuperate from birth shock, which should be distinguished from another concept, "birth trauma", used by several psychologists, most notably Otto Rank. Birth trauma is a stronger concept than birth shock, chiefly because it suggests that the trauma of birth becomes a significant factor in the *emotional* development of the individual. This is not my contention, as the evidence indicates that despite the severity of the birth process it does not leave lasting psychological effects on the normal child. Despite the infant's ability to recuperate (which is one of his major characteristics) birth shock exacts considerable strain on the system of the infant as well as the mother. In all likelihood the human body encounters few system-shocks during the normal life span more intense than birth shock.

Let us briefly reconstruct an image of the sheltered environment of the thirty-six week old fetus. His body is softly cushioned in the mother's uterus, protected from bumps and jostles by a liquid shock-absorbing system. He is partially free from the effects of gravity and therefore can move about without concern for it (a much greater concern is finding space in which to move). Nutrition is automatically funneled directly into his system via the placenta and umbilical cord. The 100 degree temperature of his domicile is subject to minimal variation. No other people compete with him for basic goods (except in the case of twins, triplets, etc.) or create hassles in general. The fetus does not breathe, receiving the oxygen he needs from the mother. He never experiences punishment, nor is he ever faced with demands to be anything other than what he is. No standards must be met or lived up to and, perhaps best of all, no mischievous brothers or sisters have to be coped with. This is the normal environment of the fetus: tranquil, predictable, rather uneventful, even somewhat envied by adults of limited ambition. However, the fetal environment is not at all like the buzzing, changing environment of the newborn, and eventually the shock of changing from one to the other must be experienced. The transition from tranquil intra-uterine to hectic extra-uterine existence takes place during a very brief yet highly critical twenty-minute period. To achieve greater appreciation and understanding of birth shock let us look at some of the demands which are immediately made upon the biological system of the newborn baby.

During the second stage of labour the fetal head is forced through the mother's cervix into the outside world. If the delivery is normal the balance of his body will follow shortly thereafter. To deliver the baby a force equal to the weight of almost one hundred pounds is required; the infant's head receives the brunt of this pressure and is able to do so successfully only because five major bone plates in the skull are pliable. The process of forcing the child out of the womb is taxing to the mother as well as to the infant, but constitutes only one phase of birth shock. The reflex which converts the baby to an *air-breathing* creature is instigated by a rather crisp blow to his posterior and, for most infants, this will be the most profitable spank ever received, but certainly not the last. The infant's first gasp of air is not easy, requiring five times the effort of ordinary breathing because air must be taken in to expand the uninflated air sacs of the lung. Breathing passages are not cleared of mucus for several days, making breathing irregular during this time. Almost all of the newborn's body cavities are filled with fluids or mucus at birth which must be removed if he is to survive in his new environment. (This is one reason for yawning, coughing, sneezing dur-

34

ing the first hours of extra-uterine life.) Though still reeling from the shock of birth, breathing, and slap, the newborn concurrently experiences the thermal shock of a 20 to 25 degree environmental temperature drop. His eyes are instantly assaulted with brightness, and this takes some getting used to after being protected by months of darkness within the womb. The newborn is exposed to auditory stimuli of greater intensity than he has ever experienced before, although this is made easier for him by the fact that his ears are filled with mucus for about forty-eight hours. The neonate must rapidly adjust to consuming food via the mouth, throat, and stomach — a completely new experience. The heart is also subjected to new duties and strains as it must now pump blood to the lungs to pick up oxygen. A major valve inside the heart must close if oxygenated blood and deoxygenated blood are to be kept separate.

In addition to these staggering jolts to his system the newborn must undergo the inconvenience of fresh one percent silver nitrate administered to the eyes (a preventive against gonorrheal ophthalmia), a brisk cleansing, and lively handling by as many as five different adults during the first thirty minutes of life.

All of this adds up to the unmistakable conclusion that birth is a system-shocking experience. On the other hand, as each of us has gone through it, it seems a bit melodramatic to suggest that birth is so "traumatic" that is causes us emotional crises for the rest of our lives. Birth is only the first, although the most abrupt and intense, of many "shocks" each human goes through in the course of normal development and maturation. Shortly after birth the infant must adjust to a less intense but still critical shock — *social* living. This is a major task, and one for which the infant is provided almost no reflexes or genetic predispositions. He must learn to cope with a mother who, no matter how loving and caring she may be, is also unpredictable and unique unto herself. The infant must adjust to the shock of an environment which constantly changes (auditory, visual, tactile, and temperature stimuli vary tremendously in the course of a routine day). Before the shock of social living has subsided (for some of us it never really subsides much at all!) the infant will encounter the transition from an exclusively horizontal to a partially vertical creature. This remarkable achievement, made by few other animals, requires fundamental adjustments in social as well as physical development. Shortly before his second birthday our unfolding child will encounter another major change in life style — he begins to speak. Each of these changes is of serious consequence and requires adaptability on the part of the child; for the normal child each of these transitions eventually will be made, although for some it will entail seemingly endless tribulations. The human infant is a strong, durable specimen — he has to be merely to survive birth — and despite his inability to fend for himself during the early years, he is surprisingly resilient and sturdy. If he is fortunate enough to be born into a protective and providing environment, only a major obstacle such as illness or accident will prevent his growing strong and straight. Thus, birth shock is the infant's introduction to a world which will continue to present additional shocks. It is the price of admission into the human milieu.

Appearance of the newborn

The newborn human is an incredibly complex, though inefficient, creature. His 270-day uterine internship has primed him for extra-uterine survival with admirable precision and mystic-like anticipation. At birth all vital organs are formed, functional, and operating with refined organismic harmony, just as they have been since several months before birth. As a biological creation the newborn is a genuine masterpiece. As a work of visual art, however, he is a disaster. "Beautiful" is a word reserved exclusively for parents (usually mothers) and grandparents when describing the newborn human baby. Fortunately for the aesthetic environment in general, and our species in particular, the infant becomes more beautiful with the passage of time.

How the mother can perceive the newborn as beautiful is one of nature's unsolved mysteries. The infant head, elongated by the birth process, takes up one-fourth to one-third of the total body length and rests precariously on a scrawny neck which provides minimal support and no direction. Usually he weighs between seven and eight pounds, though this commonly varies a pound and a half in either direction. The head is partially covered by thin, finely-textured hair which eventually evolves a "monk spot" on the back. On the front side are two greyish-coloured eyes which when not hidden by squinted lids, the wrinkles of which spread diagonally to the cheek bones, are wandering randomly because of their temporary inability to fixate. These multidirectional eyes are separated by a ski-run nose frequently scathed by scratch marks from unclipped fingernails. One of the first chores of the attending nurse is to clip the nails before they do further damage. The mouth will vacillate unpredictably, depending on the position of the jaw and the intensity of sucking action, and always seems to have a tongue protruding from it. The infant's inability to smile during the first few days of life is made easier to accept once one has witnessed his vacuous toothless grin. The chin is insignificant and the forehead slanted, though given some relief by sparse eyebrows. The ears are quite innocent ornaments but during the first hours of life do not work because they are filled with amniotic fluid which, itself, is not the most pleasant of substances.

Aesthetic quality does not significantly improve as one moves downward. The chest is overshadowed by an extended potbelly, a sort of precursor of the "beer-paunch" found in adult males, connected to a meager set of shoulders the width of which frequently is not much greater than the widest part of the head. Located directly on the centre of the stomach is the stub of the umbilical cord which will remain about fourteen days before falling off to leave a scar affectionately labeled "belly button". Affixed to the shoulders are arms perpetually folded upwards, with clenched fists that always seem to be nearer the clavicle than the waist. The fingers cannot be voluntarily controlled and it will be months before the thumb has any value whatsoever. The genitals are harboured unprotectively between two bowed legs to which feet are appendaged so that the soles face each other and can easily be tucked under the buttocks. Because the kidneys of the newborn cannot concentrate urine well the entire area is liberally sprinkled as often as thirty times per day; however, as if deciding that those who care for the newborn should have some consideration, Mother Nature has kindly designed that neonatal urine be comparatively odourless. The entire body is encased in marginally transparent skin which issues blotchy colour configurations, and strawberry-coloured pressure markings; it is frequently dry or flaky, and always sufficiently loose that folds may appear anywhere. During the first days after birth the skin of all normal infants is the same colour — a light, whitish-red. In general, the newborn is a rather disconcerting sight to everyone except the adoring mother, the proud father, and a few other assorted types who consider his assemblage of disproportionate limbs and partly functioning parts to be beautiful — or at least "natural".

All in all, the human newborn is by no means a striking piece of visual art. But then again it is not necessary that he should be. He is life. He is man. He is potential. And as such he does not need to be further validated by anything else — including beauty.

The appearance of the newborn is crucial to his understanding. His physical appearance reflects his physical condition *and* his physical potential. Eyes which do not fixate precisely will obviously impose restrictions upon his visual world; bowed legs with turned under feet impede locomotion; a large, bulky head (even though it houses a cortex which soon will be the most advanced in the animal kingdom) demands time to mature and develop. The human infant, by merit of his physical structure, is the least adapted to survival of all animal offspring; he learns at a slower rate (initially) than any other animal; he locomotes less adeptly than any other species and learns from experience less readily. Infant survival is completely dependent upon the good will of older humans. For each of these reasons the appearance of the infant has special importance and requires special understanding. And for each of these reasons his appearance, unattractive as it may be, embodies unique meaning, purpose, and possibility.

As the shock of birth subsides and as he gathers greater strength and confidence in his new environment, the neonate will change in appearance. Gradually, his limbs achieve self-control and his senses become more acute allowing him to explore his world. Soon he will assume his own unmistakable individuality and in no time can be shown off to relatives and neighbours with assurance that his beauty will be cheerfully acknowledged.

Reflexes and responses of the newborn

The human newborn, helpless and fragile though he may be, comes into the world with several general reflexes and responses. These reflexes tend to be global rather than specific and, as a rule, disappear during the first year of life, causing some observers to question their importance for survival. Whether required for survival or not, this cluster of genetically-determined reflexes are the newborn's link with an evolutional past, as well as the initial behaviour upon which he will build his future. The newborn is essentially a *reactive* organism who initiates almost no goal-directed behaviour; rather, he responds to stimuli which impinge upon him. Without a repertoire of reflexes infant behaviour would be (at least for the first few weeks of life) much more restricted and much less predictable. There is no other stage of the post-birth growth cycle when the human is so restricted to reactive and reflexive behaviour as during the first week after birth.

Like the rest of us, infants must have food. Usually it comes from the mother's breast or a bottle, but in either case the infant must do his share of work if he is to eat. When cradling the child in a breast-feeding position the mother's nipple may graze the newborn's cheek; on receiving this stimulus he will reflexively turn *toward* the source of stimulation, enabling him to locate the nipple and nourishment. This elementary behaviour pattern is known as the *rooting reflex,* and can be elicited in any normal newborn by a tactile stimulus to the cheek. Once the nipple has been reached the infant's job has just begun because he must also suck if he is to receive nourishment. This requirement does not take the newborn by surprise; in fact he demonstrates some proficiency at this task having practised it during the last months of fetal development. The human baby tends to suck in short bursts, rest up for a few seconds, then continue. Because he is not capable of executing two different kinds of activities simultaneously the newborn will usually shut his eyes while sucking; by three months of age, however, this restrictive division of labour is outgrown, permitting visual exploration during feeding hours. Although the *sucking reflex* is strong enough to allow the newborn to secure the nourishment necessary for growth, some infants can be deliberate about it, causing distress to an impatient mother. At first the newborn is rather inefficient at feeding but, as in most other things, he improves with practice. Sucking behaviour is much more complex than one might suspect, involving rather precise coordination of breathing, sucking, and swallowing; it should be noted that quite discomforting consequences accrue when this sequence is not properly adhered to. Interestingly, the sucking reflex can be elicited by a wide variety of stimuli, such as a loud noise or stroking of the arm, suggesting that it has utility other than to secure food. The infant controls food intake by accelerating or slowing down the pace of sucking, stopping once in a while to rest, and stopping altogether when full. Even though the sucking reflex is part of the infant's genetic equipment it is also, to a great extent, regulated by the total environmental (internal as well as external) situation of the infant. As the infant matures he acquires greater voluntary control of his sucking behaviour until it completely leaves the realm of reflex and falls into the larger category of voluntary behaviour.

When an infant turns his head he triggers a flexion reaction on the opposite side of his body, so that when he is lying on his back, facing right, the left side of his body will show a characteristic flexing of the left arm and left leg, resulting in a pose not unlike certain "cheese-cake" poses found in men's magazines. This *tonic neck reflex* is seen in premature babies, and is also observed during the first week of life in about 60 percent of all normal infants. Like several other infant reflexes, if it persists too long it may indicate brain damage or malfunction.

When a loud noise, or any other sudden strong stimulus, interrupts the tranquility of the newborn he will manifest a *startle reflex*. This consists of extending the arms and legs simultaneously outward and suddenly retracting them, and is usually accompanied by crying shouts of disapproval. To the naive observer the startle reflex appears to be nothing more than chaotic thrashing of limbs. Investigation of this reflex by means of slow motion films, however, reveals a rhythmic symmetry. The arms invariably follow a narrow pattern with little variation, and the same is true for the legs. This reflex can be induced by such varied stimuli as loud noises, bright light flashes, sudden exposure to a cold object, or the prick of a misguided safety pin. After recuperating from the startle response, the very young infant may return to the more customary tonic neck position. The startle reflex has been observed during the third month of fetal development and seems to be universally present during the first three months after birth, but if it continues after the ninth month it may suggest retardation or some other organically-based deficiency.

Several other reflexes are worthy of mention. The *grasping reflex* permits the baby to hold tightly to anything placed in its palm, sometimes with sufficient strength to support his own weight. Even though in my own experience with children I have never seen an infant do this, it is widely reported in the literature. This reflex usually disappears before the first birthday. Shortly before the acquisition of voluntary eye movement the infant displays what Cratty (1970) calls *doll-eye* movements. When the infant's head is tilted forward his eyes will turn upward, but when the head is tipped backward the eyes roll downward. This is observed most commonly in premature infants, and only during the first few days of life in normal infants, because the ability to fixate both eyes usually takes place within seventy-two hours after birth. The *pupillary reflex* begins to operate within two or three hours after birth. Its existence permits the contraction of the pupil when exposed to strong light and its dilation in weak light, thus serving a protective as well as adaptive function. This reflex has a much greater longevity than others, lasting through adulthood. A reflex with a much less clearly understood function is the *Babinski reflex,* which causes the infant to fan his toes up and outward when the sole of the foot is stimulated. Once this reflex is lost the human responds to stroking of the sole of the foot with a downward curl of the toes. The only exception occurs among brain-damaged individuals.

Many infants manifest a *walking reflex* if held upright with their feet lightly touching the floor. As its name suggests, this reflex triggers activity which resembles walking. Some infants also display what overly-eager parents (and sometimes physical education enthusiasts) interpret as a *swimming reflex.* These rhythmic movements, strikingly similar to those employed by a swimmer, have been filmed in infants eleven days old. These reflexive arm and leg movements disappear approximately five or six months after birth, but even when at full strength could never permit the infant to swim. Swimming requires conscious control of breathing as well as the ability to keep the head above water, neither of which has been mastered by the young infant. Therefore, even though termed "swimming reflex" it results in swimming no more than the "walking reflex" results in walking.

Although it is not precisely understood why infant reflexes disappear during the first year of life, their gradual extinction is probably due to the onset of higher cortical activity as well as the activation of cortical inhibition centres sometime near the eighth week after birth. Some observers are of the impression that human reflexes are little more than behavioural remnants of man's evolutional past, a carryover from an older phylogenetic ancestor. No matter how they are understood, reflexes are a central reality in the day-to-day life of the newborn, and also provide the trained observer with information concerning the developmental maturity and health of the infant. Frequently when reflexes are uneven in strength, when they are stronger on one side of the body than another, or when nonexistent, good reason exists to suspect some sort of neurological dysfunction in the baby. Nothing is known for certain about how the infant would learn to grasp, reach, feed, look, or avoid pain without the rudimentary beginnings which his reflexes provide. During the first days, even weeks, the infant is a prisoner of reflexes which each day become less powerful, and soon he will burst free of their restrictions and enter the world of self-initiated behaviour. In preface to this, however, other changes and further growth must transpire. Nature is deliberate in granting permission to move developmentally upward, for if the child is not *completely* ready for growth he may backslide and end up less advanced than if he had awaited further maturational readiness.

Behaviour of the newborn

To the uninitiated observer infant behaviour during the first few weeks of life appears singularly uninteresting; however, for the individual schooled in the phenomenon of early infancy there is an abundance of activity to observe, most of which is preparing the infant for growth into a more sophisticated world. One reason for the apparent monotony of infant behaviour is that his most essential skills are internal rather than external and require some prior knowledge to be properly understood.

The greatest restriction upon infant behaviour is that he spends from twenty-two hours (during the first few days of life) to eighteen hours per day in sleep. This unto itself will dampen the enthusiasm of most students of infant behaviour. However, a good deal is transpiring during sleep. The body musculature, the skeleton, the sensory modalities, and the central organs all develop during sleep hours. During sleep the infant periodically will manifest the startle reflex, suck a good deal, and flail his arms about if lying in a position where this is possible. Some doctors recommend that the infant become accustomed to sleeping in a rather noisy environment to help him adjust to distraction as well as to learn to perceive selectively certain aspects of the environment. By toddlerhood, children who have learned to sleep in the midst of noise amaze adults with their capacity to sleep in the noisiest conceivable surroundings. Children who fail to acquire this capacity often become light sleepers and as a result do not sleep as deeply or restfully as their growing bodies require.

The newborn feeds proficiently although now and then he will refuse a regular feeding. Normal infants have an efficient digestive system as well as an industrious alimentary tract. Solids may be eaten for the first time near the second week, but opinion differs among doctors, mothers, and infants as to exactly when this practice can effectively begin.

The infant possesses only meager control over his limbs. He is rarely able to raise his head before the third week, and the thrill of doing so is tempered by its sudden collapse after a few brief seconds. The infant objects to this sudden shock, but in keeping with the tradition of infancy recuperates instantly. Many mothers report that their infants begin to play energetically during the second and third week, a welcome addition to his otherwise bleak routine. Fathers happily discover that the three-week baby may be ticklish. The principle of cephalocaudal development insures that the infant is first ticklish near the head (usually the neck), then progressively downward, finally reaching the toes.

The infant cannot reach effectively for objects until about ten weeks of age; moreover, those reared in barren, impoverished environments may not reach for objects until twenty weeks. His inability to reach out with precision does not prevent his loud objections when held or dressed in such a manner that limb movement is restricted. Apparently this aversion to being swaddled too tightly can be overcome, however, as certain peoples such as the Hopi Indians bundle their infants very tightly allowing virtually no limb movement, but the baby adjusts to this confinement in a short time.

The acknowledged trademark of the infant is his ability to cry prodigiously. He always cries when hungry, but frequently it is difficult to determine more exact reasons for discontent. Pediatricians report that normal infants may cry full tilt for ten-twenty minutes under normal circumstances without serious side effects, even though his angry face may turn beet red. However, cause for serious concern arises when a twelve-month old baby cries for ten-twenty minutes with the sustained intensity characteristic of the two-week infant. This is due in large measure to the fact that infant behaviour is intense and total. He has no disposition for compromise: when hungry, he is intensely hungry; when he wants a change of laundry, he wants it *now* and does not tolerate tardiness in correcting this situation. As the child matures he acquires the ability to momentarily postpone desires; this is of little comfort, however, to the young infant's caretaker. During the second month crying may stop when mother comes into view (indicating the child already associates mother with comfort and pleasure), or when he is picked up and fondled. The child compensates for the agony his crying causes parents by giving them a smile sometime around the third week. Though first smiles are the result of reflex and have no social significance to the infant, they are of tremendous importance to the parents. By six weeks it is common for a jibbering father to elicit genuine social smiles, perhaps even a gasping giggle, from his offspring. At this age, an unknown instinct compels parents to buy cameras and take reels of film which are spontaneously shown without warning to blood relatives and innocent visitors.

The *palmar reflex* permits the infant to grasp objects placed in his palm, but there is considerable difference of opinion as to what causes infants to cling firmly and emotionally when picked up and held. Bowlby, one of the most vociferous advocates of the *clinging reflex,* claims that man inherits this trait from distant evolutional cousins. Holding or rocking has comforting powers for the infant far beyond that which can be attributed to learning, and his friendly acceptance of someone to embrace has intrigued poets as well as pediatricians since the dawn of time. Infants do differ considerably, however, in their ability to be soothed, and it is generally observed that infants easily soothed by one method also tend to respond quickly to other methods of soothing. On the other hand, babies who excite easily under a wide variety of stimuli may be considerably less susceptible to soothing. From birth some babies are more excitable than others, just as some are more aware and active than others. Individual differences among newborns are very pronounced and influence their physical, mental, social, and emotional development. In no way can human behaviour be attributed solely to effects of environment. From the first days of infancy each person has his own unique dispositions and characteristic ways of reacting to the environment which *determine in large measure the impact the environment will have on the child.* The human being is never merely a passive receptor of environmental action. Environmental stimuli must filter through the child's unique personality and in doing so are modified.

The infant can be comforted by any adult during the first few weeks in as much as he has virtually no memory and cannot distinguish one human from another (a further disappointment for unknowledge-able parents).

The infant, who begins to differentiate human voices from other auditory stimuli at about the third week, may respond to the call of his name by the sixth week. He evidences further social learning when he stops crying at the *sound* of mother's approaching footsteps. This usually occurs before the eighth week and demonstrates the child has associated the comfort provided by mother with the sounds she makes when approaching. Pavlovian psychologists understand this behaviour to be an example of classical conditioning (associating a neutral stimulus with a naturally-rewarding stimulus); Skinnerian psychologists consider it an example of instrumental conditioning (associating a cue with a reinforcer); mothers understand it as proof of the child's affection for them.

At three weeks the infant may concentrate on a mobile for as long as twenty minutes without distraction. Of equal importance, he is capable of *not* paying attention to environmental stimuli which do not directly influence him. This, of course, takes practice. Let me provide an example of how the infant avoids certain environmental stimuli. When a feeding infant is suddenly distracted by a novel sound he will stop feeding, look around, pause from his routine for a few seconds, then resume eating. If the sound occurs again he will follow the same procedure with less energy and enthusiasm. Eventually, if the sound has no direct relationship to his immediate needs, he will stop responding to it altogether. This process is called *habituation* and the infant is rather good at it considering his limited equipment. Habituation, important though it is for development or perceptual acuity, is only one part of the infant's intellectual repertoire. Here, Burton White, a leading authority on human infancy, summarizes other characteristics of the infant's general intellectual capacities:

> In the area of intellectual or pre-intellectual function, two facts seem clear. Infants less than six weeks old are not easily conditioned, and their primitive behaviour repertoire consists of a series of reflex-like functions which appear to operate independently of each other. . . . It is not until the end of the infant's second month of life that researchers routinely report consistent success is establishing conditioned responses and more than very short-lived learning effects. (1971, p. 84)

All in all, the infant is not spectacular at learning. But without doubt he is better at learning than are psychologists in explaining how he goes about it!

The skills and habits of the infant are central to his proper development. As he prepares to meet new and progressively more advanced challenges with each developmental breakthrough, he cannot be understood properly except in terms of what he has been and what he is moving toward. Jerome Kagan suggests that the growth from infant helplessness involves the acquisition of *four basic abilities,* each of which facilitates the capacity to absorb human culture more completely. (1) The infant gradually acquires the ability to voluntarily control his behaviour. This is critical to human behaviour and "requires the anticipation of an outcome, the choice of a means to achieve it, and the ability to start and sustain a chosen series of acts". (2) The infant learns to control his attention so it can be directed toward problem solving rather than being determined by external stimuli. (3) He learns to execute different activities at the same time. (4) Finally, he learns to "establish reciprocal codes that pave the way for speech and other forms of human exchange" (Kagan, 1970). Thus the skills required to survive in human culture are sown and nourished, but not cultivated, during the critical six weeks following birth.

The infant is growing, and during the next few months he will exhibit startling growth spurts and encounter critical developmental periods. His limited repertoire of behaviour now is merely the calm before the storm, and many a bedraggled mother will soon look back with nostalgia on the day when the infant slept twenty hours and served as a plaything the other four.

The world as experienced by the newborn

Although there are many physical components to human *experience* it is essentially a subjective reality which does not readily lend itself to purely objective study. When investigating the experience of an adult, or a child who is old enough to speak, the psychologist can be told what a certain experience feels like or what kind of sensation accompanies it. We have no such good fortune in the study of the newborn's experience of the world. We must infer from his behaviour and from the efficiency of his sensory equipment what he feels or experiences. This is no easy task because infants vary considerably in their activity level, their ways of responding to the environment, their degree of excitability and soothability, as well as their ability to tolerate stress or show pleasure. The attempt to understand early experience is made more complex by our inability to know what meaning, if any, the infant attaches to his perceptions. Another complication associated with knowing how the world "feels" to the infant stems from the fact that parental behaviour influences infant reactions to a considerable degree. Parental nervousness or irritability frequently exerts an adverse effect on infant behaviour. Parents sometimes attribute to the infant states of mind which, in all probability, he is incapable of experiencing, such as envy, sorrow, or remorse. For each of these reasons an exact understanding of infant experience will never be achieved. However, we can list several ways to enrich our knowledge of this topic, most notably by: (a) understanding the sensory equipment of the infant; (b) recognizing his emotions; and (c) determining his likes and dislikes. We will take a brief look at each of these areas to see what can be surmised in their regard, and by doing so perhaps gain greater understanding of how the newborn human experiences the world. (It is interesting, even puzzling to some people, that developmental psychologists almost never concern themselves with the world as experienced by the *fetus*!)

None of the senses operate during the first six weeks of life with the efficiency they later acquire. The sense modality we know the most about is vision. Although born with biologically complete visual apparatus, the infant's eyes are by no means in full working order, taking a day or more for sufficient muscle development to insure that they can be moved in coordinated fashion. Initially, the infant has only pupillary reaction to various intensities of light, but he soon acquires the ability to fixate, focus, and track, and like all skills, these behaviours require practice and time. For reasons clearly understood to no one, infants show an early preference for patterned rather than plain colours, and also demonstrate greater interest in objects which resemble a human face than random environmental objects. Researching infant vision is restricted by the fact that infants are nearsighted, highly distractable, short tempered, limited in their attention span, and indifferent to the advancement of pediatric knowledge.

Babies show response to their own hands as well as to the faces of others within a few weeks. By eight weeks the child is playing actively with his hands and diligently observing his own activity. By ten weeks he may gaze about his room (as long as it does not involve rotating his head more than 180 degrees) rapidly scanning one object after another. He will actively investigate things which come into close view, and may show frustration at not being able to coordinate the rest of his body to acquire the various tempting tidbits from the surrounding area.

At two weeks of age he displays a noticeable reaction to sound emanating from the radio or television. Hearing becomes coordinated with vision shortly after birth and is indicated by turning the eyes toward an auditory stimulus. Some mothers affirm that their infants respond to the call of their names during the first month, but psychologists long ago learned to be cautious about assessing infant ability exclusively on parental information. Loud, crisp sounds invariably elicit a startle reflex in the infant, which should not come as a surprise to anyone who has experienced a sudden fright recently. From the earliest days of life a calm, rhythmic chant exerts a soothing effect on the child although the reason for this is no more clearly understood than its comparable effect on adults. It has been recently reported that the magnified sound of the heart beat has special comforting effects on the young infant, but this finding requires further investigation before its implications are understood.

Little is known about smell and taste during the first six weeks chiefly because these are highly subjective experiences. Mothers and pediatricians agree that infants show preference for sweet substances and an aversion to solutions which are excessively salty, bitter, or sour. When solids are first eaten certain vegetables are preferred by some infants even though they have had no previous experience with them. Although children can be taught to eat almost anything, all foods initially are not equally pleasant to them. Infants quickly acquire idiosyncrasies with regard to what they will eat, a habit which reaches its zenith between the second and third year of life and causes inflexible parents tremendous consternation. Fortunately, taste is somewhat linked with age and just when one thinks the child will never eat potatoes he suddenly develops a craving for them.

Infants are relatively insensitive to certain kinds of pain, probably as a result of their incompletely developed brain centres. But this could be related to the recuperation period following birth during which the system recovers from birth shock. Pain occurs for the infant only in the event of a malfunction within his system or when he is disturbed by an outside agent. Pain indicates something is wrong, and there is never doubt as to when it is being experienced as it is accompanied by loud, total, and relentless crying which does not stop, except for periods of rest, until the pain disappears. Because all crying does not indicate pain, parents must endure hours of anguish before they can distinguish a cry which comes from distress from one which is little more than a plea for attention. The pediatric consensus is that crying during the first eight weeks reflects some sort of infant distress, but later it assumes a variety of other meanings, including lonesomeness, boredom, or the desire to be played with.

If our knowledge of sensory functioning during the first weeks of life is limited so also is our knowledge of *infant emotional experience.* During the 1920s most experts believed that infants were born with three general emotions: fear, anger, and love, and that these emotions are elicited very early in life. This viewpoint was based on research conducted at Johns Hopkins University Hospital by the famous American behaviourist, J. B. Watson. Watson believed an impartial observer, properly trained, could detect which emotion an infant was experiencing. All adult emotions, such as sorrow, grief, hatred, and elation, were thought by Watson to derive from the original three inherited emotions by a process of learning and conditioning. Subsequent research has not treated Watson's concepts kindly. Studies in the recognition of infant emotions reveal that adults are significantly influenced by their knowledge of the child's environment when they determine what emotion he is experiencing. If adults know the infant was spanked recently they interpret his emotion as anger. Many observers in the experiments on infant emotion failed to distinguish emotion from pain or hunger reactions. Still others, when shown photographs of infants would attribute different emotions to the same picture on different days. For the most part there is little current acceptance of Watson's interpretation of infant emotion. The idea most widely subscribed to today claims that during the first few weeks of life there are no specific emotions, only generalized states of excitement from which specific emotions later develop. The infant's state of excitement is thought to be characterized by general moods of pleasantness or unpleasantness, withdrawal or approach, and sometimes distress (although this could be defined as a form of unpleasantness).

Before the third month definite signals of delight and enjoyment come from the infant as well as indications of fear, relief, and anger, although it must be noted that considerable disagreement exists as to when these signals are being manifested. Before their second birthday most children experience the spectrum of adult emotions including elation, sorrow, joy, jealousy, fear, disgust, love, distress, affection.

Philosophers have long speculated whether man has *predispositions* toward certain emotions, that is, if he is predisposed to learn one emotion more readily than others. Some theorists suggest that man is naturally predisposed toward love and affection, whereas others believe man to be naturally inclined toward avarice and greed. Perhaps the most popular viewpoint is that man is born without predispositions and must learn emotions just as he learns language, customs, or numbers. Little specific information has been compiled regarding this issue which remains basically in the domain of the philosophers. If and when information of this type is confirmed, major repercussions will be felt in the field of child development.*

From this limited look at the world of the newborn we reach several tentative conclusions. The sensory world of the young infant is inconsistent, unrefined, and not synthesized as thoroughly as it will be

*For a thorough analysis of philosophical issues surrounding human nature, see J. J. Mitchell, *Human Nature: Theories, Conjectures and Descriptions,* Scarecrow Press, 1972.

in a few months. His perceptions are fuzzy and certainly less global than those of an older brother or sister. His limited ability to learn from experience, along with his short memory, make it impossible for him to experience the world with the continuity or sense of expectation known to adults. Emotionally the infant is restricted, probably being limited to pleasant and unpleasant stages of arousal. Specific emotions are fully experienced during toddlerhood but not much can be assumed with certainty about the emotional life of the infant. One is strongly tempted to conclude that the prime function of the first six weeks of life is to bolster the strength and durability of the infant so he may mature sufficiently to get about the business of being more human-like in his behaviour, thought, and experience.

The dawn of awareness: six weeks to four months

The fairly predictable and routine behaviour of the early infant undergoes a remarkable transition between six and sixteen weeks. He shows significant blossoming in almost all areas of development, especially physical, social, and sensory. This is the age when descriptive terms such as "cute" or "beautiful" become perfectly appropriate. For the most part the infant is completely recovered from birth shock and smoothly making the transition to post-natal existence — although growth is never perfectly smooth for a child no matter what his age. The period of life between six and sixteen weeks is called the dawn of awareness because the child is breaking away from the limited and restricted patterns of the first six weeks of life. He is increasingly aware of the outside world and his inner compulsion is to work his way into it, to become more competent with it, to become a part of it. The young child is becoming aware of things which before went unnoticed. His body is outgrowing its reflex-dominated simplicity and surges forward into a new dawning — a dawning of awareness.

During the second to fourth month the infant requires less sleep than during the first six weeks and the experience gained during waking hours significantly promotes more advanced development. During this period he discovers his hands and begins the manipulation activities which are so essential to acquiring voluntary control of the hands and visual-directed reaching. Neither of these activities occur with much precision until late in the first year of life, but essential beginnings are established during this period.

The thumb is still several months away from being a valuable asset although it is developing grasping value. No real indication of *handedness* appears at this age although if one predicts the child will be right-handed he will be correct about 90 percent of the time. Control of hands is achieved before control of the feet, in keeping with the cephalocaudal growth gradient. Some developmental psychologists believe that long legs at this age indicate greater maturity, but this is difficult to assess with much certainty. One thing certain, however, is that between the second and fourth month the infant becomes individualized in physical appearance, temperament, and characteristic reactions to the outside world. In other words, the nondistinct baby is rapidly becoming a highly distinct person. Some of the general traits displayed at this age, such as shortness of temper, remain not only through childhood but adulthood as well. Characteristics such as temperament and disposition already have numerous idiosyncrasies associated with them, and it is not unusual for the parents to remember this as the age when the baby began to display those typical actions which become his unique trademark, and by which he can be readily identified.

Of greatest concern to most humans, including developmental psychologists, is the tremendous social growth of the baby during this period. Smiling, as well as laughing, is common and games such as peek-a-boo bring boundless joy. Four-month-olds sometimes "talk back" to a friendly voice and as a result one frequently hears rather unusual conversations in his household. Mothers become gifted at monologues. The average three-month-old greets visitors with a pleasant gurgle or a cordial grin — he is still several months away from fear of strangers. To the enjoyment of nearly everyone, the dawn of awareness is a period when the infant is highly entertainable. He laughs at funny faces, incongruous sounds, as well as at bizarre behaviour such as waving one's fingers with the thumbs inserted in the ears. He holds his head up for sustained lengths of time, following intently the social action taking place in his environment. He may also sit with support. By all standards he is becoming a genuinely social creature. He is gradually learning how his behaviour influences the behaviour of others around him — a discovery he exploits to the full in late toddlerhood. Mothers complain their baby is getting spoiled because he has learned that crying is the most effective means of getting what he wants. Hands have now outgrown the restrictions imposed on them by the palmer reflex, and the tonic neck reflex has been outlived, allowing increased freedom of motion. The infant has begun the lifelong process of phasing from one developmental level to another.

During this crucial growth spurt the infant's ability to concentrate on all parts of his environment, including himself, is greatly facilitated by increased visual acuity. He can focus rather well on moving objects as long as they are fairly close; visual convergence also is achieved; he blinks when an object too closely approaches his eyes. It can be said in fairness that increased visual development is a major factor in the infant's increased social and environmental awareness, but much greater information about the relationship between visual and social development could be obtained by more rigorous study of development among blind infants.

Shortly before the fifth month some infants go on a three meal per day diet, although many perfectly healthy infants do not do so until nine or ten months. This is a matter for the mother and child to work out together, although sometimes the advice of a sensitive pediatrician is required, especially when digestive or elimination problems occur as a result of changing the dietary schedule.

For the majority of infants the *social* environment has not begun to play the crucial role it will shortly assume. Most growth between six and sixteen weeks is the result of maturational unfolding which automatically occurs as long as minimal social and biological requirements are provided. This is not to say the environment is unimportant. Obviously this would be foolish. What is meant is that for most infants the environment into which they are born minimally influences the abilities and skills they possess at the age of four months. Certain exceptions to this generalization include understimulating environments where virtually no sensory or tactile stimulation is provided (as many child care institutions used to be), or environments which fail to provide ingredients required for proper maturation such as calcium or vitamin C.

It is encouraging to note the incredible rapidity with which most babies recuperate from physical and psychological trauma.. Illness, though serious while running its course, is recovered from quickly. It is not unusual for a child to go from the peak of a minor illness, such as a cold with fever, to normal behaviour within sixteen hours. The child recovers almost instantly from such minor incidents as a fall, even if bumps or bruises emerge; he recuperates immediately from most emotional hassles during which his feelings are hurt; spankings are immediately forgotten as long as the child's sense of integrity or belonging have not been temporarily shattered.

Human growth is inclined to be self-stabilizing. The organism tends to return to its normal *rate* of growth after it has passed through an accelerated growth such as the one experienced between six and sixteen weeks, or after a retarded growth period associated with illness or malnutrition. Because of this tendency toward growth stabilization, rarely will a child continue to increase his skills as rapidly as during the ten-week interval between six and sixteen weeks. It is imperative to keep in mind that all infants do not mature at the same rate. Even identical twins, the most biologically similar of humans, show considerable dissimilarity in growth rate, intellectual functioning, and social development. We must caution ourselves against expecting a fellow human to live up to the expectations of charts, graphs, or developmental models. This, however, does not mean we should be unknowledgeable about the predictable trends in child growth.

The infant is now on the verge of encountering several new growth requirements. Soon he will begin to move himself, to reach with direction and precision, to form lasting emotional attachments to his parents, to establish habits unique only to him. He will acquire a more keenly developed memory and a host of new intellectual skills. He will achieve greater voluntary control of his body and move closer to becoming its captain rather than merely a "passenger" within it. All parts of his body are growing, maturing, and developing, some more rapidly than others to be sure, but everywhere one looks into the life of the four-month-old one sees the conspicuous indications of growth. The glory of achievements made between six and sixteen weeks, significant as they are, seem dim when compared with those yet to come. Despite the greatness of what lies ahead, however, none of it would be possible without the foundation established during his initial period of life.

At the age of four months the infant is ready for the growth breakthrough which signals his transition from an organism who responds only to those parts of the environment which "come" to him to one who reaches out to explore the world. This transition to an *environment-exploring* creature is perhaps the most significant social event in the life of the young child, and upon it intellectual and physical growth will greatly depend. Once the child begins to actively explore the environment he is a different person altogether. At first he merely adjusts to the environment. By the time he reaches toddlerhood, however, the environment, in many respects, will learn to adjust to him.

The great leap forward: four to twelve months

The period from six to sixteen weeks is referred to as the dawn of awareness to indicate that the young infant is coming out of his reflex-dominated style of life and moving into a greater awareness of body, environment, and self. This period of expanded *awareness* is followed by an equally significant period of expanded *action* which constitutes a great leap forward in the baby's growth. During the eight remaining months in the first year of life the infant will make definite headway in learning to think; he will become mobile as well as upright; he will begin to communicate orally (though not with words); and will develop impressive social skills. As these major growth achievements can be understood as intellectual, motor, and social, we shall investigate the last two-thirds of the first year of life by means of these general headings.

Intellectual development

Piaget claims intellectual development of normal children goes through six stages during the first eighteen months of life, five during the first year. These stages can be used as general guidelines to understand normal intellectual growth; however, we shall use them more loosely than does Piaget.

First stage (birth to one month)

As emphasized earlier in the chapter, this is the time when life is dominated by innate reflexes such as sucking and grasping. The infant's prime responsibility is to become more proficient in using reflexes and to recover from the physiological complications associated with birth shock.

Second stage (second through third month)

This stage is characterized by repetitive practice of simple acts, such as sucking or flexing of limbs, for no apparent ulterior purpose. It is practice for the sake of practice, and thought by some to enhance the formation of neural "pathways" to the brain centres. Insufficient physiological maturity prevents the child from acting purposively or from recognizing that his actions create consequences in the environment. The child has no awareness of himself as a person, or even as separate from other environmental objects, and does not know that his own behaviour effects change. He is oblivious, for the most part, of the outside world. By no means is he the intellectual equal of a chimpanzee of the same age.

Third stage (fourth through sixth month)

At this age behaviour becomes progressively more purposive; the child modifies his own behaviour in such a way as to repeat those responses which produce interesting or important results. He will bang his crib because of the sound it creates, or slap at a mobile to make it move. He acquires some recognition of the fact that events do not occur randomly. This stage, which marks the beginning of systematic involvement in specific parts of the environment for specific purposes, heralds the *beginning* of the child's immature understanding of *causality*. He is forming a hazy connection between cause and effect.

Fourth stage (seventh through tenth month)

The child now solves simple problems by using the skills he has already developed. He pulls himself up in order to acquire something out of sitting reach; he removes a barrier to get at an object. His mind is sufficiently developed that he does not become distracted by every new environmental stimuli. During this stage he *begins* to recognize that objects have permanence unto themselves (referred to as *Object Permanence*), an insight which takes several months to completely evolve. Previously he has functioned on the "out of sight, out of existence" principle. At five months it is difficult to frustrate a child by hiding a desired object because once it is out of sight it ceases to exist for the baby; his world is restricted to what is visible. Undoubtedly this is related to poor memory development, but understanding that objects have their own permanence is not founded solely on memory development. When ten months old, object permanence is marginally developed and the child may actively pursue an object he has seen hidden under a blanket, or placed behind a barrier. The child exhibits full awareness of object permanence when he actively searches for an object which he cannot see but has good reason for assuming is in one particular place. A universal children's game aptly demonstrates this principle. The adult takes a ping-pong ball (or some such object) between his thumb and index finger, in plain view of the intrigued child, then dramatically inserts the ball into his mouth and, with difficulty, "swallows" it. The child will look into his mouth — that is where the ball should be. He will even look again and, when the adult unobtrusively retrieves the ball from his palm, the child will innocently play the game again not realizing he has been lured into a contest beyond his developmental level. Time works against our magician friend, however, and the next time he visits, the child may not be restricted to such narrow patterns of cognition. The significance of the child's discovery of object permanence is that he now recognizes that objects do not lose their existence merely because they are out of sight. The child is coming to understand that physical objects exist independently of being perceived. He therefore will search for an object on the supposition that the object actually exists despite the fact that its specific whereabouts is unknown. Without this cognitive breakthrough the child would be incapable of the sophisticated exploration necessary during toddlerhood.

Speech development is beginning to manifest itself with the formation of words, and at this age we observe infants who have three or four sounds in their oral repertoire which pass for words, especially if they have cooperative and imaginative parents.

Fifth stage (eleven to eighteen months)

The child now begins to actively experiment with his environment, employing trial-and-error experimentation to accomplish specific goals.

He does not stop when thwarted in his first attempt at solving a problem, preferring instead to devise *new* solutions. In this regard he has acquired a talent possessed by few other animals. He begins to gauge the appropriateness of his behaviour by observing its consequences. Although this may not seem important, it heralds a significant breakthrough in the cognitive abilities of the child.

The child demonstrates an understanding of social continuity as well as accepted protocol at this stage of intellectual development when he laughs at incongruities. This reflects at least two general principles: (1) the child has sufficient awareness of the environment to notice when something has gone awry; and (2) the child is beginning to schematize categories (of which humour is one) for reacting to events which are out of the ordinary. It is interesting to note that toddlers (twelve to thirty-six months) initially react to physical slapstick with fear; later, after they have learned means of incorporating it into their understanding of social behaviour, they appreciate it as humour.

Sixth stage (eighteen months on)

The child learns to think about the probable consequences of actions *before they occur.* We shall concentrate further on this stage of intellectual development in the next chapter.

We may now surmise that the first year of life is characterized by the following stages of intellectual growth:

1. reflex behaviour;
2. practice of reflexes, arm movements, and eye movements;
3. repeating behaviour which produces important results;
4. use of skills to solve simple problems or accomplish simple goals;
5. trial-and-error experimentation.

Speech

Speech development is less dramatic than intellectual development during the first year of life chiefly because, by adult standards, there is so little accomplishment. Close inspection reveals that the infant undergoes significant changes in "speech" during the first year but is still far from being word-oriented. At the end of the first year, only the very unusual child uses more than one or two understandable words with purpose. The median age at which children use their first word is about thirteen months, but several additional months of development are required before they string together a two-word message. Toddlerhood brings spectacular speech growth which we shall attend to in more depth when we study this period of life. Here we shall make only a brief overview of speech during the first twelve months.

Earliest vocalizations are random and have little communication value, with vowel sounds the most common. The year-old child has about nineteen *phonemes* (the most basic elements in a language system) in his limited repertoire, but it is three times the number he had at two months. The newborn has no capacity for making sounds which correspond with the letters p, b, m, w, v, t, or n, but learns them during the first year. It is unclear precisely how this learning takes place, even though it is generally understood that children of all cultures go through approximately the same *sequence* of speech development. Babbling occurs near the third month, followed in a few months by nonsense-like chatter which sometimes has intonation and inflection similar to adult speech. Although the child is doing a great deal of behavioural imitating between nine-twelve months, he is not ready to imitate word sounds. The child must await toddlerhood and the cortical maturity it brings before he can do much with words; but once words appear he never again will return to exclusively nonverbal communication.

During the first *two* years, speech usually progresses from random vocalizing of vowels to consonants, then from syllables to simple words, and finally two-word phrases.

Motor development

The most significant factor in motor development between the fourth and twelfth month is the total maturation which the body undergoes. Environment plays second fiddle to a maturation throughout the first year of life for normal infants because this period of life is radically influenced by the genetic code of our species. Maturation brings organismic changes which allow the infant to crawl, creep, and walk. Motor development during the first year of life is orderly and sequential but not totally predictable. A good deal of consistency is noted in the way *most* children learn to walk or to manipulate their fingers, but significant individual differences occur in both *rate* and *sequence* of development. Here we shall concentrate on normal trends of motor development during the first year of life.

Manual skills

At about sixteen weeks the infant's hands come together, signalling the first of several important developments in prehensile growth. If the child does not bring his hands together by the sixth month when grasping or reaching, concern about neurological dysfunction may be justified. At about six months the baby can hold his bottle with modest proficiency and at about this time he begins to drop one object in favour of another. Soon he transfers objects from one hand to another, showing neither preference nor *handedness*. Perhaps the most significant achievement between four and six months is *visually-directed* reaching. This facilitates the pursuit and exploration of one specific aspect of the environment, and as such is indispensable to localized investigation — the essential ingredient of *global* competence. At this age any object offered will be reached for and within a few seconds finds its way to the mouth. During the first year of life the mouth is one of the child's chief investigatory resources.

At about eight months finger-thumb opposition occurs, signalling another major triumph in prehensile development. At this age the index finger is employed as an exploratory prod, searching into openings, cracks and holes, nostrils, and ears; nothing escapes its probing thrusts. At forty weeks the child is reaching with even greater precision but still has little success intercepting moving objects, such as a rolling ball. At about forty-four weeks he may place one object after another into a box; he craves give-and-receive games, although he frequently gives the impression that he engages in games such as this as a form of motor skill practice rather than for the social interplay it affords. The child is obsessed with practicing incessantly every new skill — a trait retained throughout childhood.

At about the end of the twelfth month the ability to throw objects emerges — a significant event in the child's motor development as well as his social learning. At this age mothers begin to teach their child to restrict maturational inclinations. The child now understands the meaning of "no! no!" and even though throwing objects is a natural part of prehensile development this activity frequently brings opposition from mother. During feeding time throwing can be circumvented only by removing everything within reach of the child. The child's obsession with mechanical devices at this age prompts him to remove lids, unscrew caps, and unplug plugs. He derives a devious pleasure in taking apart things which he has no ability to reassemble; however, for the first time he may engage in the constructive activity of stacking one block upon another. Manual dexterity, still primitive and unrefined, is becoming increasingly sophisticated with each month. The child, however, is almost six *years* removed from efficient use of a pencil!

Locomotion skills

After the four-month-old lifts his head to visually inspect the environment, he embarks upon a crash developmental campaign which eventually allows him to walk amidst the environment rather than to be restricted to one small part of it. As is the case with manual skills, locomotion is dominated by maturation level, and occurs in a fairly predictable sequence. Again the concept should be emphasized that *all* infants do not go through *every* stage; sometimes they skip a stage altogether, but most infants progress toward locomotion via the same general sequence.

Most children learn to sit with support between the fifth and seventh month. Sitting, which is not a reflex behaviour, does not occur before the brain centres which regulate upper body muscles have matured sufficiently. This happens only after the child learns to coordinate upper body muscles with those in the lower trunk. Sitting is a major developmental achievement and with practice, usually no more than a few weeks, the child will sit alone for more than a minute, although several more weeks will pass before he can sit as long as he prefers. The first forms of horizontal locomotion, crawling, creeping, and hitching, usually begin between the ninth and twelfth month. The range of individual differences in these forms of transport reflects an important principle we shall observe increasingly throughout childhood: as children grow older the *normal* range of individual differences becomes greater. When *crawling,* the child drags his stomach along the floor while the arms and hands propel the body. *Creeping* occurs later, and entails elevating the abdomen and locomoting with all four limbs. *Hitching* is a hybrid of creeping and crawling whereby the child lies on his stomach and pushes himself forward with one foot while dragging the other. As one can imagine, hitching is great for going in circles. At ten months the child is basically a quadruped and not yet a biped. It should be noted that some infants do not creep or crawl, and seem content to forego these preliminaries until they are ready to walk; however, this is an exception to the rule.

When the child phases from crawling to walking, several interesting predicaments commonly occur. He sometimes maneuvers himself into positions from which he cannot escape, as when his head gets jammed into a corner with his shoulder helplessly pinned to the floor and his buttocks elevated above all other parts of his body. Usually he cannot seat himself when he has first learned to pull himself upright; he habitually crawls or climbs into situations that he cannot back out of because reverse locomotion is more complicated than forward movement and requires additional developmental maturity. Usually not until the eleventh month does creeping backwards down stairs or sliding feet first off a sofa occur. The crawling child can stand upright when held by his hands, but it will be a month or two before he achieves independent standing or walking. Though most children walk within a month of their first birthday, many fail to do so until sixteen months or later. Some experts claim that the age at which a child will begin to walk can be predicted by doubling the age at which the child first sits alone, or by adding 50 percent to the age at which he begins to creep (Shirley, 1931). Universal acceptance has not been accorded these formulae, however.

Most evidence indicates that extra practice does not significantly influence the normal child's ability to walk sooner than he would otherwise. Perhaps the most spectacular confirmation of the central role of maturation during the first year of life comes from studies conducted among the Hopi Indians. As part of their cultural tradition the newborn is tightly swaddled in blankets and bound to a cradleboard. This practice severely restricts all of the infant's body movements except those of the head. During the first three months of life the Hopi child is only momentarily unbound from the board, and not until the last half of the first year is much freedom of movement allowed. Despite this constraint Hopi children go through the same general walking sequence as do other children and they also begin to walk at about the same age as other children (Dennis, 1940). During recent years the practice of "cradleboarding" has been abandoned by some Hopi, making it possible to compare the onset of walking-age between those infants reared in the old tradition and those raised in the new. The evidence indicates that there is no significant difference in the ages at which these two groups of Hopi children walk. Research of this kind provides an example of "nonsignificant" findings which, in the study of human growth and development, are highly significant from a theoretical point of view. The fact that there is no significant difference in the ages at which these two groups of children walk lends support to the notion that confinement to a slab of wood for the better part of the first six months of life has little effect on the child's subsequent walking behaviour. An interesting corollary to this finding is Spitz' discovery that absence of mother-contact *during the first six months of life* does not lead to irreversible damage; however, if the deprivation continues through the last six months of the first year there is a strong chance the child will suffer harmful emotional effects (Spitz, 1965). In other words, the child is not as much influenced by environment during the first six months of life as he is during the second six months of life.

Walking before the average age does not indicate that the child has more than average intelligence *or* that his motor skills will continue to develop at an accelerated pace. Highly intelligent children do not begin to walk any sooner than normal children, although severely retarded children begin to walk considerably later than normal children (see Dennis, W., 1943 for further data). Blindness and deafness also adversely influence the onset of walking although the reasons are not completely understood.

The California Infant Scale of Motor Development lists the following skills as critical to normal child development between four and twelve months.

Test Items	Age Placement in Months
1. Begins thumb opposition	4.1
2. Sits with slight support	4.6
3. Turns from back to side	5.0
4. Partial thumb opposition	5.1
5. Sits alone momentarily	5.7
6. Pulls to sitting position	6.2
7. Rolls from back to stomach	7.0
8. Complete thumb opposition	7.6
9. Partial finger prehension	7.8
10. Sits alone with good coordination	8.5
11. Raises self to sitting position	9.4
12. Pulls to standing position	10.5
13. Stands up	10.6
14. Walks with help	11.6
15. Sits down	12.5
16. Stands alone	12.5

Social development

Social change during the first year of life is less under the direct control of maturation than either intellectual or motor development. Nevertheless, a good deal of commonality may be observed in the social patterns of all one-year-old children. As a rule, they love to be the centre of attention, and enjoy themselves thoroughly when in pleasant company. The one-year-old experiences fear, anger, sympathy, anxiety, and jealousy. He likes music, has a sense of humour, and is making commendable strides in acquiring independence and autonomy (Gesell, 1940, p. 28).

The most conspicuous difference between the four and twelve-month child is that the former is only marginally social whereas the latter is highly social. The four-month-old seems content to get along with minimal attention or interaction with other people as long as his biological needs are taken care of, as most of his energy is absorbed by the demands of a reflex-dominated body with little left over for social behaviour. The twelve-month child, on the other hand, will complain bitterly if deprived of human company for lengths of time; he may even show signs of fear if convinced there is no one nearby. His feelings can be hurt by a sharp verbal rebuttal or even an unusual facial grimace from a parent or guardian. Few things are enjoyed more than fondling, and a year-old will resort to almost any measure to be the centre of attention. His need for human contact comfort is significant, as is his need for assurance and play. He likes others, he needs others, he complains and suffers in their absence. There can be no doubt that by the end of the first year of life the human child is a distinctly social creature.

A major social change occurs around the sixth month (sometimes as early as the third month) when the child begins to distinguish strange from familiar faces. Initially he greets strangers with a blank, noncommittal stare, which gradually gives way to withdrawal and avoidance, and finally to a definite fear of strangers. Stranger anxiety becomes one of the paramount realities in the young child's social life, but in as much as its major implications are not reached until toddlerhood we shall only allude to it at this time.

During the last third of the first year of life the child begins to develop strong emotional attachments, usually to mother and father, but also governesses and full-time babysitters. Whether emotional attachments emerge because the child has an inborn need for affection, or if it is a consequence of being treated affectionately is a matter of theoretical dispute. It is not disputed, however, that after the first year of life affection becomes one of the most important human psychological needs. When emotional attachments are being formed infants suffer distress when separated from their loved ones. This distress, referred to as *separation anxiety,* also will receive further attention in the next chapter.

Social interaction is a two-way street for the one-year-old. His behaviour exerts significant impact on the environment (he can bring an entire household to attention merely by knocking over a lamp or by uttering a recognizable word). However, the outside environment directly influences him also, as when an older brother snatches a desired plaything, or when mother fails to provide food on schedule.

The most important people in the life of the one-year-old are parents; they are the agents most instrumental in development of basic trust and also are the means by which he negotiates all requirements beyond his control. Behaviour, moodiness, confidence, and assertiveness are influenced, though not determined, by parent reactions to the child. Some psychologists, including Freud, claim that events during the first year of life seriously influence the adult personality.

The one-year-old child loves to play and explore. Chasing and hiding games are universal favourites and all cultures have some variation of hide-and-seek and peek-a-boo. At twelve months the habit of repeating whatever is laughed at is developed, fostering a creative, though an inevitably boring, performer. The concept of ownership and property sprout during the first year and are manifested by the child's objection to having anyone else play with his special toy, or by struggling against someone else's desire to share a commodity. Children must be *taught* to share and it is a kind of learning which does not come easily. The word "selfish", as commonly used by adults, is descriptive of the one-year-old. Psychologists, however, prefer the term *egocentric* which denotes that the child's "world" is limited to his own personal needs, desires, and perceptions, and is only marginally influenced by their equivalent in others. The process of teaching a child about the rights and needs of others is a slow and tedious one. The one-year-old reminds us of the classic Hobbesian man, but to the consternation of those who believe man incurably selfish, the child loses much of his intrinsic selfishness in favour of altruistic sharing. Even though the child is basically selfish during the first years of life, many psychologists are of the impression that the child is psychologically and genetically predisposed toward sharing and cooperating. They maintain that the fundamental requirement of social interaction is *cooperation,* and that man is predisposed toward accepting group rules in the same way that herd animals place group needs above individual needs.

Near the end of the first year it is possible to scold a child merely by casting an appropriate scowl; however, this should not be abused lest the child infer that *he* rather than the behaviour he is engaged in is being disapproved of. This point deserves special amplification because of its implications for child-rearing. Very frequently the young child fails to draw a distinction between scolding (punishing) for inappropriate behaviour (the typical reason for punishment), and punishment reflecting parental rejection or hatred. The one-year-old shares with all children the need to know *why* he is being punished. If, in the child's mind, a specific behaviour does not account for the punishment he receives, he is apt to infer that it reflects parental hatred or rejection. As we shall observe throughout this book, feelings of rejection constitute a psychological burden which few children can bear without some impediment to their psychological and social growth.

One cannot arbitrarily distinguish motor, intellectual, and social developments from one another — they overlap too much. The child acts out his social needs by grasping, holding, jousting, crying, and playing — all motor activities. The child cannot distinguish a pleasant parental reaction from a disapproving one without intellectual maturity and the ability to benefit from experience. Every developmental category interacts and influences every other; to suggest otherwise leads to a counterfeit understanding of the growing child. In this section distinctions have been drawn between motor, intellectual, and social development, but the intent has been to point out the intricate and delicate manner in which they each mutually depend upon the other.

The formation of basic trust

During the first year of life the infant develops patterns of trust which significantly influence the remainder of childhood and perhaps even reach into the adolescent and adult years. *Basic trust* means the infant has come to a positive attitude toward himself and his social environment, and that he has garnered a sense of self-confidence which will enable him to cope adequately with challenges yet unencountered. The infant's sense of trust is most appreciably influenced by treatment he receives from his mother and other adults. The mother who is warm and comforting to her child, who nurtures him with consistency and care, who radiates affection and concern, and who attends to those things causing distress will contribute to the infant's formation of basic trust. On the other hand, the mother who unconsciously resents her child, who treats him with aloofness and coldness, who tends to share minimal time with him, and who makes him the brunt of her hostilities and anxieties may instil in him an intuitive suspicion that the world is tense, cold, unpredictable, and insecure. The extent to which the child develops a sense of trust, or mistrust, will determine the outlook he takes into toddlerhood, and perhaps even into adulthood. Case histories of many neurotic adults indicate the fundamental source of conflict was unresolved problems of infancy.

One is tempted to ask why a mother would behave in such a manner that her child would develop a basic attitude of mistrust toward himself and the world. Erik Erikson, whose work pioneered the concept of basic trust, suggests several factors. Motherhood is not always a welcome status. Many mothers resent the restriction imposed upon them by child care and frequently release this frustration onto the child. Occasionally the experience of pregnancy and delivery is sufficiently unpleasant (physically as well as psychologically) to predispose the mother negatively to her child, which further serves to remind the mother that her future is restricted for some time to come. Finally, comes the role the baby itself plays. Many infants are unpleasant to be around. A distressed child may cry incessantly, constantly demand attention, have highly irregular feeding and sleeping schedules, and project few overt displays of affection. Each of these factors may contribute to the kind of child-mother interaction which fosters mistrust rather than trust.

The *absence* of basic trust (which always results in the presence of mistrust) has several general effects on infant development. Perhaps the most consequential effect is that mistrust destroys the child's confidence in his ability to cope effectively with his environment which, in turn, stifles normal development of curiosity and exploration to learn about the world — a world which for him is almost totally unexplored. Mistrust also makes it difficult for the child to relate spontaneously and openly with others, drastically reducing his opportunity for praise, recognition, and achievement — each essential to the one-year-old human. Surprisingly, some parents unconsciously prefer a certain mistrust in their child. It keeps him closer to parental bonds, and assures the parent a central role in all aspects of the infant's social and emotional life; it also prolongs parental dependence by stifling the child's sense of self-reliance. For some parents, who are usually incomplete in their own psychological development, this is unconsciously rewarding.

The *presence* of basic trust permits a greatly expanded freedom toward the environment. It *causes* few activities, but an attitude of basic trust frees the child to follow inclinations natural to his age which mistrust would have thwarted. In this respect the formation of trust accomplishes little other than allowing the child to follow the developmental ground plan natural to his species (known as the *epigenetic principle*). This, however, is important to the continued growth of *any* organism. In some respects the formation of basic trust can be compared with being immunized against polio. Immunization does not assure that other aspects of one's life will continue smoothly; one can still go bankrupt, lose a job, be injured in an automobile accident, or require surgery. However, if a person is so immunized, he will not contract polio. In other words, even though immunized from a particular disorder one is still freely exposed to others. So it is with basic trust. The trusting child may be immunized against certain kinds of free-floating anxieties or environmental fears, but he still must confront a host of other crises related to normal growth. Trust allows the infant to toddle headfirst, literally as well as figuratively, into the coming years; it provides the confidence and optimism to concentrate wholeheartedly on the requirements of continued growth. It does not assure that the child will learn to speak more clearly or to walk more swiftly. It simply means he will have the trust, confidence, and optimism to maximally explore the world within the biological limits nature has seen fit to impose upon him. As we shall observe time and time again in the next chapter, exploration during the toddlerhood years is contingent upon a sense of confidence, trust, and willingness to "gamble". The type of psychological courage required to cope with life between the ages of one and three can blossom in a child only when he has some assurance that the strain and pain of growing is justified by love and trust from those with whom he lives. Whether a child *grows* through toddlerhood or merely *endures* it is in large measure determined by the extent to which he has trust in the environment and those who share it with him.

Summary

In our overview of the first year of life we looked at the infant from three different ages each of which has unique developmental characteristics. The first age, birth to six weeks, is characterized by recuperation from birth and reflex-dominated behaviour; the second age, six to sixteen weeks, is characterized by an expanded awareness of self and environment and diminished dependence upon innate reflexes; the third age, four to twelve months, witnesses active advancement of intellectual, motor, and social development and the tendency to explore and become competent with the environment.

The central concepts stressed in the chapter include the following:

1. Birth shocks the newborn's system and requires a recuperation period during which little socially significant growth takes place.

2. Reflexes dominate the first weeks of life but they soon lose their strength and finally disappear altogether. The initial behaviour patterns of the infant, even though dominated by reflex, constitute the primitive beginnings of later complex behaviour.

3. The appearance of the newborn, visually unpleasant, is a function of his biological equipment, his fetal history, his species characteristics, and certain developmental principles such as the cephalocaudal growth gradient.

4. Early infant behavioural abilities are largely a function of maturational development, and are only marginally influenced by normal environmental factors.

5. The newborn experiences the world via incompletely developed sensory equipment and a limited emotional repertoire which is probably restricted to states of pleasant and unpleasant excitement.

6. During the first six weeks of life the infant has very little ability to learn from experience and is dominated by specific biological demands.

7. The infant experiences greater awareness of self and an expanded interest in the environment between six and sixteen weeks which alters his overall behaviour and makes him much more "human-like".

8. Between the fourth and twelfth months, significant growth

takes place in social, motor, and intellectual abilities of the child and, as a result, he explores the environment and benefits a great deal from the exploration. Social maturity moves the child, who is assuming childlike features and dropping some infant-like traits, toward greater social interaction and responsibility.

9. Speech development during the first year is critical for future ability to use words purposively, but results in little use of "words".

10. All growth during the first year is influenced by maturational and environmental factors. Assuming that the child lives in an environment which provides the basic requirements for survival, maturational factors account most for development during the first year of life. This maxim does not hold for later stages of development however.

11. The formation of basic trust is greatly influenced by how the child is treated during the first year of life; its formation facilitates future social and psychological growth but has no known effect on biological growth.

12. Development during the first year of life influences all subsequent development, but to what degree is a matter of theoretical conjecture. Some psychologists claim it is the most important year of life, others are of the impression that most problems which occur during the first year are outgrown and recuperated from in time.

13. It is impossible to comprehend the major developments of toddlerhood without some understanding of the major developments during the first year of life.

First Year
and
Toddlerhood

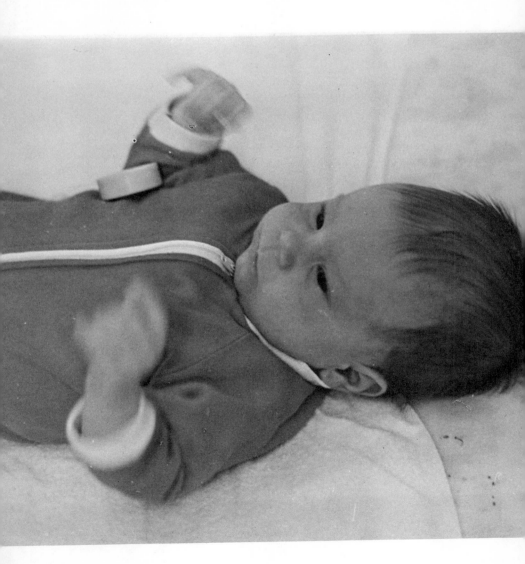

Transition stage between horizontal and vertical.

The mouth —
a most efficient testing apparatus.

Discovery of cultural tools.

The toddler enjoys cuddling and caressing — the rag doll meets this need *and* the need for role-playing.

The toddler's growing musculature and coordination opens vast new realms of physical activity.

Chapter Four

Toddlerhood

The child between the ages of one and three years has been called many things, some of them not the least bit flattering. In this book we shall refer to children of this age as "toddlers" even though any number of other labels would suffice almost as well. Toddler has special appeal because it is both colloquial and descriptive. The toddler really does toddle. He walks with short tottering steps and displays a walking gait which can be confused with that of no other developmental age. Toddler, because it is an expressive and familiar term, keeps us close to the fundamental nature of children between the ages of twelve and thirty-six months, for they also are expressive and familiar. Thus, toddler is the term we shall settle upon when describing the child between his first and third birthdays.

During toddlerhood five centrally important developments take place which mark the child's transition from a comparatively helpless creature to one who looks after a considerable number of his own needs and requirements. Each of these developments becomes a unifying force around which the child's energy and activity crystallize during the toddlerhood experience. Proper growth through these five learning processes to a great measure determines how successfully the child will adapt to the preschool years which are around the corner, and also will determine his ability to adjust to regulations imposed by society in general, and his household in particular. If liberally understood, it can be said in fairness that the main "purpose" of toddlerhood is to facilitate the following five developments.

1. *Learning to walk.* A toddler would not be a toddler if he could not toddle. Walking is the most important of all motor achievements for normal children because it converts the environment from a narrow, confined area to an open, expansive laboratory for investigation. The toddler is dominated by the urge to explore, but without ambulatory skills his curiosity would be severely curtailed. Learning to walk heralds the onset of many social behaviours from which the prewalking child is

excluded, such as strolling in the park, or outside play with neighbour children. It is almost self-evident that the impact a child makes upon his household is directly related to his ability to walk. The converse relationship is also important: the impact of the *environment upon the child* depends upon the child's ability to move through the environment and learn from it. The advent of walking greatly expands the extent to which the environment can affect the child because he is now more fully exposed to it.

2. *Learning to talk.* Speech is one of the crowning achievements of man, and as far as we currently know (evidence gathered from the study of porpoises included) no other creature in nature shares man's advanced capacity for speech. With words come symbols, and with symbols comes an entire new realm of vicarious existence. With words comes verbal communication, and though it is not a perfect form of communication, it does seem to have definite advantages over the alternatives (evidence from sensitivity-training included). With words comes the ability to express thoughts and feelings as well as the ability to benefit from the thoughts and feelings of others. The toddler works hard at acquiring the skills of speech. He is an adroit learner, a diligent and conscientious worker. He is not reluctant to ask, to quiz, to interrogate anyone who might provide a morsel of information. The toddler gives the impression that he is under "direct orders" to learn language as quickly and masterfully as possible, so eagerly does he pursue it. The onset of speech affects all other toddler developments, even walking. With speech he will walk or stop on command; he can be guided from one place to another with the spoken word; and, he can move himself to that particular spot in the environment which will allow him to most advantageously ask questions or present arguments. The ability to use words also has a positive effect on mental growth.

3. *Learning to think.* Children *learn* to think, though some of their intellectual abilities *unfold naturally* with only minimal environmental influence. Toddlers cannot engage in thought processes beyond their maturational level any more than they can walk or talk with proficiency beyond their biological limits. The thought process of the three-year-old is not only different from but superior to that of the one-year-old. The three-year-old possesses powers of abstraction, memory, perception, recognition, and invention far beyond either the one-year-old *or* the two-year-old. The progression of mental thought from one level to the next is one of the most intriguing aspects of toddler development as well as one of the most significant. Though it is unfair to draw an artificial distinction between learning to think and learning to speak (because they are so mutually dependent upon one another), it can be

said in fairness that learning to think is more critical to the child's development than is learning to speak. Perhaps the most convincing support for this statement comes from observations of children reared in nonspeaking families, who adjust rather well to the demands of life with one exception — they do not learn to speak. The *normal* child, however, does not experience the artificial distinction between thinking skills and speaking skills because they blend together imperceptibly.

4. *Learning to control elimination.* Humans, at no matter what age, prefer social gatherings where the participants do not spontaneously eliminate waste material. In our society it is expected that each individual will take care of his elimination requirements with minimal inconvenience to others. During the first year of life no demands are made upon the child in this regard because he is not biologically ready to account for himself. By the time he reaches his third birthday, however, he is expected to have acquired toilet habits fairly similar to those of adults. Like all major developments during the toddlerhood years, sphincter control depends upon biological maturation as well as learning. The child can be toilet-trained only when he is maturationally ready. However, many children who are maturationally ready for sphincter control are not as yet toilet-trained. This is where learning comes into the picture. Learning can facilitate *or hinder* biologically-based developments. If the child learns to feel guilty or dirty about the natural activity of elimination it may actually interfere with what would otherwise occur in fairly routine fashion. The toilet-trained toddler is basically no different from the untrained toddler except that the latter is more of a nuisance to adults. The extent to which the parent makes the toddler feel inadequate or inferior *because of* his nuisance value is an important factor in the child's life. In any event, the preschool child is expected to have control over bowel and bladder, and for the vast majority of children this capacity is acquired during the toddler years.

5. *Learning independence.* Toddlerhood includes the "terrible-twos" and, as everyone knows, two-year-olds are indeed terrible. Unfortunately, this is one of those circumstances where what everyone knows is only partially correct. The two-year-old is the epitome of autonomy. He insists upon making his *own* decisions, even if he makes the least advantageous one available. He insists upon doing things for himself, even if with only half the proficiency of mother or father. He is finicky, and may insist upon unswerving patterns of ritual (making preparation for bedtime a nightmare unto itself) for reasons largely unknown to the parent. Part of the toddler's unpredictability is based on the fact that he has only marginal skill at guessing the outcome of different possibili-

ties. His insistence on putting his trousers on backwards does not stem from his desire to originate new clothing trends but from his inability to anticipate the outcome of what he is doing. If there are only two choices with regard to a given issue, one fairly sensible and the other not, the toddler usually will choose the former. If, on the other hand, mother makes the more reasonable choice *for* the toddler, the only way he can exert true autonomy is to select the less desirable alternative. Being no hero, however, the toddler may change his mind the minute undesirable consequences accrue from a poor decision. Then again, he may choose to suffer through the entire event, deriving a faint sense of triumph from the indirect control over his parents which his suffering brings.

The toddler's independent nature registers firm impact on most of his social, emotional, intellectual, and physical behaviour. Parents, as well as students of the childhood years, often fail to recognize that autonomy quickly deteriorates into stubbornness, orneriness, or contrariness if improperly handled. One primary reason for adult-child conflict during toddlerhood is that the child often refuses to pay attention to the adult *even though the adult is correct.* Toddlers place little premium on correctness. They prefer to be wrong on their own rather than correct because of compliance. The toddler reminds us of the tavern brawler who rarely fights over a matter of technical accuracy; rather, he fights when he feels he has been treated with impropriety. The toddler rarely fights because of an inner conviction that he is correct. It is more important to him *to make his own decision* than for the decision to be a correct one. Wise parents recognize the caprice of toddlerhood; mothers seem especially gifted at tolerating childish gestures of self-assertion, probably because they have been living with an adult who displays a striking resemblance to the toddler in the matter of self-assertion: the North American male.

The toddler is not an easy subject for study, although one must admit that he is more open to study than our two previous subjects — the fetus and the one-year-old. The major problems associated with studying the fetus or the one-year-old are their comparative inaccessibility and their inability to speak. The toddler speaks and is accessible, but he is more *complex* and more *free* than the pretoddler.

During toddlerhood the child becomes "his own man". He acts purposefully; he acts with forethought and strategy (especially during the last half of toddlerhood); and he acts with his own interests in mind. As the toddler is not passive, to think of him as a sponge-like miniature adult who soaks up all habits and practices to which he is exposed is thoroughly incorrect. The child "soaks up" his environment, but not passively. He discards certain things and retains others; he likes certain things and dislikes others; he adapts readily to certain kinds of learning and flounders with others (his speaking skills may be accelerated beyond his chronological age while at the same time his ability to control nighttime bladder may be considerably behind that of other children his own age). The toddler is no mere blank slate upon which the impress of experience moulds a child. Neither is he a computer whose behaviour is merely a reflection of how he has been programmed. Neither is he helpless, fragile, or weak. The toddler is a young human who acts upon the world and in turn is acted upon; he actively participates in his own programming but certainly is not responsible for all of it; he can take care of himself with amazing deftness as long as he lives in a safe environment and has his basic survival needs provided; he is sturdy and durable and, if unpampered, not uncommonly is the most emotionally stable and physically healthy member of his household.

Despite his strengths, the toddler, by biological necessity, is a dependent creature. He must be cared for. He must be tended to. He must have an environment which gives him special attention and sanction. When the environment falls short, or does not live up to its end of the two-way exchange, the toddler is in trouble. In our society the force which moulds the environment so that it corresponds with the needs and inclinations of the toddler is supplied by the parents. Negligence on their part is costly. Excellence, however, is rewarding.

The toddler does not have a conscience. Neither is he very talented at distinguishing reality from fantasy. Thus we can readily see that special concessions must be made in his regard. We do not burden him with *moral* responsibility (quite different from household or social responsibility), nor do we rigidly insist that he make a clear distinction between fact and fiction. These will come with time — predictably and naturally. Gesell, with his customary insight, offers an interesting twist to understanding the toddler. He suggests, "It is helpful to think of him [the toddler] as a preschool edition of a slightly confused adolescent who has not yet found his way." Perhaps this is not so far from being correct. However, the toddler, unlike the adolescent, is much more dependent upon the parent for factual guidance as well as firm discipline (although one periodically wonders whether the adolescent wouldn't benefit from it also).

Toddlers hate being ignored. They rebel, almost as if upon instruction, when they cannot make an impact upon the environment. When unable to accomplish the tasks they set for themselves they become frustrated and anxious. Toddlers are constantly thwarted by their own impotence. Ambitions always seem to be slightly ahead of capacities.

But from this disparity they cultivate an essential skill: they learn to tap information and secure assistance from others. If the toddler is gifted at "getting into things", he is a genius at getting others to bail him out of the havoc which comes from it.

How does one go about studying the toddler? Obviously there are many ways. In this chapter we shall look into those aspects of toddlerhood which affect social, emotional, and intellectual growth. We shall also pay special attention to the ways in which the environment moulds the child, as well as the ways in which the child moulds the environment. We shall keep an attentive eye on the parents, for they, more than anyone else, influence the total development of the child. Finally, we shall try always to understand *natural* growth and the extent to which it is influenced by environmental conditions.

One further comment before embarking on our sojourn into toddlerdom. Throughout the chapter the reader will observe reference to "early toddler" and "late toddler". This is due to the elementary fact that fundamental differences exist between the skills of the twelve to twenty-four month child (early toddler) and those of the twenty-four to thirty-six month child (late toddler). Intellectual skills of late toddlerhood are not only more advanced than those of early toddlerhood, but qualitatively superior. This makes it difficult to say that the *toddler* cannot do this or that, because the truth is that he cannot do such and such in early toddlerhood but may be completely capable of it during the latter half of toddlerhood. Hopefully, this will not bog us down with undue specialization. It has been stated that modern science is already so specialized that right-kidney surgeons cannot converse intelligently with left-kidney surgeons. We shall avoid such excesses of specialization in this text despite our cleavage of toddlerhood into two halves.

The Toddler as Housewrecker

Quite obviously there are societies in which the toddler creates considerably less havoc than he does in ours; and it likewise is readily apparent that the toddler's role as housewrecker varies within families and among social classes in our own society. However, despite these relative variations, there is one statement about the toddler which can be made with absolute confidence: if left on his own, unsupervised, the toddler will eventually inflict damage upon his immediate environment as well as upon himself. Because of this inescapable fact of life, the toddler must be protected from the environment and the environment, in turn, must be protected from him. We shall explore several of the developmental conditions which lead to this state of affairs during toddlerhood.

When attempting to understand the behaviour of the toddler we must bear in mind that his is the *first* developmental level in the life cycle when the human has the ability to act upon impulses or to search out and explore those realms of the environment which are not immediately visible. *The fundamental growth obligations of the toddler are exploration and experimentation.* These are the means by which knowledge is gathered, tested, compared, and verified. In this regard the toddler is scientific in the ideal sense of the word. Unfortunately, the toddler is a victim of a disorder which is also shared by contemporary psychology — his method is much more impressive than his theory. The toddler has a very meagre theoretical orientation toward his world; most of his knowledge is based on first-hand experience or observation; he benefits only marginally from vicarious learning. The toddler is forced to experiment in order to understand how the world works, and the majority of this experimentation is trial-and-*error* (please reflect upon this last word). He is startled to discover that objects fall when dropped and sometimes break when they stop falling; he is amazed to find that things tip over, but frustrated when they fail to right themselves. Since the toddler knows nothing of the physical laws to which all earth objects, including himself, are subject, the process of learning about them is slow, tedious, and, for the parents, costly.

The *limitations* of toddlerhood dictate the deficiencies of the one-through-three-year-old, but the strengths of toddlerhood dictate its growth (as well as destruction) potential. The toddler can walk, climb, and jump, and he does; he can reach, grab, and retrieve, and he does; he can calculate, anticipate, and expropriate, and he does; he can investigate, confiscate, and judicate, and he does. In fact, the tribulations of toddlerhood are as anchored in abilities as in the lack of them. In some respects the toddler is the victim of nature's caprice because his physical skills are much more advanced than the intellectual skills which police them.

Most critical to understanding the toddler's penchant for household destruction are the following factors:

1. the onset of walking and the general increased mobility which comes with it,
2. the centrality of curiosity, exploration, and competence in the life of the toddler and the investigatory habits which always come about because of them,
3. the learning of personal, social, and psychological limits,

4. the extent to which the household adjusts to the growth needs and developmental limitations of the toddler.

We shall now overview these four aspects of the eternal feud between the toddler and the household which nurtures him.

The onset of walking. The impact a toddler makes upon his household is directly proportional to his ability to move himself from place to place. Except for physically handicapped or severely mentally retarded children, walking during toddlerhood is a distinct ingredient of social and physical development. For most families the toddler's first shaky step is a memorable event; as with most "firsts", however, the glory is greater for the parent than the child. Maturational development and physical growth during the first year of life set the stage for walking, but it is during the next two years that it becomes an artful form of locomotion. Walking is a complex phenomenon and though we could not infer it only from observing toddlers, man executes it with greater precision than any of the primates.

While learning to walk the toddler moves through several notable sequences. Initially he can stand upright only when held by the hands, or if holding on to a support. Later he is able to issue forth a few choppy steps when assisted. After this follows independent standing and walking, but several weeks of practice and maturity are required before the child can sustain the momentum of movement and not be purely at the mercy of his own body physics. Between the first and second years the toddler learns to stop or change directions while walking; these refinements entail numerous spills and tumbles which ultimately contribute to his resilience and toughness. (It cannot be emphasized too much how sturdy the normal, nonpampered toddler is. His durability is spectacular.) With the onset of walking the once restricted environment suddenly becomes not only more available but more complex: stairs, inclines, crevices, and barriers appear everywhere forcing the child to add variety to his walking repertoire. He must learn to straddle, suspend, drop, circumvent, and avoid; he also must learn to register proper control against the effects of gravity and uneven distribution of body weight. Upon mastering these requirements of locomotion the child immediately encounters others, such as attending to environmental obstacles while walking (two-year-olds are notorious for banging into protrusions below knee level and above shoulder level), and executing independent mental functions while walking, such as remembering the purpose for movement from point A to point B. The entire walking sequence is dependent upon maturation of brain centres, and though practice is required to refine walking behaviour, it does not account for its onset during toddlerhood. The toddler practises walking because he is maturationally ready. He is not maturationally ready because he has been practising.

During toddlerhood the child matures from an awkward, sloppy walker to an exuberant and flamboyant (for some reason flamboyance seems to accompany excellence during toddlerhood) runner, jumper, and skipper. At eighteen months he can walk up stairs one at a time using one free hand as a balance, but must resort to crawling or bumping down them; he is bipedal whenever possible, but has only marginal stamina and still must be carried a good deal. At twenty-four months he can jump off edges, kick a ball in stride (a rather formidable task), dance, climb book cases and linen shelves, and walk for hundreds of yards without rest. At thirty-six months he runs with assurance, accelerates and decelerates, copes with corners while running (but because he is constantly preoccupied, often encounters unanticipated objects or humans right around them). By now he knows well his limits, and rarely will hurt himself by jumping from too high or failing to stop with sufficient promptness. He can efficiently operate a tricycle and a few three-year-olds are taught bicycle riding with the assistance of balance wheels and persistent parents.

With walking comes mobility and explorational freedom, increased competence and the ability to execute it, an expanded physical environment with new enjoyments and hazards, and, perhaps most important, an entire new realm of existence in which to learn about the environment and its relationship to humans. Aside from prodigious mental growth, walking is the crowning achievement of toddlerhood upon which all future skills come to depend and rely.

Curiosity, exploration and competence. The human child, like all infant primates, is insatiably *curious* and possesses an inherent drive to *explore his environment*. Both of these traits are so thoroughly embedded in the child that it takes virtually inhumane punishment to extinguish them during the first three years of life. Not until age four or five can the child partially discipline his demand for instant knowledge, and rarely before the age of seven can he restrain himself from bombarding adults with countless questions and hypothetical situations which require solution. Curiosity and exploration are as essential to optimal child growth as calcium or vitamins; the only basic difference is that deficiency of the latter produces more obvious and more easily detectable consequences.

Competence is somewhat different from curiosity and exploration. Each child possesses a basic, unlearned drive to acquire competence with those aspects of the environment which affect his life. In order to enhance environmental competence he will acquire information, solve problems, learn skills, and master exercises. Curiosity and exploration drives greatly facilitate global competence, but they are subservient to it in that they tend to decrease as competence increases.

The focal points of the toddler's curiosity, exploration, and competence urges are the physical and social realities of his own household. There are two major facets to the toddler's investigation of the household: (1) the impact of the toddler upon the household, and (2) the impact of the household upon the toddler. Since most psychologists are "household" theorists, they pay most attention to how the child is influenced by it. Most parents seem to be "toddler" theorists, who are most impressed by the extent to which the household must adjust to the toddler. Obviously these conclusions are reached for quite different reasons.

As walking skills mature the toddler's world becomes progressively more explorable. At eighteen months everything over twenty-four inches above floor level is in an unreachable world; before his third birthday, however, only the most remote alcoves will escape his persistent and versatile exploration. Unfortunately, the adventures of toddlerhood are not without negative consequences because at this age he cannot completely anticipate the outcome of his behaviour. There are no innate mental mechanisms which inform him in advance that tugging on the cord of an iron left on the ironing board will bring it tumbling down upon him; nor can he foresee that crawling inside an abandoned refrigerator may afford no possibility of escape. Toddlerhood is the age of uncalculated exploration, blind curiosity, and global attempts at competence; only with increased experience does he differentiate high-risk from low-risk adventure, relevant from mundane curiosity, and high-priority from low-priority competence. Between the ages of one and three, accidents brought about by a combination of child exploration and parental carelessness are the number one killer of children in North America.

Most exploration, especially during the first half of toddlerhood, is completely trial-and-error: see what it feels like when a finger is inserted here; observe what happens when this is stacked upon that; taste this when mixed with that. Toddlers learn rapidly from trial-and-error exploration, quickly discerning "good" from "bad" situations, but they are highly susceptible to injury or accident during their initial experimentation. This vulnerability to environmental hazard often encourages parental overprotectiveness and the tendency to legislate against the child's natural tendency to explore, experiment, and become competent. As Levy (1943) has demonstrated, overprotective parents may actually delay the toddler's capacity for mature behaviour by discouraging his natural curiosity or by destroying his self-confidence. With a bit of foresight, concerned parents can satisfy their own desire for safety as well as the toddler's desire for exploration by constructing a comparatively danger-free environment which offers abundant opportunity for searching and probing.

Toddlers frequently are frustrated because their demands constantly outrace their abilities and their ambitions often do not correspond with their best interests. The insatiable urge to investigate mother's purse stems from the same urge to know what is inside sealed bottles or cooking ovens. The toddler's almost blind enthusiasm for assimilating new information about his world forces the parent to interdict: he hears "no-no", and is swatted on the rear more in an average day than the six-year-old is in half a year.

In toddlerhood, when the fundamental urge for exploration is being partially (sometimes inconsistently) contradicted by social rules, parents must be extra loving and reassuring. Since every child should come to *trust* in the righteousness of parental intervention, the formation of this trust is directly proportional to the love, patience, and skill of the parents. Parental trust established during toddlerhood is the foundation upon which to build future trust, one of the foremost developmental priorities of the age.

Exploration during toddlerhood is obviously not purely negative despite its negative impact upon household efficiency and its potential danger to the toddler. During these years the child's explorations and expeditions provide valuable knowledge about physical objects, geometric relationships, object permanence, causality, and gravity. He learns that things have origins and beginnings and that one reality sometimes can be reduced to another. He learns to experiment and anticipate possible outcomes. He learns that certain behaviour is more appropriate or productive than others; even more crucially, he *begins* to comprehend the reasons why some behaviour is considered better than others by adults. He is becoming *socialized* as well as educated. Because the toddler is by nature an explorer, the rest of childhood would not unfold as it does without the freedom to explore during these years when he is sheltered from reprimand and exempt from retribution. If the household must suffer because of this developmental requirement, then so be it.

Learning limits. During toddlerhood the child must learn about physical, social, and personal limits. He must acquire information about those aspects of the *physical* environment which can be manipulated or adjusted (such as tap water) as well as those which are stable and unchanging (such as the wetness of water); he also must learn about environmental objects which are useful as well as dangerous (scissors, razor blades). Once this information is acquired, his work has only begun, for he must acquire skills which allow him to deal with environmental objects in such a way that they facilitate the satisfaction of his own needs and desires.

Learning about *social* realities is difficult for the toddler because they change more rapidly and have less predictability than physical realities. Even though it is true that stoves sometimes are hot and other times not, that strange foods are sometimes sweet and sometimes bitter, it is also true that jumping on father's lap will sometimes bring a warm embrace and at other times a chastising scowl. Creative penmanship is sometimes rewarded but sometimes punished (little does the child understand that the criteria centre around *where* the drawing was done — paper tends to be OK but walls the contrary). The virtually endless social realities about which the toddler first must learn and secondly adjust to are the source of his most intense frustration and confusion. With his limited resources he must learn to distinguish when "no" really means "NO!!", and to sense when it will be followed by punishment or merely polite restatement. He must learn when his presence is preferred and when his absence is feared. He must learn about the vague distinction between being "cute" and "acting like a baby". He must learn that when certain strangers are in the house he is to be quiet and sedate, while when others are present he is to be cheerful, exuberant, and grandchild-like.

Because the toddler rapidly acquires information about the limits of parental tolerance, he prefers, for reasons not clearly understood, to take adults to the threshold of this tolerance before giving in to their demands. In families with brothers and sisters the toddler must learn not only about *their* limits but, even more complex, he also must learn that he is treated differently for the same behaviour in different contexts. Thus biting older brother is sometimes cute, but biting younger sister is an offense which draws reprimand. Parents who are not consistent in their demands, who constantly waver in their expectations, who issue punishment and praise unpredictably, add to the toddler's difficulty in learning social limits.

As parents are only human, it is unfair to saddle them with the responsibility of computer-like precision and robot-like predictability in their dealings with children; but it is fair to point out that the child's total sense of confidence is highly correlated with the security and predictability of his home environment. If his home status is insecure and mistrusting, then his perception of the social world will be similarly unstable.

The toddler must also learn about his own *personal limits* which are established in part by biological immaturity and in part by living in an environment geared for people twenty years his superior. The toddler quickly learns that some things cannot be moved, that some foods cannot be consumed without help, that some items of clothing cannot be put on or removed by himself. He also learns that some realities do not change no matter how much they are acted upon (such as the solidness of walls and the hardness of floors) while others such as towels, clay, and puzzles succumb to manipulation. Learning his personal limits is especially difficult for the toddler because his limits change almost daily — so rapidly is he maturing. A door which yesterday could be opened only by adults now responds; a cup which always spilled part of its contents suddenly pours properly; fences which formerly confined the world to one's yard are now mysteriously small and negotiable; house cats which a few months ago were as large as lions are compressed to the size of ordinary cats; precious commodities such as water and kisses which previously could be acquired only by pointing, babbling, and crying now are instantly available upon uttering a correct word; the dinner table formerly the exclusive domain of "big" people is now available for exploitation; puzzles which formerly brought only frustration fall into place almost magically; and, perhaps most importantly, the world in general, which previously was something to be sheltered from, is now a giant laboratory awaiting exploration. The toddler is intoxicated with power, reeling with buoyance, cresting with new found skills and powers. Like most intoxicating experiences, however, these are short-lived. New and more complex realities emerge. Greater and more self-disciplining responsibility is assigned by parents. The world becomes increasingly more verbal and the toddler is the least efficient of all the word-users. As the world expands beyond the household and the neighbourhood, trial-and-error exploration must begin afresh. The toddler's intoxication with power is followed by a hangover of frustration with his own impotence. Learning physical, social, and personal limits during the toddler years is hard work requiring a flexible, resilient, adjustable child.

Two additional factors require mention before we conclude: ownership and egocentrism. The toddler, no matter what society he is born into, is a selective hoarder. Certain properties (in our society — blankets, dolls, books, and trinkets are favourites) are considered his own, and he acquires unusually strong affection for them; he fights against their repossession and weeps in their absence. For this reason adults who socialize the child also have limits imposed upon them, because self-defeating vicious circles emerge when they fail to consider the makeup of the child. The toddler cannot be expected to adjust endlessly to parental demands, for he has his own internal demands and inclinations. Ownership is one of them. Many young couples who themselves believe in community ownership and universal sharing have bitter confrontations with the selfish tendencies of their toddlers who are less impressed with abstract rhetoric than their own inner impulses.

The toddler, despite his recent strides in intellectual growth, is still highly egocentric. Since he equates the perceived world with the real world, he is still convinced psychologically that the world evolves around his particular needs, wants, and dispositions. Fraiberg gracefully articulates the nature of egocentrism during middle toddlerhood:

> The magician is seated in his high chair and looks upon the world with favor. He is at the height of his powers. If he closes his eyes, he causes the world to disappear. If he opens his eyes, he causes it to come back. If there is harmony within him, the world is harmonious. If rage shatters his inner harmony, the unity of the world is shattered. If desire arises within him, he utters the magic syllables which cause the desired object to appear. His wishes, his thoughts, his gestures, his noises, command the universe. (p. 107)

This is the toddler to which the adult is entrusted!

Limits are slowly learned within the topsy-turvy world. But like all imperatives, they painfully emerge, and once present they establish the ground rules for the formation of new ones. For even though learning about personal, social, and physical limits is a major part of the toddler's life he will face their reappearance during the preschool years and again in middle childhood. There is no respite from limits, but one is well beyond childhood before one *accepts* this aspect of the human condition.

Household adjustments. It is quite within the physical prowess of the toddler to "wreck" a house. As he approaches the last months of his third year he assumes an uncanny ability to terminate the effective functioning of most machines with one thrust or probe. He can unscrew or unplug anything, can tip over most pieces of furniture (especially if it is portable), and those which resist tipping can be scratched or scarred. He can dirty anything clean or dull anything shined — he is a housecleaner's nightmare. Mothers who care for their sanity as well as their furniture must rapidly adjust. Breakable or valuable objects are placed out of reach, and if necessary out of sight. Certain parts of the house are set aside exclusively for play and exploration, and toys are purchased which create minimal damage when dropped or banged. Certain rooms, especially the bathroom and the parents' bedroom, have easily unlatchable locks affixed above toddler's reach. Crayons, water paints, jack-knives, tennis rackets, and other playthings safe within the hands of an older sibling are likewise hidden or camouflaged. The household must adjust to the mobile explorer who still is of the egocentric impression that the house was built exclusively for his own purposes. Despite the importance of adjusting the physical environment to the developmental level of the toddler, physical adjustments are less central to family life than the social and psychological adjustments which are made in favour of the toddler. After all, the physical world is merely the geographical setting for the private, existential life of humans.

Because the toddler does not operate on psychological principles identical to those of the adult, to assume he does invites catastrophe. The following are but a few of the fundamental cleavages between adult and toddler psychological functioning:

1. The toddler thinks in terms of the immediate present and has only marginal consideration for future events or consequences while adults are future-oriented and regulate most of their behaviour in terms of consequences which will accrue to it.

2. The toddler is much more easily distracted from an interest or desire than is the adult. A two-year-old who desperately wants to stay up for one more TV program can often be enticed into bed by promise of a favourite story or an evening snack.

3. Adult interpersonal relations are *verbally* dominated but the toddler's are not. Only very precocious and verbally mature toddlers can understand several consecutive sentences, therefore, they are not highly susceptible to verbal persuasion; they respond much more to tone of voice and facial expressions than to the exact words which are spoken.

4. The toddler's egocentric thought patterns prevent *genuine* understanding of contrary points of view and usually he will just give in or feign acceptance of the parental viewpoint. Adults are egocentric enough to believe that the toddler really understands — so at least toddlers do not have a monopoly on egocentric thought processes.

5. The toddler's greatest achievements are those which draw parental approval or praise but rarely are the parents' greatest achievements those which draw approval or praise from the toddler. The parent controls the child's ability to experience himself as worthwhile but no such reciprocal control exists for the child.

Each of these realities force the adult to adjust to the psychological level of the toddler, if a meaningful relationship is to arise between them. At the same time, however, the adult must provide encouragement and example so the toddler can mature beyond these limited and immature modes of coping with the world.

Numerous social adjustments within the household are made for the benefit of the toddler. Parents learn that they must adjust to the extra time required for personal and social interaction with their child. During the toddlerhood years considerable time is spent in visiting, social play, and, when the parents are so inclined, reading. As toddlers are avid listeners, they thrive on stories, poems, jingles, or rhymes, and can easily be entranced by an adult who speaks rhythmically and expressively.

When visitors are in the house the toddler receives his first lessons in social etiquette. As a rule he does not like being relegated to the status of an ordinary person if the grownups are not in the mood for his company. Usually parents will temporarily interrupt whatever social activity might be transpiring if the toddler seems to need a moment of special attention or comfort. The manner in which the parent relates to the child when he interrupts an adult social activity tells the child a good deal about how he is valued and respected. Many children form a bitter dislike for adults who, by their presence, make mother or father inaccessible.

Bedtime for the toddler, more so than at any other childhood stage, is a social event. Mother and father, sister and brother, somehow get wrangled into the process of bedding down a toddler. Very few toddlers can be tucked in for the night without making at least one plea for a glass of water, an extra blanket, or some such contrivance designed to prolong the onset of sleep and the solitude which surrounds it. The toddler's world is the social world and he leaves it with reluctance; he hates to miss anything and will go to unbearable measures to avoid turning in for the night. As this is especially true during late toddlerhood, parents upon retiring for the night are frequently startled to discover their three-year-old resting quietly, but fully awake in bed.

A mother once observed that the most important time in the life of the child is one hour before bedtime and one hour after bedtime, for it is into this two-hour span that all the ingredients of a parent-child relationship are channeled.

The Toddler as Coward

Despite the toddler's abundant talents for exploration, adventure, and occasional destruction, he is not exactly the swashbuckling daredevil one might think after only observing him in the protective and secure environment of his own household. Actually, a streak of cowardice stripes our toddler, and like the antihero of contemporary cinema, he makes no attempt to deceive others about his lack of courage. When frightened he runs away, he cries, he begs assistance, he whimpers, and he abhors conversation. The general rule which governs cowardice during toddlerhood is this: strange environments, and almost all strange adults *initially* create apprehension, uncertainty, and sometimes fear which is not overcome until the child has had time to become assured that the unknown person (or environment) is not dangerous or threatening to his security. Only when assured that everything is safe will he lose his fear and begin to engage in more usual behaviour.

The first overt signs of fear are observed during the first year of life when the infant reacts to strangers, as well as separation from mother, with behaviour which can be understood only as fear. During toddlerhood a sharp increase in general and specific fears takes place. By the third birthday the child has more fears than at any time during the first ten years of life.

Fears generally emerge as a product of learning, but sometimes surface *apparently* without any previous experience which could account for them. If a toddler is knocked over by a dog and thereafter fears dogs, we can safely presume his fear is a product of learning. However, if the child responds with fear the first time he encounters a dog we could infer two possible explanations: (1) the dog resembles a fear stimulus already known to the toddler, or (2) there is something about the dog, in and of itself, which initiates fear in the child. During toddlerhood it is quite obvious that both kinds of fear are manifested.

It is not surprising that fear plays a central part in the life of the toddler; after all, he lives in a world which is a hazy mixture of science and magic, pleasure and reality, known and unknown. He is constantly confronted by environmental hazards for which he has no coping resources. He dwells in a Lilliputian world filled with noisy monsters, whose house pets are as large as horses and whose powers are so great he can be swept upward into their arms at any unknown second. Under such conditions periodic cowardice is, if nothing else, understandable.

Toddlerhood cowardliness will be viewed in this chapter from four perspectives: (1) fear of strangers; (2) fear of separation from one's base of security; (3) the base of security and what it means; and (4) some general fears common to toddlerhood.

Stranger anxiety. As pointed out in the previous chapter, fear of strangers begins to manifest itself during the first year of life, sometimes as early as the third or fourth month, but most commonly between the seventh and ninth month. At first the infant reacts to strangers (any unfamiliar person) with a blank, empty expression more suggestive of uncertainty than fear. This reaction soon changes to apprehension, then to outright fear. When frightened by a stranger the infant will clutch vigorously to the mother, or guardian, and turn sharply away to indicate in no uncertain terms he wants nothing to do with this unknown intruder. Some psychologists believe that stranger anxiety comes into existence when the child learns that the presence of a stranger signals the departure of the parents — as is the case with a babysitter. From this perspective, fear of strangers is understood as distress over the prospect of losing one's source of comfort and security. Other psychologists, and most parents, are not of this viewpoint, however, claiming instead that fear of strangers is often exhibited *before* the infant has experienced any unpleasant relationship in their regard. Many mothers have found themselves explaining to a doting grandparent: "He has never acted like this before. I can't imagine what is wrong with him today!" Mothers who keep baby diaries frequently observe that their infants first begin to respond to strangers with fear and distress near the sixth month. Individual differences are discernible in this reaction, and some babies do not exhibit *at all* the standard stranger anxiety pattern. Adults, much more frequently than children, elicit anxiety in the toddler. When another child is brought into the room, the toddler rarely responds with the fear or apprehension generated by an adult.

Stranger anxiety continues well into the second year (frequently the third); consequently, it becomes a relevant ingredient of the toddler's social life. Stranger anxiety can be understood best from two distinct frameworks: (1) coping with strangers when mother is present, and (2) coping with strangers when mother is absent. (It deserves brief note at this time that "mother" refers to the adult who has the basic responsibility of caring for the child, especially his love and affection needs; quite obviously this could just as easily be "father" or "guardian". In our culture, however, it most frequently is mother.) Coping with strangers when mother is present is much easier for the toddler, therefore we shall discuss this aspect of stranger anxiety first.

When an unfamiliar person enters his room, the toddler, after a quick but fairly thorough visual inspection of the visitor, will scurry via the most direct route to mother, whereupon he will latch on to a leg or indicate that he wants to be held. The mother may not respond to this latter request but usually will allow the toddler to cling long enough to re-establish his sense of security. If the stranger proceeds directly to the child he will receive a dismal greeting at best and tears of fright at worst. The mother will then attempt to reassure her offspring of the intrinsic worth of the tactless visitor. (How would you respond if a stranger entered your home and upon being met with retreat and disapproval still approached you as though everything were perfectly routine?) Within a matter of moments curiosity will get the best of the toddler. He will slowly disengage himself from the protective confines of mother's arms and work his way, ever so cautiously, in the direction of the visitor. Eventually, he will reach the visitor and may even consent to being propped upon his lap, although in our culture the price for this gesture of reconciliation is usually a sweet of one kind or another. Confidence in the visitor is still tenuous and a sudden burst of laughter or an unexpected facial grimace may send the toddler scurrying back to mother. In most cases the normal toddler will overcome his fear of strangers within five minutes, especially when his trust in mother is sufficiently potent to assure him that her protection will be available when needed. Because trust in mother exerts tremendous influence on the life of the toddler, stranger anxiety is only one example where the willingness to venture forth and explore new situations is directly related to the toddler's feelings of trust and security.

The toddler's reaction to strangers in the absence of parents is a different matter unless a substitute base of security can bolster confidence and self-assurance. Toddlers near their second birthday have been known to sustain a fear reaction to an unfamiliar person for several hours in the absence of parents; this is unusual, however. Establishing rapport with a frightened toddler requires an overt gesture of trust. And, as hospital attendants and pediatricians know, the most direct route to the toddler's heart is through his stomach. Trust has been purchased from an apprehensive toddler more than once with a chocolate bar! After a child has been left with a stranger he associates stranger presence with parental absence. This learned association reinforces his natural fear of strangers and makes its effects even more intense.

All children do not experience stranger anxiety equally, but there is no theoretical consensus as to why this is so. Margaret Mead was one of the first contemporary social scientists to observe that a child's fear of strangers seems to be inversely proportional to the number of adults he meets each day. That is, the more adults he encounters during the course of normal living the less fear he displays to yet another adult; contrariwise, the fewer adults he encounters daily the stronger is his initial reaction against them. This tendency has also been observed in the kibbutzim of Israel. It is unclear if the number of adults encountered actually engender in the child greater trust and security, or whether the child just learns to quit noticing them so much. To keep the topic spicy, however, we occasionally observe a child who spends each day at home alone with mother who shows no trace of stranger anxiety whatsoever; in fact, he may greet strangers with openness and typical toddler curiosity.

Stranger anxiety is not restricted to fear of people. Toddlers frequently display an edgy restlessness when encountering a strange environment such as the neighbour's home or a subway. After an initial period of checking things out, however, the toddler goes about the business of expanding his knowledge bank through exploration and manipulation. In general, toddlers have at least a mild apprehension of the incongruous, the novel, or the different, while at the same time being intrigued by it. Stranger anxiety, as a specific developmental reality, tends to gradually dissipate before the fourth birthday, eventually to become shyness, timidity, or merely childlike reserve.

Separation anxiety. During the last third of the first year of life the infant begins to form strong bonds of relatedness and love with his parents. This relatedness is the foundation upon which all future love and sharing relationships are established, and its depth and durability is possibly the single most important factor (other than nutrition), in the episode of life known as toddlerhood. The parent, most commonly the mother, is the child's life-line to the outside world as well as his protection from it. The child clings physically and emotionally to this precious source of strength, without which he is as helpless as a fetus without placenta. The bond between mother and child eventually becomes so strong that the child fears separation, even for short lengths of time, from mother. The anxiety which sweeps through the child when separated from his mother, or when he thinks he is about to be separated, is called *separation anxiety.* John Bowlby, British pediatrician, is perhaps the most vociferous advocate of the importance of this toddlerhood phenomenon and here we shall overview separation anxiety from his perspective.

Bowlby has formulated the hypothesis that separation from the mother will automatically elicit an anxiety response in the infant if he is over twenty-eight weeks of age. Bowlby feels separation anxiety occurs not only because the child briefly loses his need gratifier (which of course is true) but because the child has instinctual predispositions toward clinging and following, which when cathected to the mother create a bond of love and affection: if the bond is temporarily severed, as in the case of separation, the child will *automatically* experience anxiety. Separation anxiety is considered by Bowlby to be a *primary* human response which is not necessarily reducible to other factors. In this respect he distinguishes himself from those psychologists who stress the learned components of separation anxiety.

In his hospital study of children brought in for surgery between the ages of fifteen to thirty months, Bowlby found that certain consistent behaviour patterns develop upon separation from the mother. The pattern follows a sequence of (a) *protest,* (b) *despair,* and (c) *detach-*

ment, with each stage having its own unique characteristics. Bowlby comments: "Should his stay in a hospital or residential surgery be prolonged . . . he will in time act as if neither mothering nor contact with humans had much significance for him. After a series of upsets of losing several mother-figures to whom in turn he has given much trust and affection, he will gradually commit himself less and less to succeeding figures and in time will stop altogether taking the risk of attaching himself to anyone." These tendencies merge into an overall personality pattern characterized by disinterest in people, non-affectivity, and a type of neutrality toward life in general. This syndrome is similar to that among institutional children described by Spitz (1965), although not nearly as acute.

Perhaps the most dramatic example of the effects of separation during toddlerhood are those documented in Bowlby's hospital studies. Even though these situations are exaggerated and unusual, the sequential progression of the child's reaction to separation from his mother is especially interesting. Here we shall observe a classic example of the effects of parental separation on Laura who, at age thirty months, was brought into the hospital for a minor operation. Bowlby describes her attitude-behaviour change during her brief eight-day hospital stay.

1. The first day she was cheerful as she met the admitting nurse. Upon bathing, etc., she began to scream and cry for mommy. She became calm after a few minutes. When alone she appeared calm, but when a friendly person arrived her feelings became known. Throughout the *first day she asked for mommy* and showed anxiety and apprehension.

2. During the second day she began to look strained and sad; she gave little response to the nurse. Her parents visited her thirty minutes after her operation. *She reached for mother* and cried "I want to go home." She was subdued because of her stitches. She waved slightly upon the parents' departure.

3. The third day she was quiet, nondemanding, spent much of her time clutching her teddy bear. She cried for mommy after the nurse played with her for a while. This reaction was very consistent — whenever she was by herself she displayed passivity and detachment, but when a friendly person played with her she would become remorseful and cry for her mother. When mother visited, it took Laura fifteen minutes to "warm up to her". When mother left, Laura was remorseful, *but did not show it by crying.*

4. During the fourth day she played wildly with her doll. Her mother did not visit.

5. On the fifth day the mother visited again and there was a thaw-

ing period. When the mother left Laura *she cried lightly but soon stopped.*

6. The sixth day another child was admitted who cried a great deal. Laura said "You are crying because you want your mommy . . . she'll come tomorrow."

7. On the seventh day both parents visited. Laura *showed no excitement* when the chairs were being set up, even though she knew what this meant. Laura made *no attempt to go to her mother* when she entered the room. She remained subdued. When they left the room Laura mumbled quietly, "I want to go with you." She seemed *to almost ignore the departure of her mother.*

8. Laura cried heavily in the morning. She had been told the night before that she would be leaving in the morning. She remained cautious when her mother arrived. Not until her outdoor shoes were placed in the room did she accept the fact that she was really going home. She demanded that she be able to take all her "possessions". On the way out she was seen walking *apart from her mother.*

Removing the child from his home and placing him into a hospital full of strangers where he is then subjected to surgery is a rather extreme circumstance in the life of a toddler. For this reason Bowlby's example of hospital-induced separation anxiety is beyond the scope of normal social living. In the course of ordinary day-to-day existence the toddler manifests anxiety when separated from his mother by whimpering and attempting to follow her; this latter behaviour accounts for the fact that the toddler (especially between twelve and twenty months) will reflexively follow the mother from room to room during the course of the daily activity. When the young toddler realizes he is in a room by himself it may matter little to him, but he is just as likely to begin searching for mother, and usually shows relief and pleasure upon locating her.

Separation anxiety reduces with time (as does stranger anxiety) and the best rule of thumb in their regard is to let them follow their individual patterns while at the same time encouraging their extinction. Because separation anxiety and stranger anxiety are part of the normal developmental process they do not *unto themselves* cause psychological trauma or disturbance beyond the coping resources of the normal child. _The base of security_. Professor Harry Harlow's world famous studies with young monkeys are perhaps most widely known for their contribution to understanding the importance of contact-comfort during the early years of life. Another major finding, unfortunately often overlooked, deals with the importance of the mother object as a psychological base of security. A description of one of Harlow's numerous experiments will clarify this concept, and serve to illustrate how the toddler's source of strength in moments of "crisis" derives from his base of security.

A young monkey going about the business of being young and being a monkey is usually engrossed in environmental exploration or robust play, which helps burn up the surplus energy instrinsic to his normal condition. In essence, he is doing the same general kinds of things as does the human toddler. However, if this scene is suddenly interrupted by the intrusion of an artificial fear stimulus, such as a giant plastic spider or ant, the young monkey will promptly halt all recreational activity and flee to mother (or in the case of the Harlow studies, a cloth-covered mannikin which served as a mother substitute). The flight to mother is fast, intense, and uninterrupted: the monkey is frightened and he demands protection. Upon reaching mother he jumps upon her, pressing against her front, holding tightly to her arms and shoulders, and rocking up and down the front part of her body. In time the intensity of this panic action subsides, but quite obviously the monkey is still not completely at ease; he begins to glance about, visually inspecting his stationary but fearful visitor, refusing to venture forth. A sense of reduced tension begins to show itself, and though not relaxed the infant monkey is no longer in an acute state of panic. He clings less tightly and stops rocking altogether, his head moves away from the breast. Eventually he climbs down from mother, partially bolstered by the courage she has transmitted to him. Cautiously he moves toward the inanimate fear stimulus, still fearful enough that sudden activity from another part of the room will trigger his flight reaction. Within less than a few minutes of the invasion of this plastic monster the young monkey will be disassembling its put-together limbs and chewing obliviously (not maliciously) on its antennae. In this brief span of time he has been transformed from a quivering, frightened coward to a normal, curious explorer. This transformation is made possible by the fact that he has available a base of security by which he restores himself to normal functioning after a frightening experience. It is especially instructive to note that in Harlow's studies those monkeys subjected to this open-field "terror" experiment who did not have a mother to run to in this moment of crisis remained in a state of fear much longer than monkeys for whom a mother was available. Young monkeys who had never known the strength of mother comfort hid face down in corners, regressing to the fetal position or autistic rocking.

The significant conclusions extracted from these studies are threefold: (1) the mother-figure has the ability to instil courage and confidence in the young monkey after he has been frightened; (2) the young monkey automatically, perhaps instinctively, flees to the mother in an emergency situation and clings to her until confidence has been rekindled; (3) those monkeys who have never known mother security (even an artificial cloth mother) have virtually no capacity to cope with environmental adversaries of any kind, including the plastic, motionless, insect-like creatures used in the Harlow experiments.

Anyone who has spent much time in the home of a toddler knows that the prowess of motherhood is not restricted to monkeys or other of man's evolutionary cousins. To the distressed toddler mother provides more than sanction — she transmits a fresh reservoir of confidence and assurance which was drained by something fearful. Mother is a base of security. When anything threatens the security of the toddler he returns to this base to have his depleting supply of confidence recharged. Throughout the toddlerhood years mother serves as a base of security. For most children its peak is reached between eighteen and thirty months. To the *toddler* mother is much more than merely nutrition and protection, more than need gratifier and comforter: she is the source of strength required to live in an unpredictable world that relishes frustrating the weak. The toddler, blessed with a mother of psychological strength who also provides a base of security when it is needed, is well on his way to mastering the fundamental growth requirement of toddlerhood — adventurous exploration.

General toddlerhood fears. Mussen (1963) reports that fear and anxiety in the two-year-old have four origins: (1) anticipation of being physically harmed, or of pain in general; (2) sudden changes in stimulation; (3) lack of congruity between what is expected and what actually happens; and (4) anticipation of loss of people who provide love, comfort, and security. These fears partially account for the fact that between eighteen and twenty-four months the child is at the peak of dependency on parents. At this age his base of security is one of his most valued assets.

The months immediately near the third birthday show the greatest incidence of fears of the entire childhood period. Girls reach their greatest incidence of fears at about thirty-six months, boys at about forty-two months. This is congruous with girls' slightly more advanced development during the first ten years of life. At age three, dogs are feared more commonly than anything else; by age four this distinction is usurped by fear of the dark. Near the fourth birthday the number as well as variety of fears begins to drop continuously until about age nine or ten (Macfarlane, 1954).

Relative size is not a major factor in toddler fears. A persistent insect is likely to trigger a fear reaction of greater intensity than a howling locomotive. Children who are mentally advanced tend to have fears correspondent with their mental age rather than their chronological age.

Because it is difficult for the toddler to distinguish between real and imaginary objects, during the third year a significant increase in fear of imaginary creatures occurs. Most normal three-year-olds spend many sleepless bedtime hours watching fearfully the weightless, transparent, wave-like movements of "creatures" who at any moment may crawl right into bed or merely dart away, later to return. Reassuring the toddler that there is no realistic basis to his fears lends some assistance and makes him less fearful. This is not because he becomes convinced of the nonreality of night creatures, but because the brief moment the parent spends in conversation serves to bolster his *general* courage and confidence. As the toddler grows older he learns about the social stigma associated with letting fears be known to others, and as a result becomes progressively more reluctant to discuss them. This phenomenon does not influence the child to a great extent before age three but it does play an important role in the life of the preschooler, as we shall observe in the next chapter.

Toddlers invariably become frightened if they sense that their parents are frightened; in this regard parental fear is even more contagious than parental confidence.

For the toddler *specific* fears (fear of horses or ladders) do not inhibit social growth nearly as much as *general* fears (fears of darkness or adults); but most destructive of all to continued growth is the subterranean (unconscious) fear that the *world* itself is dangerous. This fear, more than any other, stunts psychological, social, perhaps even physical, growth during the critical formative years of toddlerhood.

We must conclude that the toddlerhood years have their share of anxiety and fear. Though fears are, to a large measure, a function of developmental maturity (or lack of it) one cannot effectively deal with (or even theoretically conceptualize) the nature of toddlerhood without taking into consideration the unique cowardliness of this stage. But it is a short-lived period of cowardice, and during the preschool years we shall observe a renewed aura of confident optimism.

The Toddler as Computer

In our day and age it is fashionable to draw parallels between human behaviour and computer behaviour; psychologists refer to human functions in such terms as "sensory input", "memory bank", "electronic circuitry" or similar terms derived from cybernetics. It is also acceptable to use computer imagery when describing human behaviour; therefore, we read about "her computer-like efficiency", or "the old man was as disciplined and predictable as a computer". In many respects the comparison of the toddler to the computer is a fair one. Computers are made up of input sections by which they receive information and instructions, memory banks where data and instructions are stored, control sections which coordinate the activity of other computer sections, arithmetic and logic sections where calculations are carried out, and finally, output devices where the results of internal workings are presented in such a way that they can be understood by another computer or by a human. These have parallels in the human child. The senses serve as *input instruments* and process sensory stimuli which impinge upon the child's perceptual apparatus; the human memory serves much the same function as the computer's *memory bank,* except computer memory is less prone toward error; the human brain serves as the *control section* which regulates (either voluntarily or involuntarily) the functioning of all body sub-systems; the cortex serves, among other functions, as the anatomical location for *arithmetic* and *logic activities;* and finally, speech and behaviour serve as an equivalent to the computer's *output system,* allowing the person to be understood and his inner workings be made known to other humans. In addition to these technical similarities between the toddler and the computer there are several others. Computers are different from one another and can be highly individualized; they have their own unique idiosyncrasies and unpredictable breakdowns, and they can be changed or modified if they do not perform as expected or if expectations of them are changed by their human masters. The toddler shares these traits with the computer. Quite obviously there are several similarities between computers and children; therefore, drawing analogies between them or pointing out similarities in their theoretical "construction" is a helpful tool in gaining further understanding of the child.

However, several crucial *differences* between the toddler and the computer must be noted; if lost sight of, or even momentarily forgotten, the child may suffer. First, the computer is indifferent to the opinions, attitudes, or sentiments of humans and in no way do they affect its functioning or efficiency. The toddler, on the other hand, is not only sensitive to the feelings of others, but his efficiency and emotional stability are inseparable from them. Disastrous psychological consequences occur when the toddler is convinced that others *perceive* him in the *same way* they perceive a machine. Man, as well as his children, resists dehumanization and nothing more dehumanizes man than to tell him he is but a flesh-encapsulated machine. Secondly, and considerably less emotional, the toddler is capable of much more sophisticated activity than any computer devised thus far. True, the toddler cannot solve problems of calculus or instantly sum numbers, but calculations of this variety are completely programmed beforehand into the computer and the brilliance of such achievements belongs to the programmers, not the computer. Computers, as yet, are not capable of *spontaneous* invention of ideas for which they are not programmed; they cannot retrieve something which has not been stored; they cannot resist orders, and even though they frequently malfunction this is not due to self-generated resistance but rather to electronic imprecision. Toddlers, however, daily engage in all three of these activities beyond the power of the computer. Third, perhaps most important, computers do not inspire the love of adults, nor do adults inspire the love of computers. The fundamental nature of man-machine relatedness is mechanical rather than personal, whereas the fundamental nature of man-child relatedness is personal rather than mechanical. Therein lie three basic differences between toddler and computer which under no circumstances should be lost sight of in our investigation of the first ten years of life.

The toddler does share some common features with the computer, just as he is similar in some respects to all air-breathing and vertebrate animals. Similarities, however, must never be confused with identities nor should they blind us to fundamental differences.

In this section of our overview of toddlerhood we shall probe the nature of *mental development and speech development*. The maturation of mental and speech functions ushers the child into the adult world, and this, possibly more than anything else, prepares the child for socialization and entrance into the world of culture and humanly unique realities.

The urge to know and understand. Even during the early months of life when motor and intellectual skills are grossly immature, the child displays an inherent urge to know. In many respects it is similar to his inherent drive toward exploration and competence (as described in "Toddler as Housewrecker"), but differs in that the urge to know permeates all behaviour whether it be physical, social, experiential, or intellectual; it matters little to the toddler whether what is being focused upon relates to his personal life or not. A toddler will watch a spider dangle from the invisible suspension which only spiders possess with the same enthusiasm and involvement he musters while watching daytime educational TV. The urge to know has few hierarchical priorities, but it can become narrowly concentrated whenever so desired. So powerful is the toddler's urge to know and learn about his world (especially between twenty-four and thirty-six months) that he cannot restrain himself from this impulse. When he discovers that a clothespin can be placed inside the mouth of a jar he is compelled to insert pin after pin into the opening. Later, when he discovers that by tipping the jar upside down the clothespins will fall out, he executes this discovery over and over. When speech begins to exert a major force (usually near the second birthday) the toddler will spend hour upon hour talking, chattering, bandying about vocalizations which are part word, part jumble, and part chant. As the third birthday approaches, our toddler talks to himself, to imaginary companions, to parents and visitors. He wants to practise and become proficient in every aspect of language; when the words in his limited vocabulary fail him, he invents new ones, some of which are grammatically coherent.

The urge to know is constantly reinforced in everything the child does. He *discovers* new play arenas or edible goodies; he *masters* objects which previously caused only frustration (such as door knobs or small glasses); he is *praised* by parents for maturity or recognition when he learns that busy streets are off limits. The almost hourly reinforcement which the child receives for learning about the environment perpetuates his natural drive for understanding and knowledge. Though it is possible to extinguish the urge to know and understand, it succumbs only when a *negligent* or *punitive* environment surrounds the child. One never observes a toddler raised in normal environmental conditions who lacks a powerful urge to understand and know. Sometimes it is camouflaged or below the surface, or maybe even a bit rusty from lack of encouragement, but always the urge is there ready to be resurrected at the slightest prompting.

The urge to know and understand is an inseparable ingredient of toddlerhood. Several years of environmental or parental abuse will dissipate or weaken it, but it is not until the preschool years that the urge to know and understand begins to lose some of its dominance over the child. Nature is far too discerning to allow such a central requisite for human growth to be so delicate that it could be extinguished under anything less than subhuman conditions during the critical formative years of toddlerhood.

Intellectual transitions during toddlerhood. The twenty-four months of life encapsulated by toddlerhood witness significant intellectual expansion, and few other periods equal toddlerhood in importance or quality of intellectual growth. The one-year-old and the three-year-old possess vastly different modes of intellectual functioning: they operate on different principles; they have radically different degrees of freedom; and they have disparate backgrounds into which they may integrate new knowledge and experience. In summary, the one-year-old has meager capacities for learning and the three-year-old has sophisticated capacities; the one-year-old is narrow, almost determined, and the three-year-old is expanded and almost free. Here we shall overview several of the more central mental growth transitions intrinsic to the toddlerhood years.

1.   *Problem solving skills emerge.* On his first birthday the child has minimal ability to solve problems and usually must rely upon chance, randomness, or good fortune (trial-and-error) for problem solution. During toddlerhood, problems are solved first by means of active experimentation, and later by means of mental combinations or abstract thinking. *Insight* develops during toddlerhood as does knowledge of *causality;* the toddler comes to recognize his own role in causing certain events. Although we could never so infer by watching the three-year-old, the twelve-month-old child does not recognize himself as an instrument of change or of environmental influence. Therefore he usually does not approach the environment with strategy or intent.

2.   *Verbal and representational thought come into existence.* Intellectual growth and language development exist side by side in symbiotic relationship; as one grows, the other directly benefits. Words open an entire new realm of intellectual adventure, and serve as catalyst for hundreds of discoveries and intellectual breakthroughs. Symbolic thinking permits the child to use one stimulus to represent another (a doll can be "daughter", "mother", or whatever the mood calls for) and introduces the pleasure world of fantasy as well as the abstract world of thought and conjecture.

3.   *The environment becomes increasingly differentiated and compartmentalized.* The toddler learns to fragment his environment, and to break it down into small workable units. He learns to concentrate on one aspect of his world to the exclusion of others; he also acquires the ability to use one environmental object to secure another. By the end of toddlerhood he will walk across a room, pick up a chair, and return to his original location in order to reach a desired object beyond normal reach. The child learns to manipulate the environment to his advantage rather than merely being captive within it. And he learns that all parts of the environment are not available to his caprice — he learns to differentiate those parts of the household, nursery, or neighbourhood which are open to adventure and those which are closed.

4.   *Specific mental skills mature.* The toddler's attention span almost doubles between the eighteenth and twenty-fourth month. There is no comparison whatsoever between the attention span of the one-year-old and that of the three-year-old. The ability to inhibit impulses, or to

dampen body activity, missing at twelve months, is dramatically present at thirty-six months. Growth toward intellectual maturity is profoundly experienced in the child's increasing capacity for reflectiveness, thoughtfulness, and premeditation.

5. *Recognition of number and quantity develop.* The world of the one-year-old is thoroughly singular. He manipulates one object at a time; transports items in isolated, repetitive fashion; attends to one thing at a time; and can concentrate only on one stimulus at a time. The mature toddler, expanded by cortical growth and environmental encouragement, deals in big number theory. He builds towers of five or six blocks; arranges blocks in orderly sequences; and rarely will allow a single block to remain isolated from the others which give it continuity as well as utility. Frequently the three-year-old can count to ten, but this is basically a gesture of rote memory and does not signify an underlying knowledge of number. The early toddler is isolated and singular, the late toddler is aggregative and plural.

6. *Sensory input becomes integrated into a progressively more complex information bank.* The child learns from experience in direct proportion to the retentive powers of his memory. During toddlerhood memory is growing in quality and quantity almost monthly. The child learns from negative as well as positive events, but by late toddlerhood he is capable of omitting behaviour which has unpleasant consequences. The one-year-old has no such capacity except in a general, conditioned sense.

7. *Strategies are developed for coping with environmental obstacles.* The late toddler learns to "attack" his environment; to manipulate it to his advantage, and to use it for his own purposes. (Make no mistake about it, the toddler is an egocentric creature!) He can pursue problem-solving by *active* experimentation (try Plan 1 and if it fails devise another) or by *mental* experimentation (what would happen if I tried this?), but no such strategies exist in the earliest part of toddler life.

8. *Acquisition of language.* Learning to speak is one of the most important accomplishments of toddlerhood. Language is more than a tool of mental development, it also is a *source* of mental development. Speech and thought cannot be separated because each benefits from the other; increased mental development facilitates more complex speech, and expanded speech skills open new intellectual horizons. Language allows the child to benefit from the wisdom of adults; a problem quite beyond the cognitive capacities of the toddler can be easily solved if he comprehends an adult's spoken command to "turn it the *other* way".

Toddlerhood is the time of growth, and grow the child does. His mental growth is prodigious, sequential, and, in most regards, moderately predictable. Perhaps of greatest import to the student of human development is the fact that the intellectual prowess acquired during the toddlerhood years sets the stage for the capacities, interests, and intellectual talents of the preschool years.

Mental development during the second year of life (twelve to twenty-four months). Before twelve months of age the human child has few intellectual skills upon which to draw. General motor maturity is awkward and many children have not yet begun to walk. Memory is exclusively short-term, therefore, the ability to benefit from experience is minimal. The pre-one-year-old possesses a primitive notion of causality, but does not recognize himself as an instrument of causality (he will strain to lift a blanket which he is standing upon). During his second year, when these deficiencies are outgrown, the child discovers a completely new world of cause-effect, and begins to understand his role in causing events to happen.

Between the twelfth and eighteenth month the idea dawns upon the flowering toddler mentality that there is a connection between his behaviour and environmental happenings. He learns that certain behaviour commonly produces certain results, for example, that released objects fall downward and make a crashing sound when they hit the floor. This elementary observational tidbit produces at least four crucial items of information for the early toddler: (1) objects leave the hand when grasp is released (although he has known this for several months); (2) objects invariably move downward when released unless there is an artificial barrier, such as an incline, to interfere with gravitational effects (the child is into his third year before he can properly anticipate the stopping point of an object dropped on an incline); (3) objects make a sound when they strike the floor; and (4) parents make a sound immediately following the sound of a dropped object. The important kernel of wisdom which the toddler extracts from all this is: *repeating* particular behaviour causes particular results. Thus the child learns to act with intent and with some awareness of probable consequences. After this crucial discovery he eventually recognizes that adding *slight variation to the particular behaviour will produce slightly different consequences.* In other words, the child finally has stumbled upon the most fundamental item of knowledge required of an environment-manipulating animal; changes which occur in the environment are directly related to how the environment is acted upon.

The rudimentary groundwork for understanding causality is now begun, and from it flow remarkable life-changing events. The child learns to *experiment* with the novel and to *systematically* explore the unknown. He learns to *modify* his approach if unsuccessful in procuring a desired object with the first line of attack, he learns to consider himself an *active influence* in the total environment, and comes to *regulate* himself in *anticipation* of future events. He swings from reactive to self-directed active.

Despite these intellectual breakthroughs, behaviour is still primitive and little evidence of abstract thought or problem-solving is presented. Learning is still trial-and-error, mostly error, but growth in memory helps to eliminate endless repetitions of experiments which were conducted the day before. Some examples of intellectual behaviour at this stage of development (twelve to eighteen months) are provided by Flavell (1963, p. 117). An object out of reach rests upon a support such as a blanket; the infant draws the desired object toward himself by pulling on the blanket. He also learns that an object may be secured by pulling the string which is attached to it. In each of these behaviours the child achieves a desired end by employing a secondary strategy. At this developmental level the child also learns to tilt long objects in order to draw them through the narrow bars of his playpen; he learns that objects will not go through openings too small to accommodate them; and he learns how to make flexible objects pass through a narrow opening. All things have their beginnings, and here we witness the beginning of cause-effect knowledge.

Thus far the child is restricted to solving problems by *active* experimentation. He must *try* to squeeze a four-inch ball through a two-inch opening before he learns that it will not fit. Although he does acquire a fluid and expanding reservoir of information *as a result* of active experimentation, he is unable to acquire *new* information without some form of experimentation or observation. In this respect toddler intelligence at eighteen months is similar to that of other lower animals including horses, cats, and *young* chimpanzees. During the last six months of the second year (eighteen to twenty-four months), as the supremacy of man's genetic code begins to exert itself, the child advances to a new and more advanced stage of mental development; he begins to cope with the environment by means of *mental combinations* (abstract thinking). The first stage of mental life comes when the capacity to *invent* solutions without going through the process of *active* experimentation is achieved. Here Flavell describes this intellectual breakthrough:

> This important new pattern can be summarized as follows. The child wishes to achieve some end and finds no habitual schema which can serve as means. . . . However, instead of fumbling for a solution by an extended series of overt and visible sensory-motor explorations . . . the child "invents" one through a covert process which amounts to *internal* experimentation, an *inner*

exploration of ways and means. Unlike any previous stage, the acquisition of something genuinely new can now take place covertly — prior to action, instead of through, and only through, a series of actually performed assimilations and accommodations. (1963, p. 119)

In other words, the child learns to devise ideas for solving problems *which he acts upon after they are thought of,* rather than vice versa. Some examples of this sophisticated thought process will help clarify its nature more fully. A child attempts to rest up against a stool, but each time this is tried the stool scoots backwards. After several unsuccessful attempts to lean comfortably against the sliding stool, the toddler gets up, takes the stool, and places it against a sofa, and then leans against it with justified assurance that it will not slide backwards. In carrying out this activity the capacity to invent an appropriate solution without benefit of active experimentation is demonstrated. (It is here assumed that the child has had no previous occasion to learn about propping the stool against the sofa.) In providing us with another example of the toddler's capacity for abstract thought Piaget relates the following story.

Jacqueline arrives at a closed door — with a blade of grass in each hand. She stretches out her right hand toward the knob but sees that she cannot turn it without letting go of the grass. She puts the grass on the floor, opens the door, picks up the grass again and enters. But when she wants to leave the room things become complicated. She puts the grass on the floor and grasps the doorknob. But then she perceives that in pulling the door toward her she will simultaneously chase away the grass which she placed between the door and the threshold. She therefore picks it up in order to put it outside the door's zone of movement. (Flavell, p. 119)

During the second year other intellectual developments are taking place in addition to the child's two-part trip through active and mental experimentation. A strong interest in completion of an event develops around eighteen months, indicating the ability to differentiate completeness from incompleteness — a perceptual distinction which holds absolutely no fascination for the pre-fifteen-month-old child. Several geometric relationships are mastered, and the child does not expect square blocks to roll or triangles to remain upright when placed on their apex. At twenty-four months the child actually gives the impression of being a thinking animal, and sometimes his moments of reflection are almost as painfully obvious as those of the preoccupied, eccentric professor. At the end of the second year, attention span is greatly increased over eighteen months as evidenced by the fact that block towers double their height during this six-month span. Many two-year-olds remember events from yesterday although their vocabulary does not yet permit precise time distinctions. And everywhere there are words, words, and more words.

The middle toddler outgrows his numerical restrictions and deals with plural events rather than merely singular events.

> He has an interest in many and in more. He likes to assemble the many cubes into a pile or to disperse the pile into the many cubes. He likes to store and to hold four, six, or more cubes which are handed to him individually. In comparison, the 1-year-old is single- and serial-minded. The 1-year-old infant has a typical one-by-one pattern: he takes one cube after another and places it on the table or platform in a repetitive manner. This is a genetic anticipation of counting. The 18-month-old infant cannot count, but he has a vigorous interest in aggregates, and that also is a developmental prerequisite for a higher mathematics. (Gesell, 1940, p. 31)

Mental development during the third year of life (twenty-four to thirty-six months). The second half of the toddler's intellectual career is characterized by growth of all previously acquired skills as well as the spontaneous development of several additional capacities. Manual, perceptual, and verbal discriminations become considerably more precise as the last quarter of toddlerhood is approached. Exploration and investigation are greatly enhanced by refined prehensile skills and the child is presented with a continuous flow of information from the consequences of his manipulatory activity. Random and disorderly activities are partially outgrown, and we observe an almost universal tendency in late toddlerhood to arrange and tidy environmental objects. Play blocks often are grouped into geometric or colour classifications, and doll clothes may work their way into a specially designated alcove. Now the child easily solves three-hole form board tasks, and invariably triangles, squares, and circles are placed in those slots which correspond to their geometric shape. At about age two-and-a-half, when notice is taken of configurations which are incomplete, some toddlers experience emotional distress upon observing a torn picture or a statue with a dismembered limb.

Several aspects of the child's social life reflect his evolving intellectual prowess. He becomes susceptible to bargaining and trading. Though not talented at bartering, he is capable of assimilating the notion that one object is traded for another; however, his aversion to being completely responsible allows him to change his mind capriciously a moment or two after the transaction has occurred. As future time becomes conceptual he is able to negotiate about future events; at this age mothers learn that a promised dessert or some such treat will seduce the child into "good" behaviour. Such bribery is impossible at eighteen months because at this age the only "real" time is present time. Late toddlerhood also witnesses the onset of *cooperative* work because the child now recognizes that two people can work together to accomplish a desired goal, although for the most part parents or daytime guardians are the only ones capable of getting much mileage from the toddler in these endeavours. Toddlers are rewarded for their attempts at coopera- tive labour (it is one of our society's most highly prized values), and it is not unusual for parents to invent activities which require cooperation to further entrench the importance of it in the toddler's world view. Parents compulsively reward youngsters for sharing, helping, or any behaviour of a cooperative, altruistic nature. Before it may effectively begin, there must be something tangible in it for the toddler (altruism comes ever so slowly).

The verbal world dominates late toddler life as never before. Not only is a great portion of each day spent in practising and rehearsing previously acquired words, but new ones are constantly assimilated and periodically invented. Toddlers track through the house naming, cate- gorizing, classifying, and otherwise describing every object which comes into view. "Whazzat?" is the North American universal interrogative which normal toddlers cannot avoid because it is the term which more than any other precisely states what they want to know: "What *is* that?" The most significant influence of language upon the social life of the toddler is that behaviour now becomes controllable (in some cir- cumstances) by verbal command. The child responds when spoken to and is able to adjust his own internal set to that of another person. When this occurs the child becomes an irrevocable social being, and henceforth will never again be able to act consistently from a *totally* egocentric posture. The most significant *intellectual* influence of language upon the life of the toddler is that he can directly benefit from the experience of others. He learns about the world by the spoken word as well as from personal experience or representational thought. The advent of language as a *dominant* toddler reality signals his readi- ness for teachability in the unique human tradition: the transmission of *abstract* knowledge from generation to generation.

By the last third of toddlerhood *representational thought* becomes a central part of mental activity. Representational thought is the ability to represent in one's mind the possible (or probable) consequences of a given action. It permits the thinker to anticipate in advance the influ- ence of A upon B. In representational thought one is able to grasp the relatedness of an *entire sequence of separate events*. For example: if suddenly it strikes our toddler's fancy to sneak a chocolate bar from the kitchen counter he immediately recognizes that a chair is needed in order to reach it; upon discovering the chocolate bar is still out of reach he might employ a spoon to scoot it forward. While engaging in these activities he is aware that if mother discovers him he will be in trouble; therefore upon her unexpected entrance he may "freeze" in *anticipation* of her verbal wrath, he may run away, or he may even challenge her right to uphold ridiculous rules which forbid indulgence in sweets whenever they are desired. The crucial consideration here is that the child is able to *simultaneously* represent the following thoughts:

1. the chair and spoon can be used to reach the chocolate bar;
2. eating the chocolate bar may meet with mother's disapproval;
3. mother's disapproval will occur only if *she* discovers what has transpired (this point is critical because it signifies the ability to distinguish between general knowledge and private knowledge, or stated differently, the toddler now knows that everyone does not know what he knows);
4. mother's disapproval, like the chocolate bar, must be approached with some kind of coping strategy.

It is not a wonder that by late toddlerhood many mothers describe daytime routine as a war of wits.

Although representational thought greatly expands the child's interaction with his environment, he still has a rather shaky notion of causality. During toddlerhood thought is better described as *correlational* than as causal. Event A is associated with (or thought to be caused by) event B because they occur in the same temporal span. The child may believe that blowing branches or moving clouds *cause* wind because these events occur simultaneously. Or he may infer that ice cream vendors are special family friends because they give the kind of prized treats only characteristic of true friends. Flavell again provides valued assistance in understanding the workings of the toddler mind:

> If one asks the reason for A, the child will supply a B as cause, B being simply some element which co-occurred with A in perception and has hence co-fused with A in a global, syncretic schema. Since cause-and-effect requirements are so lax for the young child, anything and everything must have an identifiable cause. One interesting consequence of this orientation is that he is unable to form a genuine concept of chance or probability. (1963, p. 161)

Sometime during the third year *logic,* embryonic though it may be, makes its presence felt on the child's mental processes. The earliest examples of logic are referred to by Piaget as *trans*ductive to indicate that it is neither purely inductive nor deductive in form. Transductive reasoning proceeds from particular to particular, and is not rooted in a concept of causality. Thus if the cat is furry, all furry creatures are cats. If dogs have four legs, all four-legged creatures are dogs. If daddy is male and adult, all adult males are daddy (to the embarrassment of every mother this latter example of transductive reasoning inevitably is verbally executed in the presence of a former male companion). Ultimately this stage of reasoning is outgrown, but its importance should not be underestimated in the daily behaviour of the toddler. Causal equations which are unique to toddlerhood come about as a result of this thought process: blanket is equated with security, and the absence of blanket with insecurity; departure through a door might signal "gone for the day", rather than gone for a moment; "Johnny" may signify brother and no one else, and brother may signify Johnny and no one else. Transductive reasoning is outgrown in the preschool years, but its obsolescence can be hastened by calmly and patiently explaining to the child one fundamental rule of logic: A may equal B, but it may *also* equal C, D, E, etc. The human mind takes readily and easily to logic and, as we shall observe, more sophisticated forms progressively unfold during the childhood years.

The young child's use of logic is a constant source of amazement to adults. Parents frequently resort to displays of power or authority in order to cope with the helter-skelter nature of toddler logic; for those not so inclined, a *tolerance* of faulty logic allows them to deal with the toddler on terms which jibe with his mental skills.

> Parents who try to reason with young children often find themselves sinking in a quagmire of rapidly changing premises, logical inconsistencies, unforeseen implications, word magic and dissolving obviousness. Told that a toy he wants is too expensive, it follows for the child that his parents must be willing to buy him another, less expensive one. . . . The young child has no doubt that a single object can simultaneously be in two widely separated locations. A new adult encountered in the home of other children is almost certain to be classed as a parent of those children, even though this may provide them with two or more mothers or fathers. (Church, 1966, p. 77-78)

Summary of toddlerhood mental development

Toddlerhood is characterized by the emergence of several intellectual developments; some of the more important include the emergence of:

1. problem-solving skills;
2. verbal and representational thought;
3. more differentiated and compartmentalized environment;
4. increased maturity of mental skills;
5. number and quantity;

6. a rich and complex information bank;

7. environmental coping strategies;

8. language.

The toddler's inherent urge to know and understand pushes him through the two major stages of thought in the second year of life: (a) active experimentation, and (b) mental experimentation. During the third year of life transductive reasoning, representational thought, and language-based abstraction are added to the child's mental skills in addition to the refinement and advancement of all previously existing thought processes.

We are now ready to look into speech development during toddlerhood.

Speech during toddlerhood. Between the twelfth and thirty-sixth month of life normal children learn to speak the language of their household and also learn a great deal about the grammatical and syntactical construction of language. Before reaching his third birthday the toddler acquires spoken mastery of about one thousand words and an understanding of thousands more. English-speaking children learn that nouns usually are placed at the beginning of sentences, that objects of action follow verbs, and that adjectives come before nouns. He also learns (as do children of *all* nationalities) that words communicate intent, that definite consequences follow them, that words used incorrectly may or may not have communicative power, and that words are integrally related to affection and love. How the child comes to acquire language and grammar is not precisely understood. There is little controversy over the thesis that language acquisition is dependent upon (a) maturation of brain functions, (b) exposure to the language, (c) reinforcement for using language, and (d) man's genetic-based capacity for symbolization. The relative importance of each of these factors is controversial, however, and different theories stress various components of the phenomenon of speech. Theoretical problems related to understanding how speech is learned are compounded by the possibility that the processes which govern *understanding* speech are not the same as those which control the ability to *produce* speech. In this abbreviated section we shall concentrate on describing the speech habits and capacities of the toddler rather than analysing various theories associated with speech acquisition. The descriptive approach is used for two basic reasons: (1) as far as most adults are concerned, the crucial factor in child speech is the *sequence* involved in learning to speak, and (2) the child's abilities are the raw material with which adults must work and, even though theoretical understanding of abilities is helpful, it is subordinate to a descriptive understanding of these same abilities. Therefore, we shall describe the important stages of speech development, as understood within the context of contemporary research, while constantly keeping in mind the importance these stages hold not only for the toddler's interaction with the world but also for our understanding of his inner workings.

Twelve months: The child's first word, which usually occurs within a month of his first birthday, is little more than a conditioned response to an object or person. First words are difficult to distinguish from the random, playful vocalizations which the child has been making during the past few months; however, mothers seem to have a unique knack for distinguishing them. A few additional words may be acquired before the fifteenth month but it is quite within the normal range for a child not to have uttered his first recognizable word by this time. Between fifteen and eighteen months the child jabbers and chatters with intonation even though he does not use "real" words. A visitor from outer space unfamiliar with the specific words of a language might be convinced the child is actually conversing. Communication at this age is carried out almost exclusively by gesture and mannerism (as it has been since the first months of life); in a few months the child experiences considerable frustration at being unable to communicate in the verbal medium to which adults are most suited. Not until about eighteen months does the toddler experience frustration at being misunderstood, because before then words do not have explicit communicative functions. The quality of vocalization at this age may be influenced by (a) personality differences, (b) environmental encouragement or suppression, (c) the opportunity to hear adult conversation or associate with older children, and (d) inhibition based upon severe emotional experiences.

Words such as "mamma" and "dadda" now appear and there is definite indication that certain adult words as well as simple commands (Sit down!) are understood. A principle which holds throughout the childhood years already is manifesting itself by twelve months: language *comprehension* precedes language *production*, usually by several months. In other words, the child understands much more than he is able to speak (to the surprise of no one who has learned a second language!). Evidence has been compiled suggesting that a period of speech *readiness* occurs between the ages of twelve and eighteen months when the child is maximally sensitive to the acquisition of words, and conversely, susceptible to impairment of normal speech growth if subject to damaging conditions such as severe illness or acute emotional trauma (Hurlock, p. 219). The period between twelve and eighteen months may thus be considered a *critical period* in speech development.

Eighteen months: Word production increases spectacularly between eighteen and twenty-four months after a comparative slump between fifteen and eighteen months. Smith (1926) found an average increase of ninety-six words between eighteen and twenty-one months and an additional one-hundred and fifty-four words between twenty-one and twenty-four months. (This accelerated *rate* of word acquisition is similar to that experienced by an adult who has made a sudden breakthrough in learning a second language.) At about eighteen months the Broca region of the brain, which is integrally related to speech development, undergoes rapid development; also at this age language assumes a communicative function of greater importance than ever before. Spontaneous word combinations are slowly emerging; by twenty-four months the toddler will create and invent his own original phrases which express desires or describe environmental objects. (This ability to create phrases spontaneously poses special problems for theorists who assume that speech acquisition is essentially the result of imitation.) As the toddler now understands simple directions, he can carry out routine requests as long as they do not require extensive use of memory; otherwise he will forget the original message before it is acted upon. The child has a limited repertoire of words but still engages in a good deal of babbling; he may chatter *at* an adult without any attempt at communication, but also may chatter *to* them with intent and purpose. Frequently, to distinguish one from the other is difficult. Despite the increased number of words the eighteen-month-old child uses, he still has minimal capacity for two-word combinations; only among the most precocious eighteen-month-old toddlers are three-word, grammatically sound phrases used. At this age the child relies extensively on one-word sentences (called *holophrasiastic speech*) which are intended to express a complete idea. "Eat" means "I want something to eat," or "bath" might communicate that "I want to take a bath now."

Word comprehension is increasing rapidly, as is the toddler's ability to interpret the meaning of a sentence by the tone of voice used by the speaker. This latter ability accounts for the unexpected fear reaction elicited from the toddler by a playful but gruff *sounding* command. Between eighteen and twenty-four months adjectives work their way into the vocabulary, the most common being "good", "bad", "hot", "cold", and others which have direct bearing on the toddler's personal world. Retardation in speech acquisition has been observed among institutional children (especially those who have minimal exposure to adults or speaking children), mentally deficient children, children late in showing hand-preference, and children who have experienced severe illness or emotional shock.

Twenty-four months: By the second birthday the child has progressed from random vocalizing of vowel sounds to consonants to syllables to elementary words. Interest in virtually every aspect of language increases near the second birthday. Two-word phrases are spontaneously formed by almost all children. For the most part they relate either to the child's immediate needs ("Go potty"), or describe a visible environmental object ("Dog big"). It is not unusual for the child to invent words (*neologisms*) which allow him to express an idea for which he does not possess sufficient vocabulary. Some toddler neologisms include: "fator" (food is in the refrigerator); "uvkiss" (give me love and a kiss).

During the next six months toddlers experience considerable frustration in attempts to communicate because words now have definite purpose and are intended to elicit specific responses. For the two-year-old the verbal world is analagous to the Tower of Babel with understandability randomly permeating the stream of words which ricochet throughout the household. The two-year-old, by merit of his ability to tolerate the frustration associated with living on the periphery of a verbal society while he possesses only the most rudimentary verbal skills, is testimony to the discipline and endurance of the human spirit.

For most children, usable vocabulary is approaching 200 words. Pronouns are introduced for the first time, indicating the movement away from exclusive preoccupation with nouns, verbs, and adjectives. "I", "me", and "you" become differentiated, though "I" and "me" remain juxtaposed for some time. Because "my" and "mine" come before other possessives in the toddler's vocabulary their communicative function is asserted whenever someone tries to confiscate an object the toddler considers his own. Many toddlers still use the proper name when referring to themselves or others rather than the correct pronoun. Investigators who have tabulated the vocabulary of two-year-olds report ranges from 5 to 1,212 words; at thirty months the range extends from 30 to 1,509 words. This serves to remind us that *individual variation* is the normal condition of speech acquisition. Some children seem able to name everything in their environment while others lack this capacity. Occasionally a child considerably below the norm in speaking skills at twenty-four months will make an impressive breakthrough and by thirty months be an average, or perhaps even precocious, speaker.

Thirty months: Prior to this age speech has essentially been "telegraphic" in that the child speaks as though he is sending a telegram and eliminates all unnecessary words. Messages are usually direct, precise (if you consider the unspoken elements), and to the point; they have little literary merit, and allusion and metaphor are nonexistent. At two-and-one-half the child begins to mature beyond purely descriptive speech, but it will be another year before he is very good at it, and fully two additional years before he can speak extemporaneously with sufficient skill to hold the attention of a group of adults. At thirty months new words are added every day and the child will go out of his way to learn the proper verbal label for an object or person. He enjoys rehearsing speaking skills and will flit about a room naming object after object. The toddler engages in this kind of behaviour even without praise; it is commonly done in the absence of company. He is developing a new skill, and like all newly emerging skills, it demands exercise.

At thirty months there is little babbling; phrases usually have communicative intent, and sentences may be five words or longer. The child understands rather well what is said to him. At this age parents teach the child that verbal commands, even complex ones, are to be acted upon. Words acquire definite inhibitory power and the child is expected to discipline his desire for dessert because mother says "Not now," or "Dessert will come later." Words have praise value and the toddler will go to painstaking efforts to receive a "What a *good* boy," or "You are my most wonderful helper." Children especially enjoy the *gestures* of affection which accompany verbal praise, but willingly accept spoken praise even in the absence of embrace or caress.

As one would expect, the inherent superiority of females during the early childhood years is manifested in their greater facility with words. At three years girls surpass boys in virtually all areas of speech development including vocabulary size, length and complexity of sentences, and general communicative ability. The developmental difference between normal girls and boys at this age is about three to six calendar months. Even for girls, however, words are not used to precisely differentiate reality from fantasy and the only way to determine whether the thirty-month-old is talking about a dream or a specific physical event is to contextualize his words and his emotional frame of reference.

Thirty-six months: The child now has about 1,000 words in his working vocabulary and thousands more in his comprehension vocabulary. His speech is intelligible even to strangers, and grammatical complexity is roughly that of colloquial adult language (Lenneberg, 1965). At thirty-six months the child may *introduce* the main points of his message with appropriate comments rather than stating *only* the exact message. He will spontaneously initiate conversations which have no purpose other than the social pleasure intrinsic to conversation (this habit reaches unbearable extremes in middle childhood as we shall shortly observe).

Despite achievements in the acquisition of language, the toddler still has a great deal of trouble with prepositions such as "above", "below", "under", "in", "on". Sending a child on an errand in which a prepositional term is central to its proper execution ("Get the paper *under* the table.") inevitably meets with failure unless the child is able to contextualize the message and thereby know that father wants a paper which is *somewhere* in the vicinity of the table. Much toddler comprehension results from contextualization as is evidenced by his willing attempts to act upon a command which makes no sense. If the mother says "Go in the bedroom and bring me the . . ." she might be startled to observe that the toddler will go into the bedroom and search for something. He does so because from the intonation of the sentence he knows it is a *command;* and from the particular words he knows that he is expected to *retrieve* something. Lack of cortical maturity prevents him from realizing that the first part of a command is meaningless (or at least ambiguous) without its conclusion.

Perhaps the most significant breakthrough at this age is the ability to talk cogently about nonpresent events. The three-year-old talks freely about past events although future happenings are discussed in more restricted terms. Compound and complex sentences emerge and usually *plurality* as well as *past tense* has been mastered. The toddler is quite creative at inventing past tense words which are grammatically sound, but technically incorrect, such as "runned", "swinged", "bath-tubbed", "eated", and "wented". The child is still a year away from the metaphysics of future time, and questions such as "Where do I go when I die?" are awaiting further intellectual growth before they surface from the toddler's fertile imagination.

In the span between the eighteenth and thirty-sixth months the child completes the transition from a nonverbal to a verbal organism though, to be sure, further refinements continue to occur. Thus, in 540 days the human toddler accomplishes what nonhuman primates have been unable to do in more than one million generations. The transition is unfathomable if one merely considers the toddler as similar to the computer.

In order to equal the speaking capacities of a three-year-old child, a man-made computer would have to be capable of *inferring the intent* of ambiguous messages; *contextualizing words or phrases* which do not make sense or for which the computer is not programmed; *omitting* words not central to the verbal message being sent or received; *reconstructing* the meaning of a sentence when it is used in a humourous vein (frequently adults use words playfully in which case the intended meaning is opposite to the *spoken* meaning, i.e., "My, my, I don't think I like you anymore. No sir, no sir, I really don't."); *spontaneously invent-*

ing new words; *delineating* pretend words from real words; *distinguishing* between words used for explicit communicative purposes and those used only for recreational or play purposes; and finally, learning when one sentence *cancels out another,* i.e., "O.K., I've changed my mind, it is alright to go outside and play." All of these abilities found in toddler speech are nurtured by toddler intelligence. Upon discovering this, the scientific investigator once again is humbled by the awesome complexity and sturdy intricacy of childhood and its wonders.

The Toddler as Environmental Pollution

Despite the lack of pending federal legislation against their pollutant tendencies, a very good case can be made that toddlers are the number one source of household pollution in those domiciles which house them. In addition to their proclivity for housewrecking (which we have already discussed) toddlers have at their command a host of other mannerisms and habits which serve to make impure, unclean, and dirty the environment in which they live. Despair over this intrinsic condition of toddlerhood is unnecessary, however, because just at the time when one is getting accustomed to the residue of toddler existence the developmental immaturities which most account for it are outgrown. As the child approaches his third birthday we observe that the three major sources of his environmental pollution are responding to the demands of socialization and the benefits of advanced maturity.

Three developmentally-based behaviours account for much of the toddler's pollutant prowess: (1) his *plumbing equipment,* bestowed by nature, is immature, impulsive, and comparatively immune to social constraint, and it is rarely before twenty-four months that the child is able to take advantage of the instrument modern man devised expressly for the purpose of reducing human waste pollution: the toilet; (2) his *play* is exploratory, ambulatory, and adventurous, and periodically it can not be distinguished from malicious vandalism; and (3) his *eating habits* are messy, imprecise, and capricious, and even though they are the least potent of his pollution potential, eating habits contribute to the general aura of quaint messiness which characterizes toddlerhood. Because of the centrality of these three domains of toddler existence we shall briefly investigate not only their social implications but their developmental genesis. First we shall describe toilet-training during toddlerhood, then play habits, and finally eating habits. Hopefully by doing so we shall achieve greater understanding of the inevitability of toddlerhood pollution but also come to an increased appreciation of the transitory and developmental nature of it.

114

Toilet-training: Bladder and bowel control, like all neuro-muscular activity, require maturation and practice before effective functioning begins. However, there are few anatomical developments which create such impact on the external environment as those involved in toilet-training. Urination and defecation are facts of life for all animals, but those which live within sheltered confines (man is not the only example) must learn to deal with the discomfort as well as the disease associated with the elimination of body waste. In humans the process is rather simple for the first eighteen months of life: the child eliminates whenever he needs to and someone else tidies up and disinfects after him. Largely because of this latter aspect of elimination parents rejoice when the toddler is able to control elimination voluntarily. The ability to control eliminative functions is a complex achievement which depends primarily upon maturational readiness and partially on training and practice. Urination (also called *micturition*) is controlled by both voluntary and involuntary muscles: the detrusor muscle is involuntary and is stimulated to contract by impulses from the spinal cord, but the external sphincter is voluntary and its control becomes possible when the child has achieved maturational readiness, which for most children is between eighteen and thirty months. Appreciation for the time required to learn to control elimination can be enhanced by recognizing that it takes the child more than one year to learn to open and close his hand voluntarily, and fully five years before fingers can be rapidly moved to and from the thumb.

As with most childhood achievements, a good deal of folklore exists about the precociousness of some children in being toilet-trained. Stories of children who are toilet-trained by their first birthday invariably prove to be incorrect. What usually is meant is that the child will defecate when placed on the pot; but this is because the mother has been alerted to the imminence of this activity by some cue from the child and hurriedly places him at the proper location just as nature is carrying out its responsibilities. The ability to defecate or urinate upon locating the correct place for such activity is only one aspect of toilet-training; the most significant part deals with voluntarily controlling the anal and urethral sphincters so that elimination can be *temporarily* postponed.

Despite tremendous individual differences as to the age when bladder or bowel control is achieved, there is a predictable sequence to which control of elimination almost universally adheres: (a) walking occurs before bowel control; (b) bowel control occurs before bladder control; and (c) daytime control of bowel and bladder takes place before nighttime control. The sequence takes place between eighteen and thirty-six months for the majority of normal children. Some toddlers are extremely regular in their elimination schedules whereas others are not; however, those who are most regular make it easier for an adult to act in time to get the child to the bathroom.

Although all developmental psychologists do not agree that there is a critical period when the child is most susceptible to being taught sphincter control, most agree that this process is most congenially and efficiently learned within six months of the second birthday. Stone and Church (1968) state their viewpoint straightforwardly: "There seems to be a critical period roughly between ages one-and-a-half and two years or so in which toilet training happens quite easily (provided the baby's life is going well in general), and outside which it can be very strenuous" (p. 135). Despite this apparent precision to the advent of toilet-training it is crucial that the child's physical as well as temperamental individuality be taken into consideration during this important maturation-learning process. The general rule of thumb suggested by psychologists is not to make toilet-training a source of excess stress and anxiety for the child, because these conditions themselves adversely affect elimination activity, and also increase the chance that the toddler will associate elimination with psychological distress.

By middle toddlerhood bowel control is achieved, and when accidents occur they really are accidents. Daytime bladder control is fairly well mastered by most children before the end of the third year, but the child still occasionally fails to make it to the bathroom, often stopping just a few feet short after a desperate sprint from the playground or basement. Despite the high esteem in which bathroom urination is held by parents, for some toddlers the bathroom is little more than an innocuous inconvenience. Many toddlers prefer to wet their pants rather than leave the social hubbub of the community sandbox, even though they are perfectly capable of making it home. For the most part, defecation is a different matter, and whether due to parental censure or merely personal inconvenience, most toddlers show considerable self-displeasure after soiling their pants.

Nighttime bed-wetting (also called *enuresis*) is a fact of life for many children well into their preschool and even early school years. This is of importance for two reasons: (1) bed-wetting among children five years and older can signal emotional distress, and may even be a means of showing hostility toward parents, and (2) as the child ages he becomes progressively more self-conscious of the connotations of immaturity associated with bed-wetting. Some children go to startling lengths, such as changing sheets in the night, to prevent parents from learning about their inability to control urination during sleep. Because of the large number of normal children who *periodically* urniate during sleep it seems feasible that bladder capacity is a major factor in its occurrence. As urine accumulates, the bladder wall stretches stimulating sensory nerve fibres to transmit nerve impulses to the spinal cord, which are then relayed to the brain where the impulses are interpreted as the desire to urinate. Keeping this in mind, we can note at least three factors which contribute to toddlerhood bed-wetting which have nothing to do with psychological tension or hostility: (1) the child may be a deep sleeper and therefore the brain does not respond to bladder impulses; (2) the bladder may accommodate less than normal amounts of fluids and therefore require more frequent drainage; and (3) the child may go to sleep with a comparatively full bladder, thus insuring need for relief before morning. This latter viewpoint is widely adhered to by parents of children for whom enuresis chiefly occurs when the child is not taken to the toilet in the middle of the night, or when he drinks a good deal of liquid early in the evening. For most children bed-wetting is a physiological rather than a psychological matter.

Contemporary psychology is highly preoccupied with the emotional and psychological repercussions associated with toilet-training, chiefly because of the influence of psychoanalytic theory and several of its historical off-shoots. In this book we shall make little note of this alleged relationship for two reasons: (1) the evidence which suggests that *normal* toilet-training has concommitant emotional trauma is meager at best, and (2) toilet-training, like all other toddlerhood requirements, is handled within the context of living, and the tensions associated with it are absorbed into the general coping strategies of the toddler. We can say with good cause that the *major* trauma associated with toilet-training takes places within the perfectionist, obsessive psyche of the adult far more commonly than in the mind of the normal toddler. Of more than passing interest is the observation that pediatricians, mothers, and teachers historically have never understood normal toilet-training procedures to influence the psychological makeup of the child until *after* Sigmund Freud constructed his ingenious, but almost totally unverified, theory of anality during the first third of the twentieth century.

Bernard (1970, p. 227) provides seven suggestions concerning elimination training which are generally accepted by developmental psychologists:

1. Haste, shame, pressure, and anxiety should be avoided during toilet-training.
2. The matter should be left largely to the baby.

117

3. The child should be kept clean, dry, and comfortable so he is able to notice the difference when he is wet or soiled.
4. A comfortable toilet which adjusts to the measurements of the child should be employed.
5. Interest and approval should be shown at the child's successes, but he should not be of the impression that it is the most important event in the world.
6. The use of enemas or suppositories should not be used except with a doctor's advice.
7. It is the total family atmosphere that is the most important factor in achieving the developmental task of controlling elimination.

The preschool years bring the treasured respite from elimination pollution that parents (especially mothers) have been dreaming about for several years. We shall soon observe, however, that this respite is merely illusional because the environmental pollution created by undisciplined elimination habits is infinitely easier to cope with than the household pollution generated during the course of the day-to-day life of the preschooler.

As we have previously noted, the toddler contributes to environmental pollution in many ways other than by unpredictable toilet habits — his play and eating habits also create their share of problems.

Play habits: There is a certain ambiguity surrounding the topic of toddlerhood play because by adult standards virtually everything the toddler does, outside of the requirements of daily living such as eating and sleeping, is considered a form of play. If everything is understood as play it obviously cannot be distinguished from other activities such as work, learning, or competence building. Play during toddlerhood can be understood as pleasurable work, but just as easily it may be thought of as the most efficient means by which the child can learn about his environment. Play is enjoyable, thoroughly absorbing, but often frustrating for the toddler. Inevitably the child acquires *some* growth-fostering benefit from all forms of play.

Numerous psychological and developmental factors influence play during the toddlerhood years, and to a large extent they determine its *content* as well as *procedure*. The following are some of the more central factors which influence the nature of child play between the ages of one and three years:

1.   The child is able to engage only in play activity commensurate with his mental and physical maturity. During the second year he can

118

construct block towers, string beads, and repeat over and over simple tasks which he has previously mastered; he cannot participate in play which requires extensive use of memory, manipulation of very small objects, or respect for abstract rules.

2.   The child *tends* to engage in play for which he is rewarded and to avoid that for which he is consistently punished. For most children the consequences of this principle (the *law of effect*) do not accrue until the preschool years, and it is then that wide differences in preference for verbal or reading play as well as rough and rowdy play are most noticeable. Individual differences in play preference usually are rooted in the reward-punishment schedule the child has been receiving in his household; some psychologists, however, assert that the child's *predisposition* for such activity as rowdy play exerts greater influence on the type of play he prefers than does punishment or reward.

3.   Toddler play is influenced by the mathematics and geography of the household. If five brothers and sisters share his household, the toddler will receive less parent playtime than if he is the only child; likewise he will experience a greater amount of sibling play if this is the case. If his home is spacious and "child-proof" with an open outdoor play area, possibilities and freedom are available to him that are completely lacking in cramped apartment quarters.

4.   The *impulsivity* characteristic of toddlerhood behaviour influences play patterns. The toddler is quite capable of quitting right smack in the middle of a given play project, even destroy the fruits of his labour with no regret or remorse. He has little sense of finality and it matters little to him whether or not he completes what he starts. This will undergo radical change during the preschool years when he becomes obsessed with perfection and completion.

5.   Toddler play is influenced by adventurousness and boldness and a sense of basic trust. Aggressiveness of play is directly related to the toddler's psychological feelings of security and confidence. (It should be borne in mind that the relationship between security and aggressiveness is not static, and in later years a converse relationship develops: the child becomes more aggressive as his feelings of security diminish, as is usually the case with the neighbourhood bully.) The parent who fosters security and trust in his child also fosters in him carefree exploration, adventurous curiosity, and spontaneous disorderliness — each of which makes its contribution to environmental pollution.

6.   Toddler play is regulated by the permissiveness of the household and its willingness to tolerate inconvenience and damage.

From these principles we readily observe that toddler play does

119

not surface from a vacuum, but is modified and given direction by environmental, developmental, and psychological factors.

There are several *kinds* of toddlerhood play which can be categorized as (a) body-contact play, (b) sense-pleasure play, (c) competence play, and (d) role-rehearsal play.

Activities such as bouncing, jostling, holding, hugging, tickling, embracing, pretend-wrestling, and just plain frolicking are forms of *body-contact play* in which child and parent continuously engage. Body-contact play usually has no motive other than the pleasure, fun, and laughter which it brings the participants. As a result of it, however, many important developments take place within the growing child. Body-contact play is the most ancient form of play and virtually all mammals, especially primates, revel in its pleasantry. Human infants spontaneously enjoy robust frolicking as long as they are of congenial temperament and sound health; by toddlerhood it has become an integral part of their play repertoire. During the first year of life when the child has minimal attention span and dismal body coordination, body-contact sport is one of the chief forms of parent-child interplay. Body-contact play is not *essential* to the growth of the child but does contribute significantly to his sense of love and security. It also facilitates the child's ability to synchronize body action with social interaction.

Sense-pleasure play is activity which produces clearly pleasurable sensory experiences, but differs from body-contact play in that it centres around inanimate objects or body responses: "Play with raw materials, water, sand, mud, foodstuffs, whatever — can be viewed as a sense-pleasure play, as can masturbation, swinging, bouncing, rocking, scribbling, humming, listening to music, and smelling flowers and other aromatic things." (Stone, 1968, p. 251) Toddlers crave sense-pleasure play and spend hours engrossed in dawdling in the sandbox, splashing in the bathtub, rolling down grassy slopes, swinging swings, teetering totters, or even sucking on a finger or forearm. From sense-pleasure play the child learns about body experience and how it is affected by different environmental elements.

Competence play is play which increases the child's general environmental competence. It is somewhat of a misnomer because, in one way or another, all play contributes to the child's general competence. In the more narrow usage of the term, however, competence refers to the attainment of skills which directly relate to day-to-day living requirements. The toddler who spends an hour scribbling on a wall board is practising skills required in manipulation of writing utensils; the child who stacks block upon block is practising vertical construction as well as eye-hand coordination; and the child who sits attentively observing mother is acquiring information about household routine, division of labour, even sex role differentiations. Competence play is a favourite of middle-class families because it yields growth dividends from pleasant activity which, one must admit, is an enticing circumstance. Middle-class North America supports hundreds of corporations which specialize in competence play equipment such as peg-boards, moulding clay, bouncing balls, tricycles, story books, large figured puzzles, imitation clocks, chalk boards, miniature athletic kits, water colour paints, kiddy cars, and an infinite array of skill games.

Competence play is an excellent means of practising emerging skills when the child is maturationally ready for them. Because of this they have high interest value as well as practice value. Contemporary education encourages teachers to employ competence play to its maximal educational advantage — a trend which has been heartily welcomed by students of all ages.

Role-rehearsal play is a combination of fantasy and dramatic play in which the child acts out roles and activities central to his life. In North American culture this includes playing "house" which involves mother, father, sister, and brother roles, and a variety of monologue games where several different roles are assumed simultaneously, one of which is usually himself. Pretend activities such as answering the telephone, greeting visitors, combing hair, spanking or scolding inappropriate behaviour, praising exceptional conduct, commenting on the excellence of food are examples of role-rehearsal play. This type of play reaches its zenith during the preschool years when the child has the advantage of a more mature imagination as well as an enriched vocabulary to assist him in his contrivances. Frequently role-rehearsal play is the medium by which the child acts out frustrations, insecurities, or guilt feelings and consequently it assumes "therapeutic" utility as well as recreational value. Parents occasionally worry about the fantasy content of role-rehearsal play. They caution unnecessarily against unrealistic thinking or fantasizing, and thereby unknowingly exclude the child from a prime form of preparation for coming ages, when social roles are greatly expanded.

During the first three years of life social play follows a moderately predictable sequence. At first play is solitary, involving no other people (body-contact play is an exception). Near the second birthday *parallel* play emerges. At this age the child does not play directly with other children, but he does play independently in their presence. By late toddlerhood *mixed* play occurs; here play is directly influenced by the presence of others and the child will voluntarily modify his own behaviour in compliance with expectations or demands of other children. Not until after toddlerhood does genuine *cooperative* play develop; therefore any form of play which requires consistent cooperation (such as London Bridge) is doomed to failure during toddlerhood.

Play during toddlerhood is influenced by social factors outside the child as well as developmental factors within him. Sometimes these different factors are compatible and sometimes not. The child learns to adjust himself when he gets drastically out of line with his environment; likewise parents learn to adjust the environment when it does not accord with the needs of the toddler. From this delicate pattern of reciprocal adjustment the growing child will inch his way through toddlerhood — though behind him he will leave a swath of debris.

Eating habits: The maturational ground plan which regulates (but does not determine) all human growth during the first years of life exerts significant influence on the eating habits of the toddler. As do all skills during toddlerhood, eating habits undergo a stunning increase in efficiency and precision.

At eighteen months the toddler lifts a cup to his mouth and drinks rather well; he grasps a spoon and inserts it into his dish; he places the spoon in his mouth, though usually twisting it either slightly before or immediately after it enters the mouth; he may even hand empty dishes to mother with a sense of helpful accomplishment. By twenty-four months he holds a small glass in one hand while drinking, and masters the art of inserting a spoon without twisting it. A finicky eater, he may spontaneously refuse certain foods and devour others with forceful intent. He will, if allowed, turn his tray into an arena for sense-pleasure play, stirring pudding, grinding potatoes, and stuffing everything squishable into his glass. By thirty-six months, the end of toddlerhood, he pours liquid from a pitcher (though he has little discretion as to the size of pitcher he can comfortably handle); takes in food without much damage to the floor or table; and consumes most items of food without parental assistance. The three-year-old will chatter and socialize at the dinner table but must be reminded repeatedly to sit still and remain on (not around) his chair. Occasionally at this age the toddler will reinforce mother's suspicion that civilization is having some effects by offering to assist in setting the table (Gesell, 1940, p. 242).

At no time during the toddler's career can he be placed unsupervised at the table without something eventful happening. Motor skills associated with eating, especially those involved in bringing food to the mouth, are fairly well developed by late toddlerhood, but they lack the consistency and precision required at the dinner table. Parental adjustment is imperative during eating times but for them only two options emerge: (1) supervise the child and keep messiness to a minimum; or

(2) leave the child to his own resources and allow messiness to proliferate.

Eating time abounds with social learning for the toddler. He learns about sharing, etiquette, and conversation; he begins to encounter the milieu of cultural minutia which dictate that dessert *follows* the main course; that liquids are for washing food down and not for dipping food in; and that spoons, not forks, are for soup. More importantly, he learns how mother and father treat one another; how brother and sister cope with each other at the dinner table. He makes general associations as to whether mealtime is an occasion for anxiety and bickering, or pleasant social intercourse.

For most hungry children quality of food is not a serious matter, and anything which meets general taste requirements and is not of unusual colour or texture is readily taken to. We must note in fairness to the two-year-old, however, that he may at any time refuse anything because of his obsession with autonomy and his resistance to innovation.

As far as pollution is concerned the toddler *eventually* learns that food is not for recreation and dishes are not for dropping, clanging, or banging. The wise teacher keeps in mind that at certain ages environmental objects are used by the toddler not for their intended social purpose but for their unique appeal to his developmental needs and requirements. This is but one of many insights parents are brought to by the uncompromising nature of sequential development, and is one further example of the extent to which the household must continually adjust to the developmental ground plans which preside over childhood.

The Toddler as Lovable

At *one* year of age the child enjoys and receives emotional uplift from contact comfort; he is affectionate, cuddly, clinging, and has formed the beginnings of emotional attachment to other people. The formation of basic trust is well under way. The one-year-old feels anxious when separated from love objects, and gains a sense of reassurance upon their return. All of these subjective factors make the one-year-old a sensitive, loving child. During the next two years of life, however, he learns to *give* love, to reciprocate, and to contribute much more substantively to the love relationship. The toddler develops awareness that other people have a subjective and private life of their own (although this realization is not forceful until the preschool years), but that their purpose in life is not purely to look after the wants and needs of the toddler which occupies their home. During toddlerhood compassion, empathy, and sympathy become established; the toddler also learns that he significantly influences the attitude and behaviour of others toward him. Although there is nothing which can justifiably be called "conscience" during toddlerhood years, a realization emerges that certain kinds of behaviour bring censure or alienation of affection, while others have the contrary effect. Social skills are maturing rapidly. By age three the child will use charm to entice a more favourable reaction from an uninterested partner; it is this impish, innocent but almost totally "self-ish" charm to which parents and visitors so readily succumb. For the sake of brevity we may state that the toddler's major experiential breakthrough is his capacity to recognize the private subjectivity, the personhood, of the other humans — a capacity totally lacking in the twelve-month child.

Toddlerhood, witnessing the advent of love-giving rather than merely love-receiving, marks the child's entry into the world of two-way love relationships. All toddlers possess a fundamental need for affection, praise, recognition, security, love, esteem, and contact: the genetic predispositions of our species are such that all of these psychological needs are nourished and partially gratified by *embrace* and *caress*.

At no other time during the childhood years is there such open and uninhibited display of affection. However, affection is not issued promiscuously or randomly; toddlerhood affection is selective and substantive; because it is essential to the formation of depthful bonds of relatedness it is not taken frivolously by either child or parent. Nothing is more defeating to the toddler than to have his affection refused, unless it is having his affection ignored. The toddler shares with adults a tender sensitivity to the reactions of others; like adults, he can be emotionally crushed by avoidance, rejection, or indifference.

The toddler loves to give love and loves to receive love. He is, in an innocent sense of the word, completely lovable. Yet his *need* for caress and embrace has a significant developmental component, and failure to attend to it leaves us only partially knowledgeable about the nature of toddler love-ability. The developmental dimensions which contribute to the toddler as lovable are of two types: (1) developmental conditions which originate within the child and require something akin to love in order to be satisfied, and (2) developmental conditions intrinsic to toddlerhood which trigger emotional responses within the adult. Type 1 conditions include: (a) the species need for contact comfort and clinging, and (b) the formation within the child of basic trust. Type 2 conditions include: (a) the emergence of distinctive individuality, (b) the toddler's desire to be helpful, and (c) the toddler's condition of dependence and helplessness. At this time we shall delve into these developmental components of toddler affectivity, but while doing so we shall discipline ourselves not to reduce "love" to the developmental conditions related to its genesis.

All primates, including man, have a genetically-based predisposition toward giving and receiving contact comfort. By "contact comfort" we mean the tendency to experience comfort derived from contact with other members of the species. By "predisposition" is understood the tendency to readily and easily learn behaviours associated with a particular activity. Harlow's experimental studies with monkeys confirm beyond doubt the importance of contact among certain primates; and the observational studies of human infants conducted by Bowlby (1952), Spitz (1965), Goldfarb (1943), and others, provide additional support for its importance in humans. Spitz, who is perhaps the most "radical" of this group, has asserted that *continuous* lack of contact comfort from the sixth through fourteenth month may cause irreparable psychological damage, and possibly even death to the human infant. It is not necessary to go to the extreme claims made by Spitz in order to recognize the central role of contact comfort during the first three years of human life. Specialists of child behaviour concur in the belief that normal children enjoy giving as well as receiving contact comfort; that it has powers of rejuvenation, and is able to restore confidence and security. They also agree that healthy interaction between parent and child involves considerable contact *beyond* that which is required to satisfy all other physical or psychological needs. These observations about human infants are also appropriate for other mammals, suggesting that the need for contact comfort is shared by several species, but is especially powerful among primates, the order of mammals to which man belongs.

Contact, caress, and embrace have different meanings for the adult than for the child, although for both the implications are highly emotional. In the adult they commonly engender a sense of commitment as well as the experience of compassion; for the child they foster security, trust, and confidence. The experiental consequence of contact comfort is one part of the elusive sentiment our culture somewhat capriciously calls "love". Perhaps the most significant point of information is not merely that contact comfort is one part of childhood love but that it is a biological necessity of childhood which, even though gratified through social interaction, is *rooted* in genetics as deeply as the need for calcium or vitamins.

The lovability of the toddler is not completely dependent upon his predisposition for contact comfort; several situations surround his developmental level which prompt a loving reaction from those to whom his upbringing is entrusted. During toddlerhood the child assumes startling individuality which can be understood only in terms of his constitution and makeup, his own inclinations and preferences, his own likes and dislikes. When an adult treats a person on these terms, respecting him from this centre of subjectivity, the first step in formation of a love relationship has begun. The toddler, by his very nature, invites such treatment, and, like a good psychologist, he rewards those who issue it. The toddler is the master reinforcer, for even with his limited knowledge he understands that a smiling embrace, a warm snuggle, a submissive acknowledgement of powerlessness, a lingering kiss, are the most powerful of adult reinforcers. The parent, upon whom nature has imposed a special susceptibility to toddler affection, is especially vulnerable to these gestures. The toddler *extracts* love from adults and does so with a precision that ordinarily would be attributed only to an older person. Thus, part of the toddler's lovability is based upon his ability to make adults want to love him.

Another distinctive feature of toddlerhood is the movement from almost total egocentrism to partial egocentrism. The toddler is self-centred (*egocentric*), and properly so, for he has neither the intellectual nor physical equipment to concern himself with realities not central to his immediate existence. The rewarding aspect of this gradual withdrawal from total egocentrism is the increased attention and affection the toddler shows the adult. Having learned during the first year of life how to show affection and love, the toddler is now making his own gestures of love and, even though awkward, they are quite effective in communicating to the parent the special esteem in which he is held.

Ashley Montagu, who for years has served as spokesman for the natural goodness and lovability not only of children but of man in general, summarizes the child's growth toward reciprocity:

> The infant soon learns that in order to be satisfied, in order to be loved, he too must satisfy, he too must love, he must satisfy the requirements of others, he must cooperate, he must actually give up or postpone the satisfaction of certain desires if he is to achieve satisfaction in others and if he is to retain the love of those whose love he needs. (1966, p. 90)

The toddler, because he is able to share himself unashamedly with open confidence and unrestrained enthusiasm, is perhaps the most lovable of children. But then again, perhaps not. His age conspires against him, depriving him of the maturity which fosters more depthful feelings. In the world of adult "maturity" there is, however, a hunger for the surface honesty of toddler affection. Perhaps it is best merely to admit to the lovable nature of toddlerhood and leave the comparisons to others. There is too little love and too much comparison in our world as it is that we should here sacrifice the former to attend to the latter.

The Basic Developmental Needs of Toddlerhood

Certain needs and requirements assume greater priority than others at different developmental levels. During toddlerhood several needs essential to proper growth, though present throughout childhood, are especially important between the ages of one and three. The toddler shares with all humans the need for sound nutrition, disease immunization, and protection from the environment. These biological requirements are self-evident, therefore we shall not at this time investigate their importance. Our concern is with requirements related to the social, emotional, and intellectual development of the child. The following are considered to be several of the more important developmental needs of toddlerhood.

1. *The need to explore, manipulate, and become competent with the environment.* The preschool-age child cannot cope with the world in the manner our society expects if he is not free to explore, manipulate, and discover during his toddlerhood years. These needs are important not only because of the positive advantages which accrue from them but also because thwarting them contradicts the natural impulses of the child and exerts a negative effect on his overall development. The ability to interact effectively with others during preschool years is based upon the millions of fragmentary items of information stockpiled during the years of toddlerhood exploration. The child learns to accommodate to social demands, to handle physical objects, and to consider himself as one unique part of the environment, as a result of the competencies he acquired during toddlerhood.

2. *The need for trust, affection, and contact comfort.* Despite natural curiosity, the child will not optimally learn from his environment unless he faces it with a basic sense of trust. Trust, though intangible and difficult to define, relates directly to the child's sense of security and confidence. A sense of trust allows the child to explore freely and courageously, whereas mistrust instils timidity, apprehension, and general fear of the world. The child has an open need for affection and contact comfort. He not only enjoys being held but *needs* to be held. His response to affection marks the beginning of his first love relationship. The child's psychological need for trust, affection, and contact comfort can be compared with the biological need for Vitamin C. When the body is provided with sufficient Vitamin C it does not result in direct benefits for the child; that is, he cannot run faster, speak more

clearly, or think more precisely. The growth advantage of Vitamin C is that it *prevents* disorders which come about during its *deficiency*. Trust, affection, and contact comfort do not add magical powers to the child. They assure that the child will not be plagued with disorders which occur when these needs are only partially gratified. Trust, affection, and contact comfort are qualitatively different kinds of needs than, for example, the need to practice emerging skills. When the latter kind of need is satisfied the child *experiences a direct positive benefit*, but, when the former are satisfied, the benefit is indirect. One group of needs is essentially preventative while the other is *acquisitional*.

3.   *The need for a base of security.* The child requires an adult to whom he can return when the environment (or the inner world of imagination) causes him to be fearful or anxious. When a base of security is not present the child requires greater time to recuperate from anxiety, and may resort to escape or withdrawal in order to cope with fear. The child can grow optimally only through confident exploration, but the child can be completely confident only when he knows there is a reassuring base of security available to him. *How* the child is reassured is of comparatively minor consequences as long as the adult provides contact comfort and builds trust while serving as a base of security. Without the extra confidence engendered by his security base the child falls one step behind in the acquisition of social, emotional, even intellectual skills.

4.   *The need for verbal interaction and verbal stimulation.* Speech capacities develop only with practice, and *optimal* development is contingent upon the opportunity to hear others speak and to observe the impact of speech upon the environment. During toddlerhood, more so than at any other developmental stage, the child should be exposed to verbal play and given the opportunity to absorb adult language. Although the critical period of speech acquisition is ill-defined, most psychologists believe that insufficient exposure to verbal stimulation during toddlerhood has a negative influence on the onset of speech as well as on verbal fluency in later life.

5.   *The need for mental experimentation.* The child not only must exercise his capacity for mental experimentation *but must be allowed to observe the effects of his behaviour on the environment.* Only in this way can he adjust thinking processes to correspond with the real world. The child must be allowed to build, to take apart, to sample and experiment not only to learn principles which influence the external environment but to learn about his own capacities. The child who is afraid to experiment, or who is severely punished for experimentation "failures",

learns to restrict this critical behaviour and as a result restricts his own mental growth.

6.   *The need to achieve.* The child not only needs to observe the effects of his actions, he also needs to *achieve tasks and accomplish goals.* Very early in life the child associates achievement with positive inner feelings. Though most families reinforce the child for achievement activities, sound reasoning supports the hypothesis that achievement is *naturally* pleasurable. The child merely learns which kinds of achievement are most highly praised in the environment in which he is reared. The toddler should not be deprived of the right to perform important tasks or minor household responsibilities, so he can acquire a sense of *meaningful* achievement as well as group belonging. Deprived of his need to achieve and accomplish, the child feels insignificant and, even more destructive to growth, incompetent.

7.   *The need for fantasy and imaginary play.* Though given only brief mention in this chapter, fantasy and imaginary play have an important role in toddler development. During the last half of toddlerhood (twenty-four to thirty-six months) verbal and mental skills are rapidly expanding. However, the child still does not make a precise distinction between fantasy and reality (please don't ask who does!) and constantly wanders in and out of nondefined realms of imagination. It is quite an easy matter for the toddler to "become" mother or father for role-playing purposes, and just as easy to become a horse, a cookie monster, or a fire hydrant. The toddler may unwaveringly insist that a twin sister (who is unbeknownst to the rest of the family) really exists and commonly causes messes for which her twin is unfairly blamed. Toddlers, especially those who are verbally advanced or above average in intelligence, have been known to keep imaginary companions for months without the slightest suggestion that they perceive them as being any less real than their true mother or father. Imaginary companions are dismissed, though periodically recalled, when the caprice of toddlerhood dictates.

Fantasy can be used as rationalization or escape by the toddler, and it is one of the unpleasant chores of parenthood to decipher when enough is enough with regard to toddler fantasy.

Summary

In this chapter we have looked into the key developments of the normal child between the ages of twelve and thirty-six months. It has been our purpose to view the child not only from the perspective of internal drives and dynamics but also in terms of the practical effects these years have upon the child's world. We have stressed continuously that growing up is not a one-way street where the child passively assimilates cultural habits, speaking skills, and mental processes identical to those who raise him. Rather, growth is a perpetual give and take, with the environment making fundamental adjustments in favour of the child on certain occasions and holding its ground noncompromisingly in other instances. The toddler is partially bound to his own principles and dynamics and not infrequently they conflict with the principles and dynamics of society. Confrontation is inevitable but, rather than being injurious, it is the essential requirement for growth and maturity.

The topic headings in this chapter are designed to keep fresh in our minds the obvious, but mysteriously forgotten, fact that the world basically is not designed for toddlers and, especially in North American culture, a certain strain and tension will always be interwoven with these years.

Without doubt the toddler is a *housewrecker* and this is primarily due to the fact that he is learning to walk during the same chronological time span that his psychological life is dominated by the uncontrollable impulse to explore and become as competent with the total environment as the natural limits of this age will permit. *Curiosity* is at an all-time high but, unfortunately, *intellectual discretion* is at an all-time low. The inability to anticipate accurately the consequences of behaviour gets the toddler into predicaments he rarely will encounter during the preschool years. This also is the age for learning about *physical, social, and personal limits,* but again the effects of limited intellectual prowess makes itself felt on the household. All adjustments do not fall to the child — parents also encounter their share. It quickly dawns upon parents (who as a rule learn more swiftly than toddlers) that they must adjust socially, psychologically, and even physically to the presence of their growing offspring.

The toddler is also a *coward*, though in all fairness, only in certain situations. The toddler rarely overcomes completely his apprehension of strangers. During those times when his courage is being taxed he prefers to be in the presence of someone who will serve as a *base of security.* Toddlers receive strength from adult strength and though the process is not completely understood there is no doubt that it is true. Near the second birthday, when the child is most averse to separation from parents, he often will experience considerable anxiety when separated from them. Many factors influence *separation anxiety;* however, it can be reduced by social learning and parental reassurance. A definite developmental component exists in childhood fears; the months adjacent to the third birthday are the time they are most abundant. General fears tend to reduce rather predictably after this age, but some children persist in their fear of real or imaginary objects long after they cognitively understand that the fear is unfounded. Just as it is for the adult, fear for the child is essentially nonrational.

The toddler is by no means a *computer* even though it is possible to draw several parallels between these two wonders. For those writers liberal in their use of metaphor we observe the tendency to compare the toddler's prodigious mental growth with the magic of the computer. Perhaps this is justified. During the second year of life the child passes through two major mental growth stages: *active experimentation* and *mental experimentation.* Third year development includes *representational thought, transductive reasoning,* and *language-based abstraction.* Speech development is perhaps even more spectacular in its growth rate. By thirty-six months the child has an active vocabulary of over 1,000 words and conversational skills include impressive command of syntax, grammar, sentence structure, plurality, past and future tense, as well as the ability to perceive social nuances which inform the child when he is expected to speak and when he is expected to listen.

No metaphors are required to know that the toddler is not only a cause of but the epitome of *environmental pollution.* Toilet habits (actually the lack of them) are a major contributor, but rambunctious play habits as well as messy eating habits add a finishing touch. By late toddlerhood *daytime sphincter control* is usually achieved with modest consistency but *enuresis* occurs well into the preschool years for many children; in most instances its causes are physical rather than psychological and indicate no underlying emotional disturbance. *Sense-pleasure play* accounts for most toddler messiness but other forms of play, especially *body-contact play* and *competence play* produce their share.

Children at all ages are by nature *lovable* and become otherwise only when their *natural need for affection* and love has been stymied by an impoverished environment or by emotional defect. The toddler is lovable because of his *need for contact comfort,* his *need for trust* and *acceptance,* and because of his unique ability to *elicit love responses* from adults. Even though the nature of love during the early years is difficult to study scientifically, evidence gathered from direct observation points clearly to the conclusion that children function better at all levels of development under conditions of love than conditions of distrust and nonaffection.

By the end of toddlerhood the child is unmistakably acculturated not only to his immediate family but society as well. The toddler learns the language of his culture but traces of pronunciation, intonation, and word usage unique to his family will spice his speaking habits for years to come. The toddler is introduced to cultural norms and ethics

131

only as they are *interpreted* by his particular family. The toddler acquires knowledge of sex role differentiations enforced by society but he is most firmly impressed by how they are valued in his own home.

The toddler also is learning to decide for himself, to choose, to calculate, and to anticipate. Equally important, he is learning to take the consequences of his behaviour, and this allows him to assert himself unpredictably and for reasons *known only to him*. Because of this developmental fact there can never be a deterministic science of toddlerhood. As the child grows older he will come to rely more and more upon his own power of self-direction and personal freedom. The psychologist who tries to understand the child is now forced to attend to the child's capacity for *free* choice if he is to honestly comprehend the nature of childhood behaviour.

Preschooler

Consideration of the uniqueness of the child's world results in effective communication.

Five has an insatiable urge to squirm and fidget.

Preschoolers masquerade confidently and enthusiastically.

The preschooler is easily converted to an alligator or any other creature the imaginative teacher persuasively suggests.

Man shares numerous commonalities with his evolutional cousins such as the chimpanzee.

Chapter Five

The Preschool Years

The time span covering the years between the end of toddlerhood and the beginning of the first grade is called the preschool years. Psychologists are particularly fond of preschool children because they are easy to study, fairly accessible (especially with the recent boom in preschool education), verbal, naive about psychological tests, and innocent enough to declare freely their opinions, interests, or conclusions. The psychologist is also especially fascinated with children of this age because the influence of environment is becoming more easily discernible and that of heredity less predictable. Individual and group differences are much more pronounced among preschoolers than among toddlers. Noticeable differences are commonly observed; environmental effects are everywhere visible: dress, social skills and mannerisms, speech habits, and intellectual versatility are drastically influenced by the richness or poverty of the preschooler's environment.

The daily life of the three, four, and five-year-old is active and expansive. Growth is relentless, almost frighteningly consistent and persistent. The groundplan of childhood development for our species, though significantly influenced by environment, is not easily denied. During the preschool years the child blossoms physically, socially, psychologically, morally, and intellectually. The biological innocence characteristic of the toddler is outgrown and replaced by the social innocence of the preschooler.

In this chapter we shall investigate several preschool domains, hoping to encapsulate the substance as well as the spirit of these years, knowing full well that by so doing we shall also enhance our knowledge of our own spirit and substance. Of the childhood years, the preschool years perhaps exert the greatest influence on later life, and do the most to determine the direction taken during later life. During the preschool years the psychological foundation of trust and confidence is significantly structured; the social foundation for extroversion and self-

137

expansion is solidified; the intellectual foundation for investigation, experimentation, and resolution is blueprinted; and the moral foundation for conscience is germinated. The school age child is a direct product of his preschool internship, but its influence remains felt for years beyond the elementary school grades.

In our attempt to encompass the substance of the preschool years we shall traverse several different realms. The initial section of this chapter provides a description of daily activity, physical appearance, social skills, and psychological idiosyncrasies of three, four, and five-year-olds. The intellectual and educational aspects of the preschool years are discussed under the headings: "The preschooler as an educational headache" and "The preschooler as thinker". Physiological development is summarized in "The preschooler as athlete in training"; explorational activity is overviewed in "The preschooler as astronaut".

Before embarking upon our description of the preschool child, a word or two concerning age-grading is in order. There are numerous practical problems involved in describing traits of the "normal" three-year-old, or four-year-old, or any age for that matter. For one thing, all children are obviously not "normal" or "average"; some are above average or below; some are above average in one area and below average in another.

Averages come from studying large groups of children, consequently they are not always applicable to particular children. They are more appropriate for enhancing our knowledge of, say, three-year-olds as a group than for understanding an individual three-year-old. This should be as self-evident as the fact that studying one particular child does not always yield reliable information about groups of children. We favour year-by-year description for several reasons: (a) during the first ten years of life children of certain ages have a great deal in common with one another; knowledge of this similarity leads to meaningful insights about the nature of childhood; (b) many social and intellectual traits during childhood are intimately related to biological development and thus are modestly predictable by knowing the chronological age of the child; (c) age-grading provides a workable conceptualization of the skills, interests, inclinations, and capacities of particular ages; (d) by knowing the developmental capabilities of children at given ages we are able to infer what is beyond their developmental capabilities and hopefully we will avoid saddling them with responsibilities or demands which are unrealistic or harmful to future development. Bearing in mind both the strengths and weaknesses of describing children by age, we shall proceed.

The Three-year-old

Three-year-old children tend to have many things in common with one another because their physical, mental, and social development has taken them through similar growth experiences and leaves them with similar capacities, abilities, and inclinations. As with any age, we cannot say with complete assurance that all three-year-olds are, for example, highly verbal or moving into a new era of social equilibrium. We can, however, note the considerable extent to which these comments are highly descriptive of most three-year-olds. Perhaps the most significant asset of the three-year-old child is that he has outgrown many of the rigid, narrow, and inflexible traits of the two-and-a-half-year-old and has not as yet adopted the bossy assertiveness so commonly observed in the four-year-old. Tension and anxiety are part of every developmental age, but during the year between the third and fourth birthdays children commonly reach the most comfortable balance of social, mental, and physical demands of the entire preschool period. The reasons for this comparative calm are diverse. By portraying the salient features of this first year of post-toddlerhood, we will acquire a more precise understanding of the inner mechanics of the three-year-old.

Three is losing the pudginess of Two and is becoming much more streamlined in appearance and motion. Though not a creature of graceful mobility, Three moves through his environment with considerably more poise and versatility than he did only a few months before. During the preschool period, growth is fairly steady and because of this stability the child does not experience a particular period of gross awkwardness or clumsiness as does the pre-adolescent when growth outraces coordination. The average three-year-old weighs about thirty-three pounds but he adds five more pounds by his fourth birthday and another five by his fifth. Though there are no noticeable sex differences with regard to weight, boys are often slightly heavier than girls. (Boys also tend to be more aggressive, assertive, and rowdy than their female companions, but it is hard to determine the extent to which this is the result of cultural learning.) The average three-year-old is about thirty-eight inches tall and will grow another five inches during the next two years. Body proportions are undergoing change and the child gives the definite image of lengthening out. Baby fat disappears, the torso lengthens, as do the long bones of the legs and arms. The child takes on a lean, sinewy glide which stays until the long bones stop growing more rapidly than the rest of the body. With the loss of "baby" features, many three-year-olds begin to look more than ever like a parent to which they previously showed only a slight resemblance.

Three moves with new-found finesse and specialization. He shows marked increase in total body coordination and constantly startles parents with his ability to negotiate a task which six months earlier would have resulted in catastrophe. The ability to inhibit or restrict his own body movement also blossoms, much to the relief of parents who are driven to distraction by the insatiable squirmishness of Two. He runs with smoothness; accelerates and decelerates; turns corners with moderate sharpness; stops suddenly though not always predictably. Three toddles and sways less when walking than he did as a toddler. High-powered acrobatics such as standing on one foot for several seconds, hopping, skipping, or smooth backward locomotion, however, are still beyond his daily three-ring routine. Many children now scurry around the neighbourhood on a tricycle, but owing to the advancement of motor precocity over mental adroitness, they may forget the way home, although the route usually will be stumbled upon if they are given enough time. Three makes it through the day without wetting or soiling but still has difficulty with nighttime elimination. He bruises easily and has ample occasion for doing so because he runs with his head thrown back (in order to maintain balance) and frequently trips over obstructions he fails to see, or collides with obstacles which do not bend.

A spirit of cooperation and good will permeates Three which was almost totally lacking in the two-year-old. This is the age of cooperative play with parents as well as other children, but it is still highly egocentric when contrasted with play of the six-year-old. There is a strong desire to make social contacts and to have someone with whom to chat, visit, play, and, in general, be with. Each child has a need for solitude which must be respected, but at this age it is far from being a dominant force in his personal life. Nursery school teachers enjoy the three-year-old because of his desire to tell chatty stories (some of which reveal rather spicy information about activities within his own household) and to visit pleasantly and nonchalantly. Cooperative play is becoming a definite part of the child's daily routine; he is also showing a tendency to follow suggestions. He may be easily lured into the house from backyard play by saying, "Now is a good time to play inside. Come on in." Parents and nursery teachers are advised to capitalize on this suggestibility because it does not work nearly as consistently for the four-year-old, who insists upon exercising autonomy whenever possible. As Three also enjoys social imitation, frequently he will adopt the behaviour of the child next to him for no apparent reason other than to do that which seems to be working for someone else. Imitation is not restricted to the behavioural. Young preschoolers are so empathetic they may burst into tears upon observing a friend who is crying. They can as easily become angry or sorrowful if that is the dominant mood of a comrade. Three does as he sees, honestly mirroring his surroundings. Three is fun because he accepts word messages which are sung to him. Mothers, whose promising careers as Broadway sopranos were cut short by marriage and children, may happily relive their moments of glory by turning their homes into suburban operas, singing to their three-year-olds every command or comment that comes to mind. Three loves it. The specifics of daily living such as eating, sleeping, eliminating, and playing are coped with more easily than during toddlerhood. Three is becoming civilized. Despite important differences among young children and the extent to which changes occur within the same child, most psychologists conclude that Three is a comparatively delightful age.

Many of the uncontrollable anxieties and fears of toddlerhood are dissipating or at least becoming easier to handle. The child has less need for rigidness or stubbornness. Alternatives are more easily perceived; routine can be interrupted without the child sensing that it has been destroyed. Impulsiveness is reduced; self-discipline is acutely improved though still a long way from a dominant reality in the life of the child. The three-year-old becomes much more aware of the separate existence of mother, father, brother, and sister. He also learns that they have their own forms of relatedness to one another which may be different from their relatedness to him. He senses, perhaps even recognizes, that mother and father have a unique relationship which he does not share. (Some psychologists are of the impression that this awareness fosters jealousy in the child, or creates resentment toward one or both parents.) Three is sufficiently egocentric to assume that everyone naturally wants to play and visit with him. This makes him especially enjoyable when his expectations are correct, but somewhat of a nuisance when they are not — he is slow in learning just when his presence is preferred and when it is not.

Parents discover that the child can now play for considerable lengths of time at games which require self-discipline and coordinated effort. He may spend up to an hour or more engrossed in house play. It is essential, however, that play offer ample opportunity for large muscle movement. The child is still a long way from sitting still for prolonged lengths of time and, when he does, it is only because something of unusual interest is holding him down. Three-year-olds love to dart into the TV room for a quick commercial and then as quickly dart back to their previous involvement. Commercials cater to their attention span,

141

their sense of urgency, their enthusiasm for jingle or rhyme, and, frequently, to their intellectual level. As do all children, the three-year-old has a special fascination for the unusual. He does not let anything novel, incongruous, or out-of-the-ordinary slip by uninvestigated. He learns not only by becoming proficient with routine realities but also by stripping each new reality of its knowledge-generating information. This trait identifies all children, not merely preschoolers.

Three talks. He talks when he plays. He talks to himself. He talks either *to* or *at* others. He talks in bed, the bathtub, the backyard, the church, the nursery, the movies. Silence is blasphemous. What greater sin than to waste valuable practice time in refining the most essential of all social skills — conversation. Words dominate the life of the three-year-old in a way unfathomable to the two-year-old. Words have the ability to distract Three when he is involved in his own private activity. Though he usually cannot be dissuaded by reason, he can be sidetracked by the melody of words or by the secure persuasiveness of the person who issues them. (Parents like to believe that their moppet actually understands the logic hurled at them, but this is rarely the case. Persuasiveness and logic are two different ball games for the three-year-old.) Most play involves chatter, gossip, miscellaneous phrases, and comments which may or may not directly relate to the substance of the goings-on. Three identifies with authority figure roles, and periodically will arrive on the scene prepared to conduct a medical investigation, issue a ticket for speeding, or provide corrective discipline for some unknown misbehaviour. In language development the three-year-old resembles Four vastly more than he resembles Two. "He uses words to express his feelings, his desires, and even his problems. He heeds words. Suggestions take effect." He has the ability to suit action to word and word to action. "He indulges in soliloquy and dramatic play in order to hatch his words and phrases and syntax." (Gesell, 1940, 43-44). The three-year-old listens to learn and he learns to listen.

Tantrums are recuperated from more readily than before, but this is a short-lived respite as many four-year-olds mysteriously resume the kind of temper tantrum thought to have been outgrown earlier. A fairly strong realization of "wait your own turn" is forming at this age. Sharing, though inconsistent and unpredictable, is emerging; the sense of pride this generates is gracefully acknowledged by the three-year-old and he may embark on an exaggerated sharing spree where every commodity in sight is loaned, shared, or given away outright. There is a pronounced desire to conform and live up to the expectations of loved ones. For this reason Three is the ideal age for teaching general household rules and responsibilities, although obviously they cannot be too complex for the child to understand. The tyranny of the "no" still looms ominously over his daily activity, but for the most part Three has adjusted not only to its inevitability but also to its protective value.

Fantasy is becoming wonderfully expansive and creative. The marginal and constantly fluctuating boundary which bifurcates "reality" from imagination is never more fluid than at three. Fantasy can become a vehicle for social as well as intellectual expansion, however, and should not be prematurely discouraged. Three learns about his world through conversation, but he prefers conversation which centres around flying elephants rather than newspaper reports. The essentials of most social learning can be indirectly communicated to the child via examples from fantasy almost as well as by pure description. This is not true during the later preschool years, but with the three-year-old it is. The child's ability to learn from imaginary realities should not dim the parents' zest for explaining the world simply and realistically, however. Three-year-olds are not genuinely interested in causality, but they must learn that events in the external world are influenced and regulated by physical realities. This they are able to accept readily; but they as readily accept a mythical or magical explanation of natural phenomena. Although he understands that the physical world has its own permanence, occasionally the child will attempt to obliterate it by closing his eyes. In games of hide-and-seek, young preschoolers may cover their eyes in order to become invisible to those who are searching them out. This carry-over from toddlerhood's egocentrism illustrates the alternating nature of Three's cognitive patterns. Children of this age believe that everything is potentially alive; later they assume that everything which moves is alive; finally they accept the fact that only plants and animals live.

Three is full of growth, change, mystery, and achievement. It is a pivotal stage in the development of childhood. The child is not yet a *bona fide* preschooler in the eyes of most people. He is still more thought of as a toddler. Consequently he receives the benefits of extra attention and affection while possessing many abilities which permit individual growth and exploration. He is sheltered and for the most part still exempt from accounting for his behaviour. This will change during the coming year.

The Four-year-old

By no stretch of the imagination is the year between the third and fourth birthdays a period of perfect calm and serenity. On the whole, however, it is considerably more relaxed and cooperative than is the year between the fourth and fifth birthdays. The four-year-old encounters several new and difficult social realities which take their toll. Four is a more troublesome year than three. Parents come to expect more mature conduct and the pressure of aging is felt in increased demands and expectations. Maturity brings increased responsibility as well as accountability. It is generally thought by developmental psychologists and pediatricians that life for the four-year-old is marked by a considerable degree of insecurity, disequilibrium, and unpredictability. This is borne out by the fact that symptoms of anxiety become more apparent during this year. Parents often admit that their four-year-old is more belligerent and assertive than at any previous age (with the possible exception of two-and-a-half) and that temper tantrums border on the ferocious. Dodson concurs with this general picture of the middle preschooler. In describing the four-year-old, he states:

> Tensional outlets are heightened at this age. The child may blink his eyes, bite his nails, pick his nose, play with his sexual organs, or suck his thumb. He may even develop a facial tic. . . He is given to the same type of emotional extremes: shy one minute, overboisterous the next. Many children are as ritualistic at this age as they were at two-and-a-half. (1971, p. 158)

Beck (1967) reports that almost all preschoolers go through a stage of speech development when they seem to stutter. Usually this is outgrown, or subsides as life becomes less stormy.

Four is prone toward dogmatism. His thought tends to be rigid rather than flexible, at least when his mind is made up. This is partially due to the fact that he has accumulated enough knowledge of the world to be confident that certain of his interpretations and understandings are completely correct. This confidence was not justified at Three because then his information was too limited to be relied upon. At Four the child believes that the way he understands something is the way it really is. Three is of a similar impression but only because his thought processes are too immature to change easily. The world changes, however, and what was true yesterday may not be true today. Four accepts this fact grudgingly. Mother always came to his rescue at Three: not so at Four. He is now expected to become more proficient at fending for himself. He was usually given the benefit of the doubt in social dispute at Three: not so at Four. Rules at Three are made to be broken, or at least to bend a good deal: not so at Four. The world is changing. Rules are changing. Expectations are changing. The baby status of Three is rapidly vanishing. The inevitable onset of responsibility and accountability are creeping slowly and painfully into the social world of the perplexed four-year-old. Like the rest of us, Four resists change. He hides behind stubbornness and rigidity. He prefers showdowns and confrontations because in their own way they help to make conflicts more sharply defined. His ideas are more sophisticated than they were at Three, and so is speech. Four believes that he can "hold his own". Although he often feels insecure, he has a stubborn confidence in his own importance and consequently opposes those people who contradict him. He has the insight to know that he is growing but fails to recognize how limited his skills are in relation to those of his older house companions.

The social world of the four-year-old is not smooth and easy going. There is little reason to assume it would be considering that his private world is topsy-turvy. Although it is common for the four-year-old to play quite well with one other child, trouble usually occurs when three or more gather at the same time. Two of the children always seem to join forces against the third and, from this alliance, aggression (physical or verbal) invariably follows. One observer gives this description of social life among four-year-olds:

> Social life among four-year-olds is no tea party; it is stormy and violent. Outsiders tend to be excluded once a clique has been formed. There is a good deal of commanding, demanding, shoving, and hitting. Bragging is the most common form of language among a group of four-year-olds. Name-calling is also popular. Four is crude and direct. Other people's feelings matter little to him. (Dodson, 1967, p. 158)

Four is not all anguish and perhaps it is unwise to excessively dwell on its troublesome moments. Speaking is coming along nicely with many flashes of genius in this area of development. In addition to Herculean performance in acquiring and assimilating words, the four-year-old shows admirable creativity in coining words and concepts. Chukovsky (1963) informs us that he is indebted to children of this age for teaching him that a bald man had a barefoot head, that a mint candy made a draft in the mouth, and that the husband of a grasshopper was a daddy-hopper (p. 2). Chukovsky is of the impression that the preschool child is, in actual fact, a linguistic genius:

> It seems to me that, beginning with the age of two, every child becomes for a short period of time a linguistic genius. Later, beginning with the age of five to six, this talent begins to fade. There is no trace left in the eight-year-old of this creativity with words, since the need for it has passed; by this age the child already has fully mastered the basic principles of his native language. (p. 7)

Silly words and nonsense rhymes are favourites of this age. An enthusiastic four-year-old can wear away the patience of an adult with a stream of "milk-quilk," "bony-fony," "ass-frass," "gaga-gugu," "jump-rump," "cookie-lookie," "goosy-toosy," *ad infinitum*. Four also uses words boldly and experimentally. He may announce in braggadocio style that he can hold his head under water for six hours or that he can run two minutes an hour. He assumes the listener will infer the proper word whenever it has been misused or omitted. Weight may be described in minutes, "I weigh 40 minutes." Temporal terms are frequently confused, "I had a milk shake last year." Always, however, the intent is to communicate a precise message. If the words themselves are not precise, the listener must recruit the term which most accurately corresponds with the intended message. Four expects his listeners to separate the grain from the chaff. The listener should be attentive because Four will scowl at him or call him stupid if he misinterprets the message. Four-year-olds require extra leeway.

Four is rowdy, robust, boisterous, assertive, and quick. He loves to run and scamper, dart and glance. He enjoys body movement in and of itself and it is not unusual for him to roam around an empty room totally engrossed in his own body contortions and the pleasurable experiences which accompany them. Muscle tissue constitutes about one-fourth to one-third of the preschooler's total body weight. Muscle fibre is considerably more developed than during toddlerhood and greatly accounts for the four-year-old's fluidity of motion and adept body control. Because the muscles are not yet strongly attached to the skeleton, muscle fatigue is a central feature of the preschooler's daily experience. Though one could not infer it from observing him during his "peak" activity hours, Four does tire rather easily and needs rest periods during the day and deep sleep at night. Normal children cannot restrain themselves from wholeheartedly exercising their developing bodies, and the incessant flow of motion which results consumes every iota of extra energy. If forced to sit still and contain the boundless energy which sustains this flow of motion, the child has no alternative except to squirm, fidget, and generally stir about. His energy level demands it.

Physical activity obviously serves functions other than the release of energy. Activity brings experience and experience always brings learning. The body's subsystems also benefit from the flow of activity which fills the child's day.

> The preschooler's steady diet of physical activity, which naturally tends to emphasize the large muscle action involved in gross body activities, contributes to muscular development and coordination. At the same time, however, there are many other benefits derived from the incessant activity so characteristic of this stage. The respiratory system and circulatory system are clearly involved and clearly benefited by normal muscular action; their healthy growth is stimulated by the demands in-

creasingly placed on them as the child makes greater use of his muscles. Further, in the normal course of physical activity, the child's sensory processes are continually stimulated and much learning occurs as a result. (Gardner, 1964, p. 135)

Again it is helpful to contrast some of the basic characteristics of the three-year-old with those of the four-year-old. Three is an age of co-operation and helpful assistance. The child is in equilibrium with himself and with the rather limited social world to which he is exposed. He has markedly less anxiety than he did during the irritable two's and has less need of protective rituals to cushion him from the pains of uncertainty. Tantrums are less frequent and intense than during the months before the third birthday. As a rule the three-year-old is not domineering or dictatorial and has moved to a new level of social cooperation and interaction. Four, in some aspects of his social-emotional behaviour, is more similar to two-and-a-half than three-and-a-half. New responsibilities bring new pressures and new pressures bring back traditional childhood mechanisms including stubbornness, rigidity, tantrum, avoidance, withdrawal, sullenness, and orneriness. Four will defy orders, but on the other hand he also will accomplish many tasks correctly and properly. He enjoys friendly attention but also enjoys confrontations and rebuttals. He likes his own special toys but shows almost no respect for the toys of others and certainly does not believe in the property rights of others. He is of the impression that whatever he can carry off is rightfully his, but if something he owns is carried off by someone else he still believes it is his property. He appreciates co-operative play and work but lacks the social skills to assure the longevity of either. Four is a prodigious learner despite his tendency to disbelieve information which contradicts his present world view. Four is old enough to assume considerable responsibility (some walk alone for blocks in city traffic) but so craves variety that he cannot in fairness be expected to stick with one task or project for any length of time.

He is capable of lengthy and complicated conversation during the course of which he unpredictably vacillates between fact and fiction, sometimes sheepishly admitting to inaccuracy or fabrication when confronted with an obvious falsity. He takes them in stride, even humorously, as long as does the adult. He perpetrates wrong behaviour in order to entice reactions from others rather than to be malicious or ornery. His questions, which are becoming increasingly sophisticated and insightful, are asked with straightforward matter-of-factness. He expects brief answers which coincide with what he already knows. If presented with anything else, he may initially reject it, but his sense of investigation is so strong he will eventually get around to assimilating new-found information into his world view. This inner compulsion to assimilate new information largely accounts for the incredible knowledge expansion during the preschool years.

Four has a host of other fairly consistent characteristics brought about by learning and overall mental and social development. He learns to alibi and make excuses for unacceptable behaviour. (He is learning that some behaviour brings punishment but does not have the inclination to stay away from it simply because of this.) His advanced verbal skills allow him to present a credible alibi when he gets into mischief and his mental skills allow him to make it fairly logical and coherent. When all else fails, he can be depended on to say that he can't remember anything related to the incident in question. Physical aggression takes on a verbal component. Four accosts people with words. He challenges, bluffs, threatens, and accuses others with his razor-sharp, merciless tongue. Many parents have been pushed to the threshold of self-restraint when their four-year-old announces that he will kick them the next time they request that he be good. Or when their moppet replies "Shut up" when asked why he doesn't talk nicely. Despite his use of verbal aggression, the four-year-old craves the praise and attention of adults. He also enjoys acting out their roles and for this reason Four will wear father's old sweater or mother's high heels at the slightest prompting. Because sex differences are becoming stronger at this age, it is easier to get a girl into the high heels and a boy into the sweater.

In as much as Four is beginning to understand the importance of money, many children begin to save or snitch pennies at this time. Loose change frequently disappears in a household which has recently had a birthday with four candles on the cake. Preschoolers of all ages like to share discoveries and inventions with parents. Natural enthusiasm and curiosity are rejuvenated when dividends which accrue from them are acknowledged or, better yet, admired by those adults most important to the child's psychological need structure. Four especially requires praise and encouragement for his efforts. His growing awareness of his own limited abilities (when compared with those of children older than himself) makes him susceptible to inferiority and inadequacy feelings.

Four is a braggart. He likes to show off possessions at nursery school or home. He shows discretion in lending and prefers to loan only to trusted friends, a trait almost nonexistent in the three-year-old. Four enjoys children more than adults when it comes to recreation. He may refuse to play in a park which is devoid of children. Children who have never before left their yard without permission may begin to do so at this age. They can most easily be tracked by listening for the sounds which emanate from children's gatherings.

Trips to the park or the river are treasured. These excursions cater to several preschool needs simultaneously. The child's urge to explore, to be adventurous, to engage in dramatic play, to venture beyond the limits of home or school, to do what big people do are all met in one degree or another in travel outings. Four hates confinement (unless self-imposed) and delights in openness. Upon entering an open, empty gymnasium he cannot restrict his impulse to run full steam ahead. He will run till exhausted.

Four is filled with contradiction and paradox. He is assertive yet insecure. Bossy but affectionate. Adventurous yet docile. Relief is in sight, however. If Four is tense and off-balance, Five is relaxed and homeostatic (at least by comparison).

The Five-year-old

Five is an exciting age for child, parent, and teacher. Rapidly, much more rapidly than some parents prefer, the five-year-old is losing his young child identity and assuming a considerably more mature school age atmosphere. During this last of the preschool years the child startles us time and again with dramatic growth spurts, especially those related to social skills and self-control. In many respects Five is similar to Three. Both years are periods of *comparative* (it cannot be stressed too often that childhood is never completely calm or tranquil) stability and balance. The child learns to assimilate the demands of his own needs with those of his family; he learns to discipline his appetites and impulses; he comes to appreciate (not objectively understand) the sensitivity and subjectivity of others.

Whereas Four is in continual confrontation with those aspects of the world he has outgrown or those for which he is not quite ready, Five is reaping the benefits of what was learned during the turmoil of the previous transition year. On the whole, the five-year-old displays the essential traits necessary for school life: he is reliable, stable, and rather well-adjusted. Self-constraint is much more evident than at Four and many children of Five display what adults call good manners. Five keeps in mind that behaviour has consequences and he is not nearly as dependent upon experimentation for information about consequences — he thinks things through more completely than ever before. The reservoir of information built up during the less disciplined exploration of the previous year is making its presence felt. Five is growing and knows it. He takes genuine pride in his growth.

Body coordination continues to show refinement. Balance, agility, flexibility, and mobility improve. Strength, durability, perseverance, and stamina increase. Five plays on the monkey bars not only to burn off excess energy (which he possesses in ample quantity) but to execute moderately complex turns, rotations, lifts, drops, and twists. Five prides himself in his physical adroitness and unashamedly confesses that "I am really good, ain't I?". Five competes, but more because of the adult praise that comes with it than for victory (eventually, of course, the two become equated in the thinking of many children). Increased body maturity makes household life more relaxed for child and parent. Five brushes his teeth, dresses and undresses himself, sets the table, runs to the corner store, retrieves items from the freezer, tidies (in a general sense) the living room, and, perhaps most important for nervous parents, moves through the house without leaving a swath of broken vases, cracked windows, and scarred furniture.

The preschooler's love relationship with words does not diminish during this final trimester of the preschool years. Words, however, take on a special significance. They become vehicles for understanding *how* the world works as well as the means by which the child *precisely* informs the outside world how he is feeling or thinking. Infantile articulation, for the most part, is outgrown. The child uses words in the manner he later will use money: discreetly, purposefully, and intentionally. Questions conjured up by the five-year-old tend to be to the point and relevant. They are asked for a reason, usually to acquire a piece of information ("Where does daddy work?"), or to weave together a vague relationship ("How come Johnny is bigger than I am?" or, "How come old people are wrinkly?"). Three and Four speak for practice and companionship as well as information. Five is unique in that he becomes distinctly (not exclusively) preoccupied with the latter. His social maturity makes itself evident in speech when he politely prefaces a comment with "Excuse me." or, "May I talk?" or, "It's my turn!". The latter is a favourite of children who have been attending nursery school or kindergarten, where the ability to take turns is a highly rewarded virtue. Language is now essentially complete in both form and structure. "Five has assimilated the syntactical conventions and expresses himself in correct, finished sentences. He uses all types of sentences, including complex sentences with hypothetical and conditional clauses." (Gesell, 1940, p. 55).

The developing skills of the five-year-old are numerous and diverse. Not only does he build upon and refine his four-year abilities, but several new skills are also acquired. Motor control is well-matured as are speaking skills. Five talks without infantile articulation; he hops and skips; he runs with full loping strides; he speaks with calm matter-of-factness and precision far beyond that of the four-year-old. He stands on tiptoe; he uses his hand rather than the entire arm in catching a small object; he follows the trajectory of a thrown ball with fair precision; he dresses and undresses himself (shoe laces are a special problem) and may be able to completely prepare himself for bed. He is conversational and social at mealtime and listens attentively to adult conversation. Word skills continue to grow and focus is no longer only on total sentences but as well on the specific wording of an entire sentence. Five may ask for an interpretation of a particular word in a sentence rather than a restatement of the entire sentence when his understanding is stymied by only one particular word. Pencils, tooth-brushes, brooms, and magazines are handled with passable precision and the number of out-of-bounds items is reducing monthly. Conversation is enjoyed not only for the social intercourse it provides, but also as a specific means of accumulating information. Five can narrate a story with sufficient intonation and suspense to hold the attention of even an impolite adult. Cooperative play is common but the spirit of competition and rivalry is making its presence felt. Creative pursuits such as drawing and painting are approached with beforehand ideas, and the five-year-old does not have to wait until he is through drawing a picture to decide what he has drawn. He decides in advance that he will draw a man, even a particular man: father. He can be trusted to buy an item or two from the store and he can walk himself to school if it is not too far. Five becomes self-conscious about nudity and may prefer not to be seen by strangers or members of the opposite sex in his natural state.*

Toilet activities and vocabulary hold a special fascination for the five-year-old. Adult slang and colloquialisms which deal with natural functions are readily adopted. Preschoolers, quite aware of the shock value of certain words, experience a strange sense of comic power by watching adults react to them. Four-letter words such as hell, damn, shit, and other more graphic terms usually not found in textbooks punctuate the five-year-old's spicy vocabulary. Interestingly, these words are usually used in proper context and show either frustration or displeasure.

Five comes to realize that danger exists not only as an abstraction but also that he himself could be injured by accident. The five-year-old is especially curious about deformed or crippled people and wants to

* Self-consciousness about nudity seems more prevalent in North American society than most European countries. The cultural differences which account for this dissimilarity are difficult to account for. One viewpoint asserts it is the result of North American children acquiring unnecessary inhibitions about nudity, whereas a second viewpoint assumes it results from European children being taught not to pay attention to natural inhibitions about nudity.

know how their condition came about. He accepts almost any calm, matter-of-fact response, suggesting that he is as much concerned about whether there is a feasible explanation as about the explanation itself. If parents show confusion, fear, or anxiety when asked certain questions, the child tends to acquire a similar subjective reaction to these questions. Five's ability to recognize danger is only one aspect of his growing awareness of personal limitations and fallibility. He knows much more about what he can or cannot do than he did at Four. He does not boldly swagger into situations beyond his developmental level. He may become worried about death (though he does not understand the concept very well), failure, injury, or illness. Worry can be easily coped with, however, because Five is wonderfully responsive to calm reassurance. It is well within his emotional resiliency to range from fear of death to worry over whether he gets popcorn at the movie next week in a ninety-second period.

Five has only slight awareness that his thought is a subjective process and not part of the objective world. He commonly assumes that adults are able to read his mind or know when he has committed a minor trespass. The unmistakable look of guilt preschoolers wear after doing something considered wrong reflects their hazy understanding of the subjective and objective world. Five, however, is more sophisticated than Four in these matters, and many have learned to tell lies rather well by this stage. Lying is one part of the child's intellectual discovery that parents do not *always* know about things they have not seen. The child is well into middle childhood, however, before he begins to understand how parents piece bits of evidence together in such a manner as to correctly conclude when the child has done something wrong.

Fewer emotional ups and downs trouble Five than Four, but when mood swings do occur they frequently reflect a matter of genuine importance to the child. Teachers and parents should be attentive to emotional shifts at this age in a more concerned manner than required with either Three or Four. At Five, problems are more substantive, and the child's sensitivity is more stable; therefore, moodiness often reflects a more depthful circumstance than it did during previous years. Fortunately, Five is relatively stable. He also is a pragmatist and is likely to welcome mother's return from an afternoon of shopping with "What did you bring me?". If the reply is not favourable, further conversation is abandoned. Five is to the point.

Preschool children enjoy poetry. It has a pleasant blend of fact and fancy, description and prescription, metaphor and reality, each of which cater nicely to the child's mixed understanding of the world. He likes stories about the fantastic and incredible. He identifies with them and, after a particularly exciting story, he may announce that he is going to climb into the clouds or crawl inside the stomach of a whale. At another time he may teasingly announce that he has an alligator in his pocket or a hippopotamus in his closet, laughing uproariously when parents feign surprise or shock upon hearing these announcements. Five is utterly convinced that he possesses a masterful wit and he generally is the first to laugh at his barbs and the last to stop. Five readily accepts the fact that he is lovable, an innocent gesture which adds immeasurably to his natural lovableness.

Five is a moralist but only in a crude way. He hates to see anyone get away with anything. He is a chronic "tattle-tale" who considers it his duty to report deeds which get others into trouble. He constantly reminds parents when they utter a swear word, usually by blurting "AHHEMMM!". Five, however, bases right or wrong almost exclusively on specific teachings he has received. He has little concept of degrees of wrongness. Crossing against the red light is as morally reprehensible as exploiting someone's trust. Specific behaviour, which has not been defined as wrong, usually isn't classified under a similar concept of wrong. Thus the child may feel no wrong in crossing against a "wait" sign at a crosswalk, even though he understands the intent of the sign, unless he has been specifically taught that one does not cross the street against the wait sign. Six will outgrow this moral shallowness. Five is oriented toward punishment and superior power in moral matters. He gives little weight to the *intent* of an action, but rather focuses exclusively on the *consequences* of the act. This not only reflects his limited understanding of personal accountability, but illustrates that his thought process is practical rather than ideal. Five follows rules and regulations for three general reasons: (1) he is afraid of the punishment which may occur if he violates them; (2) he enjoys the praise received for following them; and (3) he perceives that the rules, when applied in his favour, have personal benefit. Five is not exactly a theologian's delight.

Despite a fairly mature vocabulary and an admirable ability to account for his own behaviour, Five still has only a limited understanding of physical causality. He may be of the impression that real people are inside the television set, or that real musical instruments are inside the radio. He does show insight, however, when he asks how they got inside such a small area. Five has little idea of how an automobile works and commonly is of the impression that it takes little more than a key and will power to move the family automobile along the freeway. Even a six-year-old has little notion of why his bicycle stops working when the chain slips off. "Pretend", one of the most important words in the vocabulary of the five-year-old, is used to indicate roughly that some things are physically plausible while others are not. He may or may not change his mind when a adult informs him about something ("a submarine is a boat which moves under water") which does not jibe with his previous understanding (boats travel above water).

Five is zesty, almost in love with life. He openly admits his awe of beauty as well as his love for people. Five jokes, ridicules, and makes fun of himself, something he could not do comfortably as a four-year-old. Five is a treat.

Some Final Observations on the Preschooler

Growth during the preschool years is not completely predictable and certainly is not the same for every child. The common denominators of child development relate to those areas of development which all children must encounter within the limitations of their biology and social environment. The similarity in biological makeup of children during the preschool years allows us to make comparisons and contrasts in this area. The similarity in social environment of children during the preschool years allows us to make comparisons and contrasts in this area. Obviously there are differences among children not only in biology but also in social environment. These differences make the similarities even more important if we are to understand the definite, but general, lawfulness of childhood.

Most of the information on the preceding pages of this chapter deals with several general categories of biological or social growth which take place during the preschool years. Let us look at some of these categories.

1. *The preschooler learns to control his bioligical as well as his social impulses.* The preschool child finalizes toilet training. He learns to control his physical energy; to concentrate it and put it to constructive use; to attend to one specific part of the environment; to share and cooperate; to stand in line; to accept "No". He learns to discipline his impulse to eat when hungry and wait until mealtime. He learns to release frustration other than by blind rage. The preschool years are filled with learning about self-restraint, with coming to grips with a personal control system of biological and social impulses. Learning to inhibit one's inner feelings is not easy for child or adult; it always entails frustration, anxiety, and anger. Growth during these three years is never devoid of frustration — in fact, frustration is definitely the normal expectancy during much of this age.

2. *The preschooler acquires greater independence.* Each child evolves his own unique sense of identity and individuality which continues to evolve and change throughout his entire life. Individuality assumes that the child has separated himself from total identification with parents.

He recognizes himself as a distinct person, and though he may be perplexed, even disenchanted with some of what he discovers, he learns to consider himself as distinct. He abhors people who do not take into serious consideration his individuality. Limited vocabulary and immature cognitive development prevent him from spelling out in precise detail this fact, but his behaviour makes the point very clear. Independence during the preschool years is intimately related to the child's feelings of self-esteem. Environment, especially parental behaviour, significantly influences self-esteem. Apparently, the factors which exert the greatest effect on a preschooler's sense of self-esteem are: (1) consistent acceptance with respect and concern, and (2) freedom and independence within carefully defined limits. The child with high self-esteem usually has experienced a combination of these qualities. Here is one interpretation of the role of self-esteem in the preschooler's world.

> Children with high self-esteem are self-assured and confident. They are not frightened or intimidated. When you speak to them, they look you in the eye and do not hang their heads or answer in a whisper. They relate well to others, adults as well as peers. They have a strong sense of right and wrong, and they know how to distinguish between the two. They are open, and if they do something "wrong", there is seldom a need to explain their erroneous behavior to them. Most children with high self-esteem are happy, vibrant, and energetic. Sullenness and withdrawal are seldom observed. Unhappiness is usually expressed verbally and repression has not become a defensive mechanism. (Felsenthal, 1972, p. 179)

3. *The preschooler learns about sex roles.* Upon entering the first grade children have very clear-cut (though limited) ideas about what men do and what women do. Their understanding of sex role differentiations is acquired at home, with peers, via the media (especially television), and through cultural folkways and mores. The child will change many of his viewpoints about what is acceptable or unacceptable behaviour; the important consideration is that he does possess them and they significantly influence his behaviour, self-esteem, pride, and feelings of adequacy. To assume that a child has not formulated opinions about behaviour his sex permits or forbids is an injustice to him. Boys *enjoy* doing what they understand as manly and girls *enjoy* doing what they understand as womanly. It is a comparatively easy task to convince a doubting boy that cooking is an activity for men as well as women, but it is virtually impossible to get the same boy to condone male cooks or to engage in cooking games *until* he is so convinced. The particular beliefs which children acquire (or come to on their own) radically influence the range of their behavioural possibilities.

There is not agreement on the matter of how sex-role learning takes place in early childhood. Spencer (1967) reports that several general theories have a certain degree of acceptance. Psychoanalytic theorists suggest that children identify with their like-sex parent out of fear. Another theory suggests that the child identifies with the parent who is an effective punisher as well as an effective reinforcer. In other words, the child identifies with the parent who symbolizes and also represents power. As stated before, our concern in this text is more descriptive than theoretical. Our interest is in the influence sex-role learning exerts on the behaviour of the child. The evidence indicates that young boys are more influenced by sex-role identification than girls. Young boys more consistently choose masculine items on preference tests than girls of the same age choose feminine items. "This acceleration in sex-role learning continues throughout the early elementary years with boys becoming progressively more masculine each year" (Spencer, 1967, p. 195). Other evidence indicates that girls reach their peak of femininity around five years of age and remain rather constant, or even decrease in femininity during the first years of school. Boys and girls show very different patterns of conflict during the preschool years, especially after age three. Boys become increasingly combative and rowdy in their disagreements with one another. Girls, however, tend to quarrel less and less after age three, and when they do, disagreements tend to remain verbal rather than physical (Stone, 1968, p. 385). Neither sex displays much poise or calm in disagreements and will resort to almost any course of action which will bring about the desired end. One favourite method is to bring in an adult who will interdict and exercise his power of authority in favour of the child who brought him in. Because this so commonly backfires, children have learned by the age of eight or so to keep adults out of peer disagreements whenever possible.

4.   *The preschooler learns about the give and take of interpersonal living.* As the child's social world expands beyond the household, he encounters the requirements of interacting with humans who do not show him the deference to which he has grown accustomed. The preschooler *learns* to get along with others, a learning task which does not come easily. The preschooler begins to understand that he, as a person, is subject to rules which have not been designed exclusively for him, but for all people or certain classes of people. The highly egocentric child initially resists rules which deemphasize his importance. Only with time and a good deal of frustration does he compromise. The compromise is not a sellout of his individuality, however, but merely a redefinition of it with greater emphasis upon his learning to adjust to others rather than vice versa.

5.   *The preschool child develops a conscience.* The internal set of impulses and guidelines which incline the child away from what he considers bad and toward what he considers good is called conscience. Its importance in human life should not be underestimated since significant behaviour is based upon it. For the most part conscience is learned, but much of what eventually becomes classified as "conscience" comes about as a confluence of external and internal forces. In other words, some aspects of a child's conscience are formulated internally and others are assimilated from external sources such as parents. The child's conscience serves as a parental substitute and allows him to make decisions on ethical rather than on purely practical grounds. Children may or may not experience guilt when they violate the commands of their conscience. Wide individual differences prevail in the degree to which conscience influences the behaviour of the preschooler. Some children are greatly influenced by conscience; others much less so. An important consideration when investigating the role of the conscience is to recognize that it represents an internal frame of reference which permits the child to cope with situations on grounds other than purely pragmatic or egocentric. He no longer bases decisions purely on his own best interests or personal impulses. The emergence of conscience adds a new set of complications for the preschooler because he now approaches the world not only in terms of what is "real" and "unreal" but also in terms of what is "ideal" and "nonideal", or, if you will, "good" and "bad". The preschooler's fluid mind must now stretch one step further and accommodate this new attitude. It is an attitude never outgrown even though the specific content of the attitude will undergo many changes throughout life.

The Preschooler as an Educational Headache

Preschoolers pose many problems for the society which nurtures them. They must have their basic needs cared for and this includes not only nutrition and housing but also education and socialization. In traditional North American culture, parents have borne the responsibility to provide the basic biological, social, psychological, and moral aspects of child-rearing. This is beginning to change. Physically and economically, parents are more mobile than ever before. They spend less time with their children than did their own parents and they relegate more child-rearing responsibilities to societal institutions than did previous generations. The social implications of these changing modes of parent-child relationship are staggering; in many respects they have caught North American society off balance and only marginally equipped to handle the multitude of problems which have subsequently arisen.

In 1970, there were approximately 26 million children in the United States and Canada under five years of age. Of the 33-35 million women in the combined labour force of these two countries, about 60 percent are married, widowed, or divorced. In 1965, in the United States, more than four million children under the age of six had working mothers. From these facts alone it is apparent that many homes are not characterized by the "housewife" and "working-husband" combination which for so long has formed the basic division of labour in our society. The number of children who spend their days away from home has increased so spectacularly in recent years that communities are forming day-care centres as well as morning nurseries and kindergartens on a scale never thought possible only twenty-five years ago. Households in which both parents are absent during the day create at least three major problems with regard to their preschool children. (1) *Where* will these children spend their days? (2) *How* will these children spend their days? (3) *Who* will supervise these children? Though simple questions, their proper solution is presently taxing the conscience as well as the pocketbook of a society which is as committed to adult economic freedom as it is to freedom of growth during childhood.

Several different methods of child day care have emerged as tentative solutions to the problem of preschool children whose parents work during the day. There is wide variation in purpose and philosophy of these centres entrusted with the care of preschool children. Some are little more than babysitting services which care little for the social or personal development of the child; others actively participate in expanding the child's social, psychological, and intellectual capacities. Some are financed by civic or federal government funds while others are privately owned and charge tuition fees; some hire only professionally trained personnel while others operate on such meager budgets they must employ only those who are willing to work for minimum wages. Here we shall briefly overview some of the more significant examples.

1.   *Day-care centres.* Day-care centres are exactly what their name implies: centres which care for children during the day. The emphasis differs from centre to centre but, as a rule, day-care centres are more custodial in nature than educational. Their primary function is to provide working mothers a place where their children will be provided and cared for during the day. Day-care centre personnel usually are not trained in preschool education. Children are given freedom to play, exercise, and frolic, but serious attempts at academic preparation or personal development are not part of the stated purposes of most day-care centres. Parents pay for services rendered; in Canada as well as the

United States, however, payment tends to be proportional to parental income.

2. *Play schools.* Play schools usually are operated in neighbourhood centres or churches for the benefit of local families. As a rule, they are staffed by volunteer workers, usually mothers of children who attend the play school or housewives who have no children at home during the day. Play schools are varied because of their small size, but the general emphasis is utilitarian. Because play schools are run by volunteer help they are especially helpful to mothers who earn little pay or who work every other day rather than full time.*

3. *Nursery schools.* Though the term has come to be used as a general expression for all forms of preschool education, nursery school refers to the first unit of the elementary education process. Nursery schools, manned by personnel trained in elementary or preschool education, are designed to blend with the first grade curriculum. Nursery schools are frequently designed to cater to the psychological, intellectual, and physical needs of the four-year-old, but this is not a rigid rule. Cooperative play, personal growth, art appreciation, and creative expression are the general goals of most nursery school programs. Wide variation pertains in the methods employed to attain these goals, however.

4. *Kindergarten.* The unit of the school which enrolls five-year-olds on a regular basis for a year prior to entrance to the first grade is defined as kindergarten. "The purpose of the kindergarten program is to further the developmental growth of the children through experiences that are of interest and help to them. This unit provides for a continuous educational experience under the direction of a qualified teacher in close cooperation with the parents" (Leeper, p. 92). Many kindergartens operate as part of the public education system, while others are privately owned and operated. The purpose of the kindergarten is educational rather than merely custodial.

5. *Cooperative nursery school and/or kindergarten.* This approach is a synthesis of play school and kindergarten, blending the volunteer help of community mothers with hired professionals who serve as directors. It is a less expensive plan than nursery schools or kindergartens and also allows parents the opportunity for more involved participation in the education of their own children. This plan is not suitable for professional parents who must work certain specific hours of each working

---

* The city of Edmonton, Alberta has designed one of the most elaborate and noteworthy play school programs in North America. Operating approximately 150 centres, staffed by volunteer mothers as well as professional staff trained and paid by the city, the program stresses social cooperation, nature study and appreciation, arts and crafts. There is virtually no emphasis on academic preparation. Though costly for the city, the program has proved popular with parents and beneficial for children.

day, but it has proved very successful in communities where there are enough volunteer mothers.

It is worthy of note that in the Soviet Union where preschool education is largely a matter of government policy, a strong trend prevails toward accepting the philosophy of the nursery school and kindergarten with less emphasis on day-care centres and play schools as they have been described in the previous paragraphs. Preschool centres are also expected to look after the health and physical development of the child; therefore, dietitians, health nurses, pediatricians, as well as physical education specialists all work their way into the Soviet preschool program. In a report on nursery schools in the Soviet Union, Cole (1972, p. 217) reports: "When we asked Mrs. Shvedova what goals Preschool 67 had for its children, she replied, 'We want them to be smart and honest. If they are honest, they will be fair. We want them to love beauty, to be real people. We don't want them to be all alike, but originality and creativity are not that important.' " Most North American parents, though having slight reservations about the last part of Mrs. Shvedova's statement, would find such a philosophy well within their understanding of what constitutes a good preschool.

Numerous philosophical questions inevitably arise whenever preschool education is discussed. Their solution is influenced not only by sound research but also by each individual's philosophy of childhood and his belief about what is in the best interest of the child. These questions centre around the purpose, the procedure, and the method of instructing children of preschool age. (a) *What is the purpose of preschool education?* Is it merely to give the child something to do while the parents are at work? Is it a time for preparation for the first years of public school? Is it a time for constructive play and social learning? Is it a time for learning about oneself and others? A time for learning about social rules and obligations? Should each of these be stressed during preschool education? (b) *By what methods should the preschool experience be carried out?* Are traditional classroom settings appropriate? Should children be expected to conform to the demands of a social setting or should rules be established which minimize group considerations and maximize individual considerations? Should the child be expected to compete with other children, or be compared with them? Should he be urged to compete with himself, to live up to his own expectations? How should children be disciplined or punished? How should they be rewarded or praised? Should parents be encouraged to drop in on the preschool or should it be like the public schools and comparatively closed? (c) *What is the best way to teach children?* With

160

regard to children, are "best" and "most efficient" synonymous? Are some kinds of teaching better than others even though they are less efficient? Is the *experience* of learning as important as the *outcome* of learning? Do certain kinds of learning increase the child's desire to learn more than others? Does the child require extraneous reward for learning? Should the acquisition of classroom skills which benefit the child upon entering the first grade be a top priority in preschool education? If children are not intellectually stimulated during the preschool years, will they be at a competitive disadvantage with children who have? What is intellectual stimulation? Are some forms of intellectual stimulation more productive than others? Should preschool teachers be authoritarian or permissive?

All of these questions require special investigation and analysis; however, the answers do not come from purely objective assessment. They are significantly influenced by one's philosophy of childhood. For the student of child development, however, it is imperative that his philosophy of childhood correspond as closely as possible to the actual nature of childhood. This is where investigation and analysis come into play.

The Renaissance of Early Childhood Education. We are presently going through a major development in contemporary education which centres around the widespread reawakening of concern with the education of the very young child. This reawakening is taking place not only in universities and institutes devoted to the study of preschool children but also in the minds of parents and in the legislation of governments. The boom toward early childhood education received its greatest impetus in 1965 when the United States federal government created and sponsored the Head Start program. This program brought more than 500,000 children into preschool programs who had never before been exposed to them. It provided incentive for thousands of university students as well as professional teachers to study the educative process for children under the age of six years. What are the factors which contributed to this Renaissance of early childhood education? Shane (1971) suggests, among others, the following.

Political decisions. In North America, funds have been made available for preschool education on a scale never before equalled. Although these funds are subject to changing priorities of different political groups, the precedent has been established. The decision to allocate funds for preschool education has been influenced by the realization that many urban and rural ghettos are potentially explosive. Some government officials maintain that one effective way of postponing or precluding explosions is to provide educational programs for the children of the poor.

Current social commentaries. The public has been made aware of the appalling conditions of many urban schools, rural communities, and ethnic ghettos through best-selling books and news coverage by the media. The national collective conscience has prompted the creation of life-style alternatives, including preschool education, for children who live in these unfavourable conditions. Pines, in her book *Revolution in Learning,* portrays an image of the educational importance of the preschool years which has received wide acceptance:

> Millions of children are being irreparably damaged by our failure to stimulate them intellectually during their crucial years — from birth to six. Millions of others are being held back from their true potential. Our severest educational problems could be largely solved if we started early enough. Yet we recklessly ignore an exciting and persuasive body of knowledge about how human beings learn. (1966, p. 1)

Environmental mediation. Most adults now accept the thesis that each child's future life can be positively influenced by an early education experience based on sound principles. Although genuine misgivings persist about the philosophy as well as the practice of preschool education, we can say that most parents agree that it can be helpful if conducted properly. So many people today take this last statement for granted that it is easy to lose sight of the fact that planned, deliberate educational intervention in the preschooler's life is a phenomenon which did not begin in earnest in North America until the 1960s.

Creating intelligence. Recent research has substantiated rather conclusively that a child's ability to perform on an intelligence test can be improved, and consequently, his I.Q. as measured by the intelligence test can be increased. Although critics suggest that this is due more to the weakness of intelligence tests than to the strengths of preschool education, one can see that children show improvement in many skills related to intelligence assessment when exposed to high quality preschool education. Many psychologists are convinced that environment is as important as heredity in the development of intelligence of young children.

Experiments in early learning. During the past decade hundreds of experiments have been conducted in the area of early learning. Results have been diverse as well as controversial. Some researchers have concluded that preschool children can learn virtually anything which an adult can learn if presented in terms they understand. Others have discovered that young children have skills and capacities far in excess of

162

what was previously thought. Less dramatically, it has also been suggested that preschool education has only negligible effects on the child and that his time could be as profitably spent elsewhere.

Intensive study of elementary school children's potential for learning mathematical concepts, though not finalized, indicates the child is much more capable of understanding geometry, higher mathematics, physics, and algebra than educators or psychologists had heretofore assumed.

Improved understanding of subcultures. Recent breakthroughs in the sociology and anthropology of subcultures has greatly expanded not only our ability to teach children from these subcultures but to learn from them as well. Preschool education no longer is attended only by middle-class children or taught exclusively by middle-class teachers. Neither are its purposes based solely upon middle-class values and ambitions. Most government sponsored preschool centres are expressly intended for children of all socio-economic groups and, though the preponderance of instructors are "middle-class" (no one really knows for sure what this term means), this is rapidly changing.

Language development. Most contemporary research suggests that language development is a critical factor in mental development and educational success. An enriched linguistic environment, that is, one which provides good language models together with variety and rewards for verbal responses, enhances cognitive development. An impoverished, dull, understimulating environment, on the other hand, seems to inhibit these developments (Mussen, 1963, p. 310). Some researchers have gone so far as to state that for culturally deprived children academic success and language skills are virtually the same thing. Bereiter and Engelmann conclude:

> Evidence was cited which suggests that lack of concrete learning has relatively little to do with the intellectual and academic deficiencies of disadvantaged children and that it is the lack of verbal learning, in particular the lack of those kinds of learning that can only be transmitted from adults to children through language, that is mainly responsible for these deficiencies. *Thus there is justification for treating cultural deprivation as synonymous with language deprivation.* (1966, p. 42)

Additional research indicates that the preschool years are extremely influential in determining the nature of speech skills in later life. If these skills are not cultivated during these critical years, the child may never develop speaking abilities as richly as he would otherwise.

Each of the above factors has contributed to the boom in preschool education. They also contribute to the diversity of ideas about what constitutes a good preschool and what is in the best interest of the

163

child. Most preschools which purport to be educational rather than merely custodial can be classified in one of three general categories: (1) compensatory education programs; (2) academic preparation programs; (3) personal-social enrichment programs.

Preschool as compensatory education. All children do not enter the first grade equally prepared for classroom activity. There is a wide range of individual differences among children in natural intelligence, emotional stability, ability to concentrate, manual dexterity, and other traits related to school work. Differences are prominent among children from various socio-economic classes. As a rule (to which there are numerous exceptions), children from low socio-economic families are less prepared to cope with the demands of the first grade than are children of middle socio-economic families. Two reasons for this are: (1) Middle-class families tend to share more common values with the school system than lower-class families. This is possibly due to the fact that middle-class individuals have been managing the public schools for generations. It may also stem from the historical relationship between academic achievement and upward mobility in the middle class. (2) Children from middle-class families, in the course of their daily living, acquire verbal, auditory, and concentration skills which more closely correspond with those required in the first years of school than do children of lower-class families.*

The attempt to compensate for the competitive disadvantage which lower-class children face upon entering the first grade is referred to as *compensatory education.* The basic concerns of compensatory education can be more fully understood by describing some of the ways in which lower-class children differ from middle-class children. Compensatory education attempts to increase those skills related to classroom activity which lower-class children lack.

Several basic differences are evident between lower- and middle-class children with regard to school readiness which give the latter a marked advantage in the school setting. Children from lower-class families tend to be weak in auditory and visual discrimination, both of which are crucial in learning proper speech and reading skills. Vocabulary differences are also noticeable; lower-class children lack abstract language and are not as adept with words used for categories, classes, or

---

* We shall not at this time enter the debate concerning the viability of school requirements as they now exist in the public school system. The substance of the debate is this: many of the demands made upon first grade children are essentially rooted in middle-class values rather than educational necessity. Therefore, low socio-economic children do not face an *educational* disadvantage, rather it is class discrimination in the guise of educational policy which hinders their progress. Here, we shall concentrate on the evidence which indicates that children of lower-class families enter the first grade with fewer classroom related skills than do children of middle-class families.

nonconcrete ideas. Middle-class families tend to be more verbal and to place a greater premium upon precision and clarity of verbal messages. As a result their children enter school with a readiness for precision of statement, and they also possess listening skills which allow them to decipher more cogently the substance of a spoken statement. Children of low-income families, however, possess exceptional skills in use of gesture and colloquialism, but they are less practiced in stating messages exactly. Stone (1968, p. 310) points out that lower-class children show little of the inventiveness, playfulness, or imagination found in the language of middle-class children. Research in personality development of the "deprived" child, though not extensive, is somewhat consistent in its findings. "The available evidence, however, does seem to indicate that the ego development of the deprived child is more likely to be characterized by lack of self-confidence and negative self-image than that of the middle-class child" (Bloom, 1965, p. 72). The negative self-concept leads the child to expect failure which, in turn, greatly contributes to its probability. This phenomenon is sometimes referred to as the *self-fulfilling prophecy*. Another factor which favours middle-class children is that the values of their household tend to correspond more closely with those of the school. Middle-class students have been reared to value future-time orientation and to strive for delayed or symbolic gratification. They learn to place a premium on self-restraint as well as on group participation. Each of these values is integral to most school programs.

Several specific consequences accrue as a result of class differences in readiness for school. Children who have less preparation in such areas as auditory discrimination, visual discrimination, verbal clarity, abstract vocabulary, delayed gratification, symbolic reward, self-confidence, and group participation soon fall behind in classroom work. Not only do they fall behind, but they tend to fall farther behind each year. Thus, a child who performed near the average in the first grade may fall slightly below the average in the second year and by the third grade may be among the lowest achievers in his classroom. This tendency to drop farther behind one's age group is called the *cumulative deficit syndrome*. Its name indicates that the child's deficit *accumulates* each year rather than remaining constant. "On the average, by eighth grade these children are about three years behind grade norms in reading and arithmetic as well as in other subjects. These effects are most marked in deprived children of average and low ability" (Bloom, 1965, p. 73).

Children who perform poorly find school not only comparatively devoid of meaningful reward and involvement but also experience a great deal of frustration and anxiety. Even in the first grade children know among themselves who is weak and who is strong in classroom activity. Though the negative stigma for weak performance is not pronounced in the first grade, it becomes so by the second and third grade. Low performing students must learn to cope with the insecurity which comes with being considered less competent than average. A common coping strategy for many young children is to learn to act so stupid that the teacher will not expect anything other than failure from them and will therefore quit reprimanding them when they perform poorly. Paul Goodman referred to this unconscious coping strategy as *selective stupidity*. Its basic value to the young pupil is that it relieves him from pressure to perform well in a situation in which he is at a competitive disadvantage. It allows him to feel at ease about classroom failure because eventually he becomes convinced that he is stupid and therefore expects no success.

The intent of compensatory education is to provide learning which the child would not experience in his home environment. This presumably will decrease the probability that the child will fall farther behind each year, and that he will not have to resort to the defense mechanism of selective stupidity. It also assumes that as a result of the learning acquired in the compensatory education program the child will more ably actualize not only his classroom potentialities but also his future social and economic potentialities. Implicit is the assumption that in compensatory education learning is a valued end in itself.

Preschool as academic preparation. Some preschools stress the acquisition of academic skills which directly relate to classroom schoolwork of the first three grades. Because the children who attend such preschools are usually four or five years old, special teaching techniques must be adapted to their developmental level. In academic preparation programs children learn to count and frequently to add one-digit numbers; they learn the alphabet as well as the more common phonetic combinations of the language. They learn about animals, especially their family and safety habits, and may be introduced to the theory of plant and animal reproduction. The proper manipulation of a pencil is taught (this is not an easy task for most four-year-olds and many five-year-olds experience difficulty in this matter); one favourite exercise is to have the child print his name, thus combining the practice of penmanship, letter formation, alphabet learning, and memory into one task. Children at this age must partake in large muscle activity, which can be combined with academic learning. Foot races may be timed, fostering in the child an awareness of time as well as its relationship to distance. Running around the perimeter of the school provides not only exercise, but in subsequent conversation creates an opportunity to casually discuss the relationship between perimeter and distance, and their relationship to fatigue if paced quickly. Most children are fascinated with art work, especially their own. The alert preschool teacher combines the play and aesthetic enjoyment of creative art with lessons about texture, colour combinations, and even the geometry of space.

Advocates of academic preparation base their reasoning on four types of arguments. (1) The earlier we start a child on the formal academic path, the earlier he will finish, thus reducing the total educational cost of the child. (2) As learning comes easy to the preschool child, we should capitalize on his eagerness for academic skill. (3) Because intellectual growth is rapid in the preschool years, education will help maximize this growth while the absence of it will curtail cognitive growth. (4) Traditional preschool is too concerned with social and personal development and insufficiently concerned with cognitive development (Elkind, 1970).

Some experts in the field of preschool education contend that the child has physiological limitations which restrict academic preparation. The most common concern is with visual maturity. Opinion is divided as to whether the child should be taught to read during the preschool years, especially before the fifth birthday. Woodward is one of the most forthright in his opposition to teaching reading before the child is physiologically ready:

> Although his binocular vision has improved and he can focus more easily, he is not yet ready for any fine work of any description. In particular he is not yet usually ready to learn to read. The physical effort for a child first learning to read is very great. He has to focus his eyes on the beginning of a line of print, take in a number of symbols, and then stop before going on to the next batch. Then he has to make a new adjustment from the end of the first line of print to the beginning of the second, making a diagonal line. Quite often he will miss the beginning of the second and go on to the third. Even an adult, when tired, will do this, so one can understand how much more difficult for a child, who has only just learnt this difficult skill of focusing, this can be. (p. 50)

Woodward comments further:

> It [reading] takes intense concentration on his part, which sometimes he cannot sustain, and hence reading may be an unsatisfactory experience for him, especially if the adult expresses disapproval. Many children are now going into the Infant School before the age of five and in many cases are expected to begin to learn to read right away; this is almost impossible for them, and even when the child is physically mature enough, periods of learning to read should be chosen by the child himself, who knows when he can no longer concentrate

enough to be successful. He may be encouraged to read or guided to read, but never pressurized into reading. (1966, p. 50)

Gesell, as early as 1940, was making similar claims about the child's ability to cope with reading. Opinion, however, is divided. Many preschool specialists do not concur with Woodward's assessment of the situation. Kindergarten and nursery school teachers are equally opinionated on the matter, with some refusing to begin reading instructions before first grade, while others launch apparently successful reading programs for four-year-olds. Preschool instructors, however, should show discretion in this matter, especially toward children who complain about reading difficulties or those who have a personal or family history of eye weakness.

Preschools designed to enhance academic acceleration differ from compensatory education programs in that they do not assume that the child comes from an academically impoverished environment. The opposite is usually assumed, and rightfully so. Programs which specialize in academic acceleration attract middle-class children largely because of the special fascination they hold for white collar, professional, middle-class parents. However, few preschools are preoccupied exclusively with academic preparation; most combine academic preparation with development of the personal-social skills of the child.

Preschool as personal-social development. This type of preschool is distinguished from compensatory education and academic acceleration preschools by comparative avoidance of skills which relate to the academic aspects of the first three years of public school. Their general purpose is to enrich development of those aspects of personal and social living which allow the child to live most fully life *at his present age.* Stress is placed upon allowing four-year-olds to cultivate and develop "four-ness". Little emphasis is placed upon acquisition of academic skills which will prove advantageous in future years. However, an implicit assumption (this is where the philosophy of a preschool program becomes important) is that by allowing the child to actualize most fully the potentialities intrinsic to his present developmental level he will develop the capacity to adjust to new demands as they arise. With regard to academic skills, personal-social practitioners usually say, in effect: "There is ample time for that later. Now we want the child to learn to appreciate art, nature, people, and himself and to enjoy doing what is right."

Competition, especially what adults commonly call "cutthroat competition", is avoided. Sharing, cooperation, and participation are stressed. Excellence is encouraged more because of the intrinsic personal reward than social praise. The school attempts to assist the child to become not only a better person, but also a better child. Preschools which stress personal-social development are to a great extent modeled after the naturalistic tradition of Jean-Jacques Rousseau who taught that children have the basics for natural growth as long as they are sheltered from adult nonvirtue and allowed to follow the course of their unique development.

Among growing factions of parents and educators recently has come a reassessment of the role of preschool in the life of the child. This is due partly to the disenchantment experienced by children and parents with academic preparation programs based upon operant conditioning and behaviour modification techniques. Although these programs are often highly successful in attaining their stated academic or behavioural goals, parents object to the dehumanized (perhaps we should say dechildrenized) atmosphere of some of these programs. The philosophy, "There is plenty of time for academic learning later", is gathering audience among professional educators not only because they sense that children are being robbed of their childhood in some programs, but also because many simply believe it to be true — there is plenty of time. This viewpoint was registered rather forcefully in a preschool program where staff members resigned and parents withdrew their children after the director announced that pupils would be *allotted* recreational and creative arts time only as reinforcement for success in other activities. Although this system has worked effectively in other preschool settings, people eventually demand to know how great a price their children are paying for what they learn.

Do preschools work? The success of any program can be assessed only in terms of what it has attempted to achieve. Since preschools have varied goals and ambitions, their success or nonsuccess must be viewed in terms of their unique purposes. Supervisors of compensatory education preschools claim that pupils benefit from them. Research supports this claim with such consistency that it is impossible to overview the evidence in this brief space. Low-income children consistently show increased scores on measures of intelligence and academic achievement. They frequently demonstrate increased powers of concentration and are able to stick with abstract tasks longer than other low-income children who do not attend special compensatory programs. Research also suggests that children who have attended compensatory preschools fare better in the first grade. Long-term studies of the effects of compensatory education, however, are not nearly as abundant or positive. Evidence does not clearly establish that preschool programs have lasting effects with regard to academic competence. Nor is there conclusive evidence that the values of lower-class children shift in the direction of those of the schools. Thus, many teachers feel that the value conflicts between schools and lower-class students are merely postponed rather than eliminated. Preschool programs which stress academic preparation or acceleration also yield mixed data. Alumni of such programs are, on the whole, more successful in elementary school than children who did not attend, but this could be expected for reasons other than their preschool experience. They are strong in the same areas in which children who enroll in compensatory education programs are weak, therefore one would expect that school work would be easier for them. We know least about preschools which stress personal-social development for two reasons: (1) their stated goals are extremely difficult to objectively measure or to assess, and (2) their concern is more with present than future effects on the child's behaviour and experience. Personal experience, as well as discussions with parents and children, however, lead most parents of preschoolers to support schools of this type.

In conclusion, it appears that the worth of preschool is determined almost exclusively by the values of parents and educators. If they value academic acceleration, compensatory coaching, or personal-social development, a good chance prevails that the proper kind of preschool will contribute to partial achievement of these goals. Because most parents in our society do value one or more of these goals we can assume with a measure of confidence that preschools of one kind or another will continue to be an integral part of the child's institutional life.

Experimental programs in preschool education. An unusual phenomenon accompanies experimental research in the area of preschool education: virtually all experiments are highly successful. The number of failures noted in the past twenty years of preschool research has been miraculously scant. Whether the research deals with low-income or upper-income children seems to make little difference in the findings. Also of little import is whether the experimenters use permissive or nonpermissive teaching techniques; whether the subjects in the experiment were hand-picked or chosen at random; whether academic skills or social living skills were the major focus of concern. How do we account for the almost uniform success of preschool experiments? It could be that experiments which prove preschools to be failures are not reported and are abandoned to die a lonesome, silent death. This undoubtedly accounts for some preschool failures but certainly cannot be the most complete explanation. The probable answer is to be found by analysing those ingredients usually present in experimental educational programs but absent in regular educational programs. Several conditions intrinsic to experimental programs in preschool education more or less assure that the goals of the program will be achieved. First, experimental programs are often financed more richly than regular school programs. Per capita allotments are usually higher and resources for purchase of special technical equipment such as audio-visual aids are more readily available. Although financial assistance is not the key ingredient to successful preschool programs, it no doubt makes a significant difference to many of them. Secondly, the teachers of experimental programs frequently are better trained and possess more professional experience than the staff of ordinary preschools. Thirdly, enthusiasm among staff members is greater in experimental programs because of the excitement which comes with innovating a new program and the natural tendency for people to want their own ideas to reach fruition. Children are, as a rule, quite responsive to adult enthusiasm. Fourthly, experimental programs in preschool education tend to be more successful than regular programs (even programs which are modelled exactly after the experimental program) because the individuals who design special research programs tend to concentrate on areas of investigation which have proved successful for them in the past. Thus, we do not see B. F. Skinner, the famous American behavioural psychologist, conducting preschool research based on the assumption and biases of his philosophical opponent, Carl Rogers. Experimental programs usually are not brought into existence unless the founder can assure those who pay for the program that it will yield positive results.

It is important to view research findings from a critical and informed perspective. A good deal of the faddish nature of contemporary education rests upon the fact that educators often are more preoccupied with the results of experimental programs than with the reasons which led to these same results.

Despite the tendency for experimental programs to be successful, in the coming years there will be increasing demand by pedagogues as well as parents for improvement in the quality of preschool and elementary education. The demands will focus on cognitive as well as personal development concerns. Specifically, the demands will stress:

1. Increasing emphasis on higher mental processes in problem solving rather than merely the learning of information.
2. Increasing emphasis on the basic ideas, structure, and methods of inquiry of each subject field rather than the minutiae of the subject matter.
3. Increasing emphasis on "learning to learn"; that is, teaching the child how to approach tasks with workable strategies.
4. Increasing emphasis on cultivating those aspects of interests, attitudes, and personality which will help the individual to fur-

ther his own growth and development, and also help find meaning and purpose in life. (Bloom, 1965, p. 3)

Summary

The importance and necessity of preschool education has been accepted during the past twenty years as never before in North American society. This stems from two general conditions: (1) preschools are more necessary than ever because of the tremendous number of working mothers; and (2) preschools are more functional and effective than ever because of the significant breakthroughs which have been made in understanding the preschool child from psychological, sociological, and physiological perspectives.

Preschools have taken the following general forms in North American society, although in other parts of the world, such as the Soviet Union, the emphasis is somewhat different.

1. Day-care centres
2. Play schools
3. Nursery schools
4. Kindergartens
5. Cooperative nursery school and/or kindergarten

The renaissance in early childhood education can be attributed to many historical and cultural factors. Most notably:

1. Political decisions to allot financial assistance to preschool programs.
2. Social commentaries which have stressed the poor living conditions of many preschool children.
3. Public acceptance of the notion that the lives of preschool children can be positively influenced by a sound educational program.
4. Research evidence that intelligence level (as measured by certain kinds of intelligence tests) can be raised as the result of preschool training.
5. Research evidence which indicates that young children are capable of much more sophisticated kinds of learning than previously assumed.
6. Improved understanding of subcultures has made it easier for minority children to be taught as well as to teach others about themselves.
7. Improved understanding of the role of language in academic achievement has prompted programs which combat ineffective language learning during the early years.

Of the preschools which attempt to develop or expand the personal and

172

intellectual abilities of the child rather than serve merely as custodial centres, three general types emerge.

1. Compensatory education programs which attempt to compensate for the lack of skills which relate to classroom performance.
2. Academic preparation programs which give the child an accelerated start on skills related to academic classroom skills such as reading and arithmetic.
3. Personal-social development programs which stress growth of the personal talents and capacities of the child.

Whether one considers preschools meaningful is almost exclusively a matter of personal philosophy, and unless one is willing to assume that one personal philosophy is better (or more correspondent with the nature of childhood) than another, no other way arises to assess the personal or social value of preschools.

Although possibly never more masterfully stated, not all modern educators agree with George Bernard Shaw's assessment of the necessity for childhood education.

> If you have a baby who can speak with Tsars in the gate, who can make Europe and America stop and listen when he opens his mouth, who can smite with unerring aim straight at the sorest spots in the world's conscience, who can break through all censorships and all barriers of language, who can thunder on the gates of the most terrible prisons in the world and place his neck under the keenest and bloodiest axes only to find that for him the gates dare not open and the axes dare not fall, then indeed you have a baby that must be nursed and coddled and petted and let go his own way.

The Preschooler as Thinker

Mental growth of such staggering significance takes place during the preschool years that it does the child injustice to speak of "how preschoolers think". The child evidences growth in all cognitive realms during the preschool years; he is vastly more adept at concept formation, memory, quantitative skills, and assimilation at age four than at three; at five than at four. Differences exist among children of the same age in thought process as well as in capacity for thought. By now we should be well aware of these variations among and within children. As always, our task is to sort out the trends, habits, and principles which most aptly characterize the child, and which most fully contribute to our knowledge of his epigenetic unfolding.

The preschool child's thinking ability is usually viewed from one of

173

three perspectives: (1) its increased sophistication when contrasted with the meager capacities of the toddler; (2) its immaturity when contrasted with the more sophisticated capacities of the seven or eight-year-old; (3) its general processes. We shall focus on the last alternative, but by doing so will inadvertently touch upon the others.

We recall that between the age of twelve and thirty-six months considerable maturity of mental process occurs: problem-solving skills emerge; verbal and representational thought come into existence; the environment is mentally schematized and compartmentalized; recognition of number and quantity begin; language is acquired and developed. The toddler, however, is remarkably restricted when compared with the preschool child. He cannot begin to match his older developmental counterpart in concept formation skills, duration or depth of memory, intensity or length of concentration, verbal mastery, understanding of the social world and the rules which govern it, insight, knowledge of causality, or richness of utilizable past experience.

Because the preschool years fall within the time span defined by Piaget as the years of *preoperational thought,* we shall describe some of the preschooler's thinking habits from Piaget's perspective. Piaget contends that preschool thought, because it falls within the preoperational stage of mental development, is egocentric. Thought is built upon the relatedness of things to "me"; outside events are interpreted in terms of principles which regulate the child rather than those which regulate the event. The early preschooler is not as egocentric as the toddler, to be sure, and becomes even less so during the later preschool years, but his thought processes betray in one way or another the egocentric nature of preschool intellectualism. A second characteristic of preoperational thought is centration. "The preoperational thinking of children concentrates on a single feature of an object to the neglect of other important aspects. . . He attends to superficial features of events, understanding only those characteristics which attract his attention." (Munsinger, 1971, p. 135). His reasoning process is thus distorted because he cannot consider those features of the situation which compensate for his exaggerated focus on one part of a larger complex of factors. The tendency toward centration, blended with egocentric thought, makes the preschool child a mixed blessing to educators. If his propensity for focusing on only one aspect of a problem is properly channeled, very impressive insights can be fostered; if new information or ideas coincide with his egocentric nature, he gravitates to them with zeal and enthusiasm. The good teacher cultivates these reflexive thought patterns of the young child. A third trait is the preschooler's limited ability to process information from several sources simultaneously. This can be understood either as a by-product of centration, or as the cause of it. When compared with the intellectual skills he will possess in later childhood, preoperational thought is superficial, rigid, elementary, and nonempirical.

A thorough knowledge of the preschooler as thinker requires that we learn not only about what he knows, but also how he comes to know what he knows. For the most part, the preschool child's concepts and ideas are not formulated in a systematic, rational, and logical way. They stem from concrete experiences, are acquired from older children or adults, or are associations of previous thoughts. The young child is prerational as well as prelogical in most areas of thought. Because he has little ability to check the internal consistency of his thought, he rarely perceives that his particular ideas are only one possible approach to a topic. Egocentrically assuming that his thought mirrors reality, he is insulted by the suggestion that it might be less than perfect. He readily accepts (experience forces this realization upon him) that his interpretations may be weak or faulty, but he resists the notion that his interpretations are the result of particular thought processes and that the viability of the interpretation can be counterchecked by evaluating the thought process which produced it. To him, interpretations simply *are*. The preschool child has few means by which to confirm or authenticate what he assumes to be true; for this, he relies almost exclusively on authority. When authorities conflict, he sides with that viewpoint most in compliance with his own. Rarely does he change an idea, thought, or conclusion because it has been shown to be logically inconsistent; however, he will change or abandon an idea if it proves ineffective or nonfunctional. Preschoolers concern themselves little with the *origin* of their own thought, concentrating instead on how well it fits their limited world view. Knowledge of the environment is based upon the concrete, personal experiences of home life. Rarely before the last years of childhood does he fully comprehend that his family routine is only one of many possible routines, or that the social world is not modelled after the relationships which exist within his own family structure.

Thought during the preschool years is comparatively rigid, limited in scope, action-based, and not subject to self-analysis. The preschool child does not take the intellectual vantage point of another person nor does he conceive that his thinking on a given subject will change in the face of new or unexplored evidence. Though his growing mind is aware of detail, he has few skills in discriminating important from trivial details. When asked to summarize a story just completed he may concentrate on the fact that the dog was yellow rather than on his heroics, which the story was about. Even though remarkably advanced when compared with the toddler as a thinker, the preschool child is strikingly immature in comparison with the seven or eight-year-old. Vast and significant intellectual changes are in store for the growing child but, for most of them, the monumental breakthroughs will not occur until after the preschool years.

Progress in most mental functions accumulates steadily during the preschool years. Memory, number skills, concentration, comprehension, concept formation, and depth of thought are more advanced at four than at three, and at five than at four. This progressive advancement is not due to age alone, as we have learned from contrasting the mental skills of children exposed to academic training at an early age to those of children who have not. Rather, the consistent progression comes about because in the course of growing older each child makes new discoveries, encounters new realities, and undergoes growth in mental maturity to which he accommodates. Because of individual differences among children, one can easily find a four-year-old who can achieve mental tasks beyond the range of some five-year-olds. However, for that particular four-year-old, present skills are more sophisticated than they were when he was three and less sophisticated than they will be when he is five. Mental growth during these years is progressive but not constant; consistent but not totally predictable; age-based but not strictly determined by age; accelerated by enriched environment but not determined by it; related to total body development but not dominated by it. Mental growth is lawful but the laws which govern it are general rather than specific.

In order to encompass more fully the nature of preschool thought we shall now describe several specific components of thought during these years. Special mention is made of the child's understanding of causality, memory skills, knowledge of quantity, awareness of time concepts, concept formation, and perception of social relationships.

Causation. The preschool child is not fundamentally interested in a scientific understanding of what causes certain events to occur. He rarely concerns himself with the cause-effect relationship of a given phenomenon, readily accepting that things are as they are. He prefers to concentrate on ways to maneuver to his maximum advantage the way things are, making him a poetic mixture of Stoic and Pragmatist. Daily life of the preschooler is filled with confusion and mystery concerning causation. Although he has limited understanding of the origins of tap water, he seldom inquires about it; he is not concerned about the destination of disposed waste material; neither does he have much interest in how human waste is formed. It is not lack of intellectual energy which postpones concern about these specific examples of the nature of causality. Rather, the child accommodates himself to what is, and utilizes his intellectual energy to build upon rather than to question. In fairness to the five-year-old, one must report that concern about causality can be taught successfully. One often encounters a child not yet in the first grade who possesses a rigorous, empirical mind, at least with regard to *some* aspects of the environment. This child, wanting to know the how and why of everything, demands explanations based upon physical causality. If he is not taught such an empirical attitude, the preschooler is equally predisposed to understand causality either *associatively* or *magically*. "Fire comes from smoke" the child associatively infers. When two events are linked temporally or occur simultaneously, the child often will assume a causal relationship between the two events. Magicalism does not *dominate* childhood thought, but even highly intelligent children are attracted by its explanatory prowess. Three-year-olds willingly accept that rain comes from weeping giants in the sky — five-year-olds, as a rule, do not. But Five is likely to believe in Santa Claus, flying reindeer, tooth fairies, and assorted other mythical creatures. The preschool child wanders in and out of different views of the physical world. This is one reason he is so remarkably creative and adaptive. Children of this age are unimpressed by the incredible tricks of magicians which confuse and startle older children possessed of more advanced understanding of causality. Lacking a coherent conceptualization of causality, the preschooler is not surprised to witness an apparently (to an adult or older child) inexplicable event. Nine-year-olds, on the other hand, are a delight to magicians, who view increduously their ability to defy chance, permanence, and other principles not yet formed in the fluid preschool mentality.

Initial attempts to understand the nature of causality include *animism, realism,* and *artificialism.* When the child believes that inanimate things such as clouds and raindrops move because they have purpose, intention, will power, feelings, and other such qualities, he is using what Piaget calls *animistic* thinking. Many children attribute physical characteristics to psychological events such as thoughts, dreams, or fantasies. This is called *realism.* A child who refuses to sleep in a room because it is filled with bad dreams is reflecting this kind of thought. Later the child may assume that all events occur in order to blend with the wants, desires, or orders of some person. It snows so we can build snowmen; the television set shows a western movie because it knows we want to watch it; the car quits running on the freeway so we can play on the nearby grass. This understanding of causality reflects *artificialism.* For the most part, children understand all events as being purposive and do not think in terms of randomness, chance, or the impersonal forces of nature. Since one fundamental obligation of childhood is to make sense of the world, what makes most sense to the child is to assume that everything operates on principles and obeys forces similar to those which regulate and act upon him. This, of course, is in line with his egocentric nature.

Memory. An amazing stockpile of information is stored in the memory bank of the preschool child's mind. When he enters the first grade he has at his command from 25,000 to 45,000 words; this indicates the reservoir of words available to recall or recognition. Nursery rhymes, jingles, poems, idioms by the hundreds are stored neatly away, awaiting only command or an associative cue to be brought into use. The bulk of material the child is able to remember startles adults. Though rich in quantity, the preschool child's memory is weak in quality. For the most part memory is associative, rote, and clustered. Though able to recite flawlessly the national anthem, the child may have little or no under-standing of what the words actually mean; though able to recall per-fectly the wording of a jingle, he may not be able to paraphrase or summarize the intent of it. The child often remembers without assimi-lating the meaning of his memories. He may or may not contextualize a message which he commits to memory.

The ability to *intentionally* remember is influenced by maturation. When asked to repeat digits which are presented at one-second intervals, few preschool children can repeat five digits without error. Thus, if given at one-second intervals, few children under the age of six can successfully repeat 8-4-9-2-6, or any such five-digit combination. The ability to repeat numbers successfully, however, is hampered by several factors, including lack of number concepts, faulty attention, inadequate auditory imagery, or hearing deficiency. Despite limited ability to recall numbers, the preschooler can repeat sentences or short paragraphs with a meaningful message. The four-year-old who could recall only three digits might be able to repeat flawlessly "The horse ran up the hill." Even at this age meaningful clusters are remembered more readily than numbers or nonsensical statements.

The lack of logical organization and mental classification which characterizes preschool thought also affects memory. Young children do not take preconceived strategy to a memory task (such as remember-ing numbers in groups of two), nor do they remember by classifying objects into more easily remembered catagories. Consequently, memory usually is spotty and inconsistent.

Despite these limitations memory is modestly impressive. Things related directly to the child's needs have memory priority (I have never known a preschool child to forget where candy was once accidentally discovered in the kitchen). Much of what the child remembers, how-ever, is merely associative. Upon meeting an adult not encountered for several months, a four-year-old may blurt out, "Where is your *brown* coat?" indicating that he remembers the coat worn on their first meet-ing. At the same time he may be incapable of recalling the adult's name or anything else about his earlier visit.

Middle-class parents, with their secret obsession with precocity, enjoy listening to their child rattle off interesting anecdotes picked up from news broadcasts or adult conversations, caring little that the child understands only marginally about what he speaks. The parent can help cultivate the child's verbal as well as reasoning skills by asking him to reformulate the message without losing the substance of it. This often meets with failure, however.

If interrupted in the middle of a memorized recital, the pre-schooler, like the spider who has been interrupted while spinning his web, must go back to the beginning and start anew. This is especially true of three and four-year-olds, but by no means are five-year-olds exempt from this tendency. Teachers and parents often are surprised to discover that some children understand no better the meaning of songs composed of words from their native language than those which they have learned from a second, unknown language. Though he remembers well, the preschooler often does not know in any meaningful sense what it is that he remembers.

Quantity. The preschool child has outgrown the naive quantitative con-cepts of toddlerhood but he has a long way to go before he grasps the basic relationships between number and quantity or shape and quan-tity. It is a fairly easy matter to tutor a three-year-old to count to ten, or a five-year-old to one hundred. More difficult is to teach them that ten is to twenty what thirty is to sixty; or that every number can be doubled. For children who have not had special instruction, numbers are memorized but for the most part lack functional utility. They are played with, used for recreation, but do not significantly influence the preschooler's daily life. This is in stark contrast to the nine-year-old whose understanding of proportions, multiples, sums, and percentages profoundly influences his day-to-day behaviour. Most preschool child-ren have not learned that total quantity does not change because shape has been altered or rearranged. Thus, they usually insist that when the contents of a tall, thin pitcher are poured into a short, wide pitcher that a greater quantity of water existed in the thin pitcher than in the wide pitcher. They do not understand that quantity remains the same regard-less of the shape it assumes. When the water is poured back into the tall, thin pitcher its heightened water level is construed by the child as proof that it holds a greater quantity. He does not see that the same quantity of water merely has been poured from one pitcher to another. This dogmatism of thought, which characterizes the mental set of pre-schoolers, by no means is restricted to issues of quantity.

Preschool children understand more and most, few and many, some and all, quite a bit and just a little. They *rarely* understand the constancy of impartial numeration such as that of a yardstick, weighing scale, or calendar. Though they know *of* these cultural tools, they do not appreciate the constancy or universality behind them, or the fact that they are based upon elementary quantitative principles.

Time concepts. Children have considerable difficulty learning the ways in which past, present, and future time is schematized in our culture. Three-year-olds have little knowledge about, or concern for, time as understood by adults. For them, time is present time with an occasional exception made for important events which are about to occur or which have recently been completed. Four-year-olds learn the days of the week but are quite detached from the fact that the name of each day is predictable and serialized. Five-year-olds know how old they are, how old they will be on their next birthday and how old they were before their fifth birthday; it is doubtful, however, that they can comprehend anything beyond a year. Children understand that some people are older than others, but at the same time may assume that they eventually will catch up in age with an older person, especially their parents. Few five-year-olds are able to distinguish past time with the correct labels. When asked how long it has been since he returned from an out-of-town trip, the preschooler may reply "two weeks", "twenty hours", "a year", "I don't know", or "fifty months". In fact, his return may have occurred three days before.

When compared with adult standards, the preschool child's compartmentalization of time is remarkably nonspecific. This is somewhat understandable in view of the fact that there is no practical reason for him to learn about time labels. Decisions about time usually are made for him. If the preschool child was punished for tardiness as measured by the clock, or highly rewarded for conceptualizing particular time schemes, we might be surprised at his adaptability. This has been the trend in all other endeavours.

Concept formation. Concept formation involves "discovering and defining the critical features common to a group of objects or events" (Mussen, 1963, p. 36). The formation of concepts is highly dependent on vocabulary as well as on experience. Events which the child has most experience with become conceptualized more easily than those with which he has limited experience. Father is a concept which comes easily to children of our culture, but the concept of an uncle who assumes the paternal role of the biological father does not. Personal experience is central to concept formation in childhood; concepts are inferred from specifics. The preschool child's limited ability to conceptualize is easier to understand once we recognize that he is essentially prelogical, if "logical" is defined as connecting facts or events in a rational, systematic way.

The ability to formulate concepts is limited and primitive during the preschool years. Although he has been formulating elementary concepts about the animate and inanimate world since toddlerhood, the first grader's conceptual knowledge of number as well as of abstract ideas is not refined. At about age eight, marked development of concepts pertaining to social objects and relationships occurs. In general, the child attains concepts in much the same way as do adults, but range of experience and organization of experience is more elementary. The preschool child employs both inductive and deductive thought in the formation of concepts; however, the inductive method is the more common. Thought progresses from particular to general; with increased age there is a gradual shift toward incorporating deductive thought (inferring from general to specific).

Until the age of six, the child's thinking is primarily egocentric and not based upon logical structure or organization. Concepts are determined by direct experience:

> Up to the age of six, the child's concepts are determined mainly by his own specific experiences and actions, and are, consequently, naive, inconsistent, diffuse, imprecise, simple, and closely bound up with the immediate perceptual features of objects. Perhaps as a result of marked improved verbal skills, a marked shift occurs at about the age of six. Concepts become more logical and differentiated, a trend that continues throughout the school years and into adult life. (Mussen, 1963, p. 39)

With increasing age, concepts undergo progressive changes. Vinacke (1954) suggests the following: (a) progression from simple to complex concepts; (b) progression from diffuse to differentiated concepts; (c) progression from egocentric to more objective concepts; (d) progression from concrete to abstract concepts; (e) progression from variable to more stable concepts; (f) progression from inconsistent to more consistent and accurate concepts. The preschool years are primarily for laying the foundation which allows this progressive maturity of concept formation rather than the period in which it actually occurs.

Improvement, however, does take place during the preschool years in the matter of concept formation. The three-year-old is not only prelogical but also preconceptual. He does not understand the nature of classes or class membership. He perceives each horse as a particular instance of "horse". He fails to understand that all horses have common characteristics which allow each of them to be categorized or classified under a general heading. The statement "Clydesdales are not Shetlands but they are horses" makes sense to a first grader of normal intelligence, but completely fails to register with the early preschooler. The rapid growth in cognitive capacity in preschool children makes generalizing about their intellectual skills somewhat precarious.

Social relationships. Older preschoolers know about and vaguely understand concepts such as division of labour, sex-role differentiations, and organizational hierarchies. Understanding is based upon the specific workings of their household and, from there, is generalized outward. The five-year-old may take it as the nature of things that mothers draw bath water, wash dishes, and buy children's clothes and that fathers shovel sidewalks, leave early in the morning for work, and fix the TV set when it malfunctions if his own household is designed upon such a division of labour. He may unswervingly assert that only men throw javelins, drive sport cars, or chase criminals and that hairdressing, gardening, and cooking are exclusively feminine endeavours. Although the preschooler's sex-role differentiations are based fundamentally upon what he learns at home, he is capable of spontaneously generating private ideas on the matter. Every preschool child knows about command hierarchies — that some people can overrule others. What he does not understand, however, is that a person at the top of one pecking order can be in the middle, or even at the bottom, of another. Thus military and other institutional hierarchial arrangements are difficult for the child to follow. The concept that father has a boss or supervisor while on the job is slow to penetrate a young mind which "knows" father only as strength and authority. Most preschool children, especially three and four-year-olds, assume that social relationships of all types are modelled after those of the family, inferring that all superiors have an emotional attachment to their underlings just as mother and father have an emotional attachment to their children. The innocence of this inference usually is exploded in kindergarten or the first grade. Eventually, understanding of social relationships expands, but this requires not only the assimilation of new ideas and information but also the *unlearning* of previous, restricted concepts.

What may we infer from this information? Of first importance is that the preschool child has ample (some claim it is awesome) potential to learn, incorporate, assimilate, memorize, conceive, and perceive. On the other hand, his capacity for thinking logically, evaluating the consistency of thought, paraphrasing or summarizing what he understands, assuming the intellectual perspective of another, understanding the relationship between quantity and shape, and intentionally applying his powers of memory are much less spectacular.

The Preschooler as Athlete in Training

The normal preschool child is a masterpiece of dynamic energy and physical architecture. Though his lines, contours, and proportions are not finalized, they are remarkably suited to his needs. He is buoyant, bubbly, and bouncy. He moves nonstop through his daily routine with only occasional pit stops for fuel and rest. Only the most physically fit college or professional athlete could match step for step the activity which fills the preschooler's average day. An ordinary adult would collapse from exhaustion if required to follow the same maneuvers, contortions, and physical gyrations which characterize the child at this age. Although the preschool span includes the years when the child learns to concentrate his energy and focus his behaviour, a great deal of random, "nervous", fidgety activity remains which, though beneficial to the child, appears to be completely unpremeditated.

The child's physical welfare is directly related to how well he is cared for and how well he cares for himself. For most preschoolers, however, the former is more important than the latter. Special attention and care must be given the developing physical body. It has special needs and requirements because it is undergoing important growth transitions. The preschooler in many respects is like the athlete in training. His alertness and physical sharpness honestly reflect the adequacy of his dietary, sleep, and exercise habits. Of these, diet and sleep habits directly relate to habits established in the home and, as such, the child's welfare is contingent upon the soundness of these rules and habits.

The preschooler's growing body, like that of the athlete, requires special nutrition, rest, and exercise. Muscles are developing more rapidly, as a rule, than other parts of the body. It has been estimated that 75 percent of the child's weight increase during the fifth year of life is the result of increased muscular development. Strength, which increases correspondingly with muscle growth, is facilitated by refined global body coordination. Large muscle activity dominates childhood behaviour, especially during the preschool years, as each child devises his own means for exercising and developing his expanding musculature. Muscle development in the legs is especially advanced because the child spends most of his waking hours exercising them. Arm strength is less developed proportionally than it will be in coming years; however, a few boys bring barely noticeable biceps to the first grade. Many boys can be distinguished visually from girls by their expanded shoulders and chest cavity and narrow pelvis. These masculine traits become progressively more noticeable with age. As the shoulders of young girls expand so also do the hips, until by adolescence a distinct hourglass profile appears if the waist is narrow. Although not usually noticeable by visual inspection, boys have longer forearms in relation to their body size than do girls. This quirk of evolution provides males with a physical advantage in activities which require arm strength or leverage, but because girls are slightly more mature than boys it will be a few years before this difference becomes significant.

Physical growth during the preschool years is moderately stable and predictable. Children who are tall for their age at two years old tend to be tall for their age when six years old. The converse is also true; therefore, children who are short for their age at two tend to be likewise at six. Chubbiness is a different matter; it is not uncommon for a chubby, rotund toddler to be of normal, even skinny, proportions by the time he enters the first grade.

Fewer activities are beyond the physiological capacities of the preschool child. The respiratory system becomes more stabilized, permitting greater endurance and stamina. Breathing becomes slower and deeper and the heart beat becomes slower and less variable. Blood pressure increases steadily (Mussen, 1969, p. 283).

Recent research indicates that the range of normal heart size is considerably more varied than previously thought. In essence, studies have discovered that heart size is related to body size. A child who has been growing fast and who is overweight is likely to have a large heart. A child who is of average size usually will have a heart which is about average. "When it comes to shape, the hearts of healthy children have differences so great that some of them suggest textbook pictures of congenital heart disease — and yet nothing is wrong. The shape of a child's heart is his own business. After he gets that shape, he is going to keep it, barring affliction with a serious disease." (Gray, 1967, p. 133).

Most parents find it difficult to keep pace with their child in an open park, and nursery school teachers must impose restrictions upon the range and rowdiness of play. Burgeoning muscles demand expression but the preschooler's limited experience does not always provide wise discretion in creating avenues for this expression. Boys are especially rowdy and boisterous in their play, but when they inadvertently arouse the anger of a female peer they may find themselves not only outclassed physically, but also outmuscled. Owing to its commonness, there is little social stigma among males for losing a scrap to a female. This comes later when male muscular dominance is more evident.

By age six the child's brain has reached 90 percent of its adult weight. Myelinization of the nerve fibres is for the most part completed in the higher brain centres during the last part of the preschool years (Mussen, 1969, p. 283).

Skeletal development is also manifesting striking growth. Different parts of the skeleton grow at different rates, therefore, some bones are growing rapidly while others more slowly (reflecting the principle of *asynchronous growth*). The skeleton is lengthening out. Long bones of the arms and legs are maturing at an accelerated pace and the drawn-out, gangly appearance of many preschoolers is based precisely on this fact. Muscles also must grow rapidly to accommodate the expanding skeleton. Even though preschoolers are growing up (literally), fewer than three percent of them are taller than 47 inches on fifth birthday and less than three percent are shorter than 40 inches at this age. Thus, 94 percent of five-year-olds are between 3'4" and 3'11". The bones of the wrist and hand are of special interest to psychologists because they show a consistent pattern in their development, serving as a fairly reliable index to the development of the rest of the skeleton (Gardner, 1964, p. 127). Children with advanced wrist development tend to have overall skeletal precocity; those with wrist development below the average tend toward skeletal immaturity for their age. At birth usually no wrist bones are evident, only soft cartilage. When wrist bones are present they are much more likely to be found in the wrist of a girl than a boy. The cartilage progressively calcifies into eight small bones; the rate of this calcification process indicates the child's overall bone development. One study reveals that by the age of five years a healthy child may have from two to seven bony centres in the wrist. The same study concludes that only 20 percent of all children have the number of bones previously regarded as normal for the preschool years (Gray, 1967, p. 133).

The preschooler, who still has his baby (deciduous) teeth, will start losing them between the sixth and twelfth year. Baby teeth are important to the child because they influence the positioning of permanent teeth. They must be of sufficient strength to insure proper mastication of food.

The pronounced reaction to infection and fever which characterizes the toddler is lessened during the preschool years. "Infections generally produce less of a temperature increase than they did during infancy, but the duration of the illness is usually longer. Moreover, the possibility of serious heart symptoms following a disease is smaller than it was during the first two years of life." (Mussen, 1969, p. 283). Some evidence points to a correlation between the levels of the blood pro-

185

teins (beta and gamma globulin) and the development of lymph tissue in the body. Therefore, when a child's blood contains high levels of these globulins he is likely to have larger tonsils and adenoids and more lymph nodes of every kind. Such children are more able to resist colds and other respiratory diseases than children with smaller quantities of these globulins (Gray, 1967, p. 135).

Muscle and skeletal changes taking place during these years are integrally related to the dietary, sleeping, and exercise habits of the child. Calcium and protein are especially critical if the growing skeleton and muscle fibre are to be adequately nourished. Rest, especially deep sleep, is necessary if the child is to recuperate from the exercise and energy drain of his normal-activity day.

Because the likelihood of malnutrition is greater during the preschool years than any other period of childhood, its significance should not be overlooked. The energy requirement per unit of body weight for the preschooler is relatively high when compared with the adult. The caloric need increases each year, making it unwise to base preschool nutritional needs on adult standards or on those which were effective for the child during the previous year. Four-year-old boys need, on the average, 100 more calories per day than they did as three-year-olds. Especially central to the child's diet is protein. The spectacular rate of muscle growth and the relatively high incidence of febrile (feverish) illnesses make an optimum intake of protein during the preschool years important. Severe protein malnutrition (medically known as *kwashiorkor*) is the most common form of nutritional deficiency among the children of the world and is not exclusively confined to developing, poor, or war-torn nations. Under ordinary circumstances if protein, calcium, and iron requirements are met, other mineral requirements will also be satisfied. If adults eat well-balanced, nutritionally sound meals, and the preschooler shares these meals, his growth requirements should be adequately met (Burke, B., 1960, p. 170-71).

For most preschoolers the day begins around 7:30 a.m., especially if bedded down before 8:30 p.m. Few children function sharply during the day if they sleep less than eight hours the previous night; many require ten hours. Sleep is a bodily function for which the child is equipped with an abundance of "body wisdom". He invariably compensates during the afternoon for rest he did not receive the night before. This provides a respite for mother in the afternoon but makes afternoon schooling rather difficult. Although many preschoolers (especially three-year-olds) take afternoon naps, during the latter half of the preschool years this practice is as much the result of habit as of biological necessity. Since many psychological factors influence sleep, the child should not be burdened unnecessarily with anxieties and phobias in this regard. Perhaps more so than any of the waking hours, bedtime should be an interim of cordial parent-child interplay and reassuring body contact. Preschoolers have a special fondness for bedtime stories and conversation which allow them to delay sleep but also provide treasured moments of parental attention. If comparatively free of bedtime anxiety, many preschoolers will voluntarily ready themselves for bed when tired or when the clock signals that bedtime is at hand. Dreams, common during these years, are often fearful, with obscure creatures or mean animals being the chief sources of terror. However, the preschooler for the first time is capable of humourous dreams, and five-year-olds may chuckle or laugh during sleep, usually with no recollection in the morning.

The preschooler eats constantly. He eats meals with the rest of the family though he may not eat heartily during regular mealtime. Since he eats between meals, nursery schools are inclined toward both morning and afternoon snacktimes. Preschoolers are finicky eaters and do not eat something merely because it has been placed before them. Rather than calmly announcing displeasure with particular food, they are prone to exclamations such as "YIICKK" or "UGGHH", thus voicing their dislike. Food which does not meet their fluctuating standards of texture, colour, or consistency may also be rejected. Firmly insisting that the child eat a certain food whether he likes it or not is sometimes successful, but equally often (especially with four-year-olds) the child will refuse to eat or will gasp in feigned desperate illness upon taking a bite.

Sweets are universal favourites and most children will eat them until plagued by upset stomach if allowed to do so. If sweets are available upon request, the preschool child will attack them almost as piggishly as when they are available only rarely. Moderation comes about during the early school years (ages 6-9) but rarely before this in the matter of sweets. Parents and nursery school teachers rapidly learn about the reward value of sweets and turn the child's sweet tooth into a manipulable asset in the regulation of his behaviour.

The Preschooler as Astronaut

The astronaut is the space traveller and planetary pioneer of the twentieth century. He explores little known pockets of the universe and strives to incorporate what he learns into what is already known. The adventure of the astronaut is found not only in the dangerous and unexpected but also in the challenge of continually coping with new discoveries, new realities, and new problems. In order to accomplish successfully what is expected of him he must learn to accommodate himself to alien terrain and to elements strikingly different from those to which he is most accustomed. He must adjust to the fact that his decisions are a matter of life or death and that an incorrect inference may have disastrous consequences. He must accept the fact that circumstances may arise when he cannot be rescued by the all-powerful control station. The astronaut, completely dependent upon the cooperative efforts of others, may suffer irreparable damage through no error of his own. The astronaut must learn to live by his wits, to cope with situations he has never before experienced or even anticipated, to encounter events which are well beyond his reserves. He must learn to blend his intuitions with the commands of others; he must develop the capacity to sense when his intuition is more likely to be correct than the command which he has received from home base. The astronaut must honestly face the fact that if he makes too many wrong decisions he will be replaced. Not only does his physical welfare as an astronaut ("sailor of the stars") rest upon his ability to cope with the demands of space travel, but his inner feelings of worth and self-respect also hinge upon his capacity to carry out successfully what is expected of him and what he expects of himself. The astronaut's burden, though specialized and highly unusual in its particular components, is not unique to him. Many people share similar psychological (though quite different mechanical) responsibilities. The analogy seems particularily evident in the case of the preschool child. In his own way, he encounters several responsibilities similar in *nature* to those of the astronaut.

The preschool child is also a pioneer in that he constantly discovers and explores frontiers never before encountered (at least not by him). Life is a perpetual series of discoveries, innovations, insights, intuitions, and experiments which yield consequences ranging from psychic expansion to physical injury. Since toddlerhood provides him with little knowledge of the outside world, the preschooler is faced with the task of exploring an alien world peopled by goliaths two or three times his height, five times his weight, who speak in a rapid-fire dialogue punctuated with idioms, clichés, and other gobbledegook, the bulk of which is beyond intelligible translation. These alien adults, sometimes friendly, or at least patronizing, at other times are neglectful, abusive, and insensitive. They are a strange species who require time and patience to be understood. The preschooler, having acquired a thorough knowledge of his own home during toddlerhood, now adventures beyond it. The neighbourhood is his first "drop-down" target. Two years will be spent learning its terrain, its boundaries and borders, its friendly and unfriendly inhabitants, its hideaways, and meaningful points of interest. When mastered, its boundaries will automatically expand. During the last of the preschool years the child will roam beyond the neighbourhood to claim territorial mobility up to one radius mile from home base. By late childhood (eight to ten years of age) the boundaries virtually will have disappeared as exploration becomes more dependent upon the means of transportation than on the distance the child will travel.

For the preschooler, decisions usually are not a matter of life and death (although thousands of children each year lose their lives as a result of immature discretion or faulty decisions) but he is rapidly learning that decisions lead to specific consequences. Some incorrect decisions, such as turning left at the corner instead of right, may create only minor inconvenience, whereas others, such as jumping into a swimming pool at the deep end rather than the shallow end, may create more serious consequences. The preschooler learns that decisions make a difference — a big difference. To learn to make "wise" decisions without losing self-confidence is one of the major tasks of the preschool years. The astronaut is not the only one for whom correct decision-making is important to psychological well-being.

The preschool child, despite his maturity of growth and tendency toward autonomy (when compared with his toddlerhood years) is critically dependent upon the skills as well as the good will of adults with whom he interacts. Guardians, teachers, babysitters, and especially parents have profound influence not only on the physical welfare of the child but also on his psychological, social, and intellectual welfare. From the adults around him the child learns how the physical world operates. He also learns about himself: whether he is worthwhile, desirable, likable, competent. He learns directly and indirectly what kind of person he is thought to be. This is where the child is most vulnerable to the influence of his elders. Adults who repeatedly chastise the child, who make him feel small and inferior, unwanted and incompetent instill into him a self-concept which corresponds with these perceptions. What else may be expected of the child? He has no other sources of information about his importance or value. He has few ways of knowing other than what he is taught. He considers himself as he has been considered. He values himself as he has been valued. The child is critically dependent upon the wisdom and humanism of those adults to whom he is entrusted. The child is his own man no more than the astronaut whose lifeline depends upon the wise judgment of a technician thousands of miles away.

Perhaps even more so than the astronaut, the preschooler must learn to live by his wits, to cope with situations he has never before experienced or anticipated, and to encounter events which may be well beyond his reserves. After all, the astronaut has the benefit of years of schooling; he has a much greater capacity to calculate and anticipate what will *probably* occur; he also has learned something about coping with his own anxiety when he finds himself in a situation about which he knows very little. The preschooler has none of these advantages. Most of his "schooling" has been the word-of-mouth variety. His sources of authority are limited, usually mother, father, and a few others. His powers of abstraction, though admirable for his age, are strikingly immature even when compared with those of the ten-year-old. The preschooler learns to explore while knowing little about where he is going or how he will return. He tackles obstacles about which he knows virtually nothing. His zeal for delving into the unknown makes the astronaut's sense of adventure appear puny: he does not radio for permission before undertaking a risky operation, in fact he has a special attraction to those terrains which have been declared off limits; he does not read in advance about what he likely will encounter during his exploits; he knows little about the probability of danger (much of his exploration is designed to determine the kind of danger involved in the exploration). Finally, the preschooler knows that the information gained in much of his exploration is destined to remain private, for disclosing it would betray the fact that he has explored and learned beyond what is expected or allowed. The sailors of the stars could learn much from the "neighbourhoodnauts".

Because the harmony of his social world rests on the precarious balance of doing what seems right at the moment and doing what is expected (usually these are in tolerable agreement), the preschooler, like the astronaut, must learn to blend his intuitions with the commands of others. Somehow, he must develop the capacity to sense when his intuition is more likely correct than the command he has received from home base. It is not by chance that the child first learns to tell lies during the preschool years — before these years, lies are not needed because the child is not held accountable for the negative consequences of his behaviour. The preschooler learns that independence, though encouraged, is a mixture of blessing and curse. This realization, of course, is never completely outgrown, but for the preschooler it holds a special fascination. During the preschool years a curious confusion arises about the way the world feels and the way it actually is.

The preschool years are no picnic for adult or child. However, as ample occasion occurs for festivity and merriment, these occasions sustain both child and adult during these years of expansion, autonomy, and individualization.

Some Basic Developmental Needs of the Preschool Years

From the information we have gathered during our investigation of the preschool years it becomes immediately apparent that inherent to this age period are certain basic developmental needs. Some of these needs are shared by children of other ages, whereas others are confined to this particular age period.

1. *The need for mass muscle activity.* The psychology as well as the physiology of the preschool child is rooted in movement and motion. Surplus energy keeps their bodies moving; insatiable curiosity keeps their mental activity alert and probing; the need for competence keeps mind and body working together. For most preschoolers, one of the first signs of impending illness is decreased activity and loss of environmental interest which lower their activity level to that of the healthy adult. Developing muscles require exercise; competence demands practice; learning demands experimentations; all of which require movement. Sedateness, motionlessness, apathy, impassivity, dullness, and nonconcern are never dominant traits of the normal preschooler's life style.

2. *The need for mental and verbal stimulation.* Mental and verbal stimulation are crucial during the preschool years because this is the time when cognitive and verbal skills intimately interact with one another. Deprived of verbal stimulation the child is less likely to develop optimal cognitive skills; deprived of mental stimulation he is less likely to cultivate optimal verbal facility. Although the relationship between verbal skills and mental development is not understood precisely, authorities accept the view that deprivation in one area generally leads to incomplete development in the other. Preschoolers naturally enjoy cognitive play, a fact which should be capitalized upon if actualization of their potentiality is desired. Since the child learns about the world through speech, the people in the child's world learn about him through his speech.

3. *Peer play and fantasy play.* The young child learns about the give and take of social living through his interchange with other children. He learns about limits, boundaries, rules, regulations, tolerance, and his own role in their formulation. In fantasy play the child explores his mixed world, blending his freewheeling, fertile imagination with the hard, cold facts of reality. Fantasy play also allows the child to act out

191

his aggression, hostilities, likes, dislikes, pleasures, and displeasures.

4. *The need for knowledge about right and wrong.* This developmental need is often misunderstood. The need for knowledge about right and wrong does not mean that the child should be taught that A, B, and C are definitely and eternally wrong, or that D, E, and F are conclusively right. Rather, the child should understand that some kinds of behaviour are more highly valued than others; that some are considered less appropriate than others; that some behaviour (such as sharing) corresponds more closely with the ideal than other forms of behaviour (such as compulsive selfishness). Without benefit of instruction the child *tends* to engage in egocentric behaviour, caring little about the feelings, sensitivity, and rights of others. Because he is prone to intellectual dogmatism, the preschooler's interpretation of ethical principles tends to be rigid, but this tendency is outgrown. The important consideration is not that the child learn *specific rules* about right and wrong; rather, that he be brought to appreciate, even understand, the general concepts of ideal and nonideal, desirable and nondesirable, virtuous and nonvirtuous. As he matures and acquires his own understanding for the world, he will fill in the particulars.

5. *The need for independence.* This developmental need is difficult to describe since the preschool child is a highly *dependent* creature, relying upon his parents for virtually all necessities of life. Independence as a preschool developmental need refers to the importance of the child's ability to explore, adventure, discover, invent, reorganize, and tinker with his environment. He must be able to assert himself independently and be comparatively free of limited patterns or rigid procedures in his day-to-day life. Only by coping with the environment, experimenting with it in spontaneous, autonomous, and independent ways does the child come to understand the nature of his competence or his ability to alter things. The child who believes that he cannot alter or modify things eventually gives up independence, freedom, and the sense of being prior to the environment, and assumes that he is merely a puppet. Fostering independence during the preschool years is relatively easy but at the same time, inconvenient, for adults. Children of this age do not learn cleanly. Like the toddler they create a good deal of havoc in their quest for independence. The judicious parent and teacher acknowledge this developmental fact and do not let their own day-to-day needs thwart those of the growing child.

Middle Childhood

Investigation of new dimensions of the world leads to assimilation of greater quantity and more sophisticated quality of knowledge.

Sibling rivalry is less commonplace than compatibility.

The elementary teacher learns to respect the child's need to show and give affection. First-graders group together in clusters; body contact is a part of their interpersonal patterns.

The world expands and shrinks for the eight-year-old. New lands are discovered and then are readily incorporated into his expanding world view.

Chapter Six
The Middle Childhood Years

The years between the sixth and tenth birthdays are the years of middle childhood. They are remarkable years indeed. The social world expands even more dramatically than during the preschool years when the child first ventured alone into the outside world. During the years of middle childhood, parents observe their child take giant strides toward self-individuation. New friendships are formed but, more importantly, the friendships embrace genuine emotional involvement. For the first time in the life cycle, the child forms deep bonds of relatedness to someone outside the family unit. The childhood years are the proving grounds for the emotional richness of adolescence which looms closer with each birthday.

The child continues to mature physically during middle childhood, but when his physical growth is compared with social and cognitive growth, it is certainly less spectacular. Middle-years children take their bodies for granted, so smooth and uneventful is their physical development. Except for the sixth year when illness and body disruption are fairly common, the body and its functions are of only marginal concern. This *laissez-faire* attitude changes markedly during pre-adolescence when body-image, mood swings, and self-concept are each affected by endocrinological and anatomical changes.

Mental skills skyrocket during middle childhood. Egocentrism is slowly but surely losing its struggle against advancing maturity; logic is improving; clarity of thought *and* precision of verbal expression are increasing noticeably; problem-solving strategies are without doubt at a lifetime high. Memory, vocabulary, and concentration are likewise advancing with predictable consistency.

Moral and ethical beliefs are becoming genuine factors in the regulation of personal behaviour. As with all growth areas, individual differences pertain in the matter of moral and ethical development. All children obviously are not Oliver Twist, however it is well within the limits of defensible theory to postulate that most children could easily be trained to follow his footsteps if the environment were right. This is not as predictably true during the pre-adolescent years when personal conscience sets definite limits on acceptable behaviour.

Following the example of the chapter on the Preschool Years, we shall introduce this chapter with an overview of the similarities, differences, and general growth trends of the years we are concerned with. Year-by-year age profiles are designed to enhance our knowledge of the uniformities of middle childhood as well as to improve our understanding of age differences during the years of middle childhood.

As with any system, we must caution ourselves against misuse or oversimplification. When we speak of six-year-olds, we do not refer to *all* six-year-olds, past, present, or future; rather, we refer to the common patterns which characterize six-year-olds *as a group;* we speak of the trends which commonly develop at this age. The attempt is not to force the child into a category, but to describe some of the age-based categories which frequently emerge in our society. Important age-based realities fill the day-to-day life of the middle-years child and by understanding these commonalities we enrich our knowledge of the child. Knowledge of the child is our objective in this book.

The Six-year-old

The world unravels in staccato spurts for the six-year-old. School is the most important experience in his social-psychological life, but undercurrents of biological change pull him into whirlpools and hurl him to rocky jetties. Physical development is not smooth: the first molars are emerging; the body is more susceptible to infection than it was at five; nose and throat-related problems increase; vision may show the first signs of strain; and gastro-intestinal symptoms become manifest. Parent-child relationships are frequently bumpy because of the child's tendency to bossiness and impudence; the impulsiveness of Six takes its toll on adults as well as peers. For most children the year between the sixth and seventh birthdays is transitional, and the strain of transition is felt not only by the child but by everyone who shares his world.

As a rule, the first year of school requires more adjustment from children who have not undertaken a year of preschool, but rare is the child for whom the first grade is a totally pleasant experience. Upon entering school the child leaves behind the womb-like protection and security of home. Although he is not anonymous in his new setting, this is the closest most children have come to the experience of anonymity. His quandary is much like that of the university freshman, hundreds of miles from home, friendless, uncentred, uprooted, and convinced that everyone, except he, is completely at home in this foreign den of learning. School stresses group rules, group participation, group rights; this does not set smoothly with the child's egocentric nature. School stresses performance, compliance, and orderliness; this does not set smoothly with the child's capricious nature. School stresses timetables, schedules, and readiness; this does not set smoothly with the child's impulsive nature. Though not beyond his resources, school creates a strain which affects his temperament and interpersonal behaviour. Following the precedent so well established by his parents, the six-year-old takes the pressures of work home with him, therefore, the household also knows when school has begun for the child.

School requires a revised understanding of self, with greater emphasis placed upon group reaction and interpersonal expertise. Personal idiosyncrasies, respected or tolerated at home, face new interpretations. Self-constraint becomes more important than usual; creative abilities are evaluated and guided. The child is learning a different life style; his mind is becoming more resilient and increasingly capable of accommodating new realities and expectations. School is perhaps the greatest of the transitions in this the year of transitions.

Partly because of school experience, but mainly as a result of advancing perceptual maturity, a growing awareness of personal limitations looms over the consciousness of the six-year-old. Exposed to the world of numbers, letters, and sentences, he quickly senses a body of thought and continuity beyond his resources; by comparing his talents with those of his classmates, he perceives his relative strengths and weaknesses. Continued unfavourable self-evaluation may contribute to a sense of despair or futility, but these can be talked through routinely and do not indicate underlying emotional disturbance or social inferiority.

Because his world is changing so rapidly and unpredictably, Six enjoys a certain amount of structure, convention, and routine in day-to-day living. He may want the table set just so, the bedroom arranged in precise format, a story told with expected intonation and suspense. His desire for routine reminds us of the regimentation of the four-year-old; the comparison is fair in that both years make strenuous demands, taxing the child's limited coping devices. Gesell suggests that several predominant traits of the six-year-old can be summarized vaguely by adjectives such as impulsive, volatile, undifferentiated, dogmatic, compulsive, and excitable. He fails to mention "tactile", which also is unquestionably descriptive of Six.

Six likes to touch, fondle, handle, grab, mix, and manipulate. He cannot merely inspect an object visually; he must touch it, seemingly as

199

though the other senses will not operate until triggered by messages from the fingertips. The first grade child demonstrates affection by touch. Novice kindergarten and first grade teachers quickly recognize that rules about clinging must be established or their energy may be drained in holding up children who cling to limbs, tug at extremities, or hang from the waist. The craving for tactile stimulation brings about renewed interest in the sense-pleasure play of the toddler; clay, mud, sand, and dirt are rediscovered.

Six is gifted in starting projects but atrocious in finishing them. It has been suggested that he would by happy if life were a continual series of beginnings. He often becomes discouraged in the middle of a project and forthrightly concludes that it should be abandoned. If left to his own inclinations, little would ever be finalized but a great deal would get started; in this regard he shows an uncanny similarity to university graduate students.

Face-saving is important for the six-year-old — much more so than at five. He does not like to be embarrassed or to be the brunt of humour. This stems in part from the negative consequences of making a mistake in front of classroom peers (most first-graders must be taught not to ridicule or label as stupid the limitations of others), but in many instances is attributable to adults who impose unrealistic demands on the child and show their disappointment when he fails to live up to them. The ability to skillfully distract the attention of a six-year-old when troublesome moments are brewing is the prized asset of any elementary teacher. Six thinks poorly of himself when so appraised by his contemporaries; preschoolers are likely to tell their peers to "shut up" and walk off undaunted.

The tyrannical reputation built by the six-year-old is rooted in his propensity for dictatorial leadership. Six loves to boss, order, authorize, supervise, and direct. Away from school and home he is a private on leave of absence. Ruled while at home and school, he assumes the role of ruler whenever the social climate permits; he never suffers a shortage of followers. Six is inexpert at handling complex interpersonal relationships, therefore, he simplifies whenever possible. Part of the simplification involves reducing social relationships to governor and governed. Despite this tendency, social play among six-year-olds is often so diffuse and unstructured that participants can wander in and out almost at will without significantly altering the course of play. In play, sex lines are not sharply drawn, however, this changes drastically during the last years of childhood when same-sex groupings are the rule.

The ability to pretend is perhaps at its zenith. Six-year-olds can be anything they want to be: butterflies, snails, flags, falling leaves, sad parakeets, frustrated mice, or punitive policemen. They lapse unannounced into and out of various roles, all the while entranced by the magic of pretense, enthralled by make-believe images. Interestingly, the six-year-old is often most organized and together when assuming the role of someone else. No doubt his own sense of selfhood is developed by sampling and experimenting with those of others. Six is more aware of when he is role-playing than he was at five, yet one cannot but wonder just how completely differentiated things are within his elusive mind.

It is easy to think of the six-year-old as a hypochondriac. He complains of ailments with greater regularity than he did during the preschool years; parents who themselves are hypochondriacal may have fits of worry over the genuine symptoms which naturally emerge in the vicinity of the sixth year of life. Muscles frequently ache, especially those of the arms and legs; mucous membranes inflame more readily than usual, and sties often develop. Throat infections frequently spread to the ears or lungs. *Otitis media* (inflammation of the middle ear) is at its greatest incidence since midtoddlerhood; common communicable diseases are encountered. Allergy responses are high, aggravated by the sensitive and easily congested mucous membranes of the nose. Girls may complain that their urine burns because of reddened genitalia which require care. Boils may appear on the face, neck, or arms. Tension mounts to a peak in the sixth year, sometimes generating outbursts of screaming, violent temper tantrums, even striking out physically at the parent (Gesell, 1946, p. 106-7). The six-year-old knows well the meaning of adversity; however, nature has bestowed him with sufficient resiliency to meet the challenges of life and still have surplus energy for growth, expansion, play, love, exuberance, and other human experiences not restricted to childhood.

The six-year-old is active, on the go almost every minute. Even when sitting he squirms, fidgets, slides to and fro, and leans backwards. The task of the educator is to find ways in which this energy can be channeled meaningfully without frustrating the child's biological need for movement. The six-year-old is not ready to sit quietly in the classroom for long periods of time as will be expected of him in a few years. He learns best when he *physically* incorporates that which he is learning into his knowledge bank, when he acts out or fantasizes, when he can see tangible benefits of his work, when his work brings praise and enthusiasm from the teacher, when he can move around and show off his work to his classmates, when he has the freedom to flit about and check out the work of other students in the classroom. Learning and movement are part of the same global process for the six-year-old.

The Seven-year-old

Most seven-year-olds learned a great deal from the realities to which they were exposed as six-year-olds. Much of what they learned is being synthesized into their burgeoning understanding of themselves and the world at large. Seven is perhaps the first year in which the child is likely to show genuine signs of pensiveness, reflection, and "deep" thought. He has a great deal to think about. His transition from a "home-child" to a "school-child" required adjustments in life style as well as cognitive patterns. The inevitable realization that home, but not the rest of the world, is geared to his individuality is not easy for the egocentric child to accept. Some openly rebel against the prospect; others postpone the realization as long as possible; others adapt readily, showing few indications of distress. At any rate, Seven synthesizes; he pieces together the fragments that a year before were an unsolvable puzzle.

> There is a kind of quieting down at seven. Six-year-oldness tended to produce brash reactions and bursts of activity. The 7-year-old goes into lengthening periods of calmness and of self-absorption, during which he works his impressions over and over, oblivious to the outer world. It is an assimilative age, a time for salting down accumulated experience and for relating new experiences to the old. (Gesell, 1946, p. 131)

Seven is active but more organized than Six; less energy is consumed in aimless wandering. His parsimony of action is reflected in questions which become surprisingly sophisticated and cerebral. He relies less on authority for solutions. "Because I said so", "Because that is the way it is", "That's the way it has always been", do not have nearly the effectiveness at seven that they had at six or five. Seven does not reason well, by adult standards, but at this age reason is used more adroitly and meaningfully. Seven-year-olds are more impressed by physical explanations than ever before and demand that answers have a certain amount of logic as well as overall sensibility. Seven usually does not perceive exactly what is illogical about a statement but he may nevertheless reject outright an illogical statement or explanation. In this regard his intuition is ahead of his formal knowledge. As formal knowledge increases the child will rely less and less upon intuition, fantasy, and spontaneous creativity — a fact bemoaned by many parents and educators.

The seven-year-old grows increasingly sensitive to, and perceptive of, the attitudes of others. He can be crushed when peers say they don't like him or when teacher scolds him. He cares much more about how people treat him than what they think about him for the simple reason that he cannot easily differentiate between the two. He does not take well to derogatory humour or gruff displays of affection. Fathers who hide their love with artificial displays of sternness often deceive their seven-year-old child who interprets overt gestures rather than hidden sentiment.

He regulates his behaviour with greater facility than he was able to do as a six-year-old; therefore, behaviour is less characterized by impulsive bursts. Temper tantrums for most children are disappearing at seven — a further indication of enhanced self-control. The pronoun "I" is being progressively replaced with the pronoun "we"; he begins to occasionally identify himself in terms of a group to which he belongs — a gesture which never occurs to the preschooler. Socialization is gradually, but methodically, registering its impact on the egocentric child. Some seven-year-olds become dramatically aware of the concept of community. Concepts of social responsibility, distribution of economic wealth, care for the ill or underprivileged are taking hold. Seven is remarkably advanced socially when contrasted with the five-year-old and, as well, shows startling differences from the six-year-old. Unmistakably, the child is growing.

Most seven-year-olds are much improved over Six at finishing projects which they have started. Some show real determination to complete an art or carpentry project. The excitement of novelty has been joined by the importance of finality. The child senses accurately that he is more thorough in thought and action than he used to be.

Conscience is developing in the seven-year-old. His ethical sense is immature and rigid, but definitely based upon the concept that personal behaviour is evaluated by criteria beyond the person. Although as a person he responds more favourably to praise than punishment, his embryonic sense of ethics leads him to conclude that punishment is the best deterrent to inappropriate behaviour. For the majority of children this viewpoint remains firm throughout childhood; even in grades 7, 8, or 9 school principals dare not let students determine the nature of punishment for those who break rules because of their ruthless tendency to dish it out. The inevitable counterpart of conscience — guilt — makes its presence felt for some seven-year-olds. When plagued by guilt for a minor violation the child needs to be reassured that what he has done is not so terrible, that lots of children his age make the same mistake, and that his value as an esteemed person is still intact. Seven, like the rest of us, finds this message refreshing and restorative.

Seven-year-olds enjoy praise from their teacher, but also have by now learned that they do not have exclusive access to her time or affection. Seven learns to accommodate to the expectations of the teacher and genuinely anticipates her evaluations and appraisals. He tends to perceive her word as infallible and frequently gives it priority when it conflicts with other sources of information. A more justified skepticism of teacher's omniscience will emerge during the late childhood years; for the seven-year-old she remains as close to truth as adults can hope to be.

Most seven-year-olds are adept with cultural tools which facilitate time-space orientation such as clocks and calendars. The seasons of the year usually are known by their correct name rather than as hunting season, basketball season, or swimming season. Many seven-year-olds differentiate half-an-hour from an hour, a distinction found rather difficult the year before. Their sense of future time is also coming more into line with adult conception of it; they do not get overly excited about an event which is still a month away.

It is difficult to avoid the comparison between the seven-year-old and the five-year-old. Both are years of assimilation and organization after a year of transition and difficulty. Seven is more sedate than Six, while Five is more so than Four. The rigid outlook of the four-year-old is more widely seen anew when he is six than when he is seven; the self-contained nature of most five-year-olds consistently reappears at seven years of age after the somewhat troublesome sixth year. This is not true for all children, but its generality demands thoughtful consideration.

Seven can be described not only in terms of what he is, but also in terms of what he is not. He is not as flighty, assertive, and impulsive as he was at six. He is more reflective, pensive, and thoughtful. He ruminates and cogitates. He is very much aware of others; he is capable of social politeness although it frequently fails him; he pays close attention to how others treat him. He is sampling different strategies for coping with school and schoolmates. He is incorporating ethics into his life style. He is taking his first *major* steps away from mother and father as the centre of his emotional universe; in a few years they will compete with the child's peer group for his allegiance. He is growing up.

The Eight-year-old

The eight-year-old is more than an improved version of the seven-year-old; new dimensions are added to his personality, his social poise and self-evaluation, his daily behaviour patterns. When he is contrasted with the seven-year-old, the trait which commands attention is the outgoing, forthright, almost aggressive nature of the eight-year-old. His lofty understanding of the world has brought him to an important insight which heretofore has eluded him: most problems yield to active probing. Eight can be viewed as a miniature exponent of the Protestant Ethic. He believes that discipline, hard work, and talent will solve most problems. Though periodically admitting that he does not possess the attributes required to cope with a particular dilemma, in the same breath he assures us that if he did, the problem would be conquered in no time at all. His belief that human skills can solve all problems leads him to idolize and glorify figures who are the best at what they do, including sports heroes, movie or television stars, scientists, and doctors. His glorification of these idols is not total, however, since he also is developing insight into the limitations and fallibility of adults, especially teachers and parents. At school, a new spirit of independence is appearing; Eight is not as dependent upon his teacher as he formerly was; she assumes progressively less significance in his emotional life.

Most eight-year-olds are considerably more outgoing than they were at seven. Social play with peers is more gregarious and boisterous; the give-and-take of childhood hassle is accepted and exerts less psychological hurt than it did the year before. Entrepreneurship, encouraged by the eight-year-old's growing awareness of the importance of money, manifests itself in the form of lemonade stands, paper routes, pop bottle hunting expeditions, and other activities which yield financial return. Many children of this age will work hours on their own to earn fifty cents, but scoff at the idea of helping mother for a short time for the same sum. Customarily, children of this age work better away from home and with far less sense of persecution.

Teachers and parents agree that Eight is less "childish" than he was at seven; this is partly attributable to his desire to be treated in a more adult manner, but for the most part his increased social and intellectual maturity lead us to recognize his progress away from early childhood. Adults treat Eight in a less condescending manner and are rewarded with behaviour of increased sophistication. In almost all areas of development the eight-year-old deals more effectively and productively with adults; he responds to their communications and even learns to put himself into their frame of reference once in a while. As Eight is very proud of his growth, acknowledgement of it at the proper time is one of his most prized rewards. He delights in presenting plausible theories as to why such-and-such occurred or failed to occur, sometimes giving the impression that he is more interested in listening to himself narrate on a topic than in the accuracy of the narration.

Intellectual curiosity is at its loftiest peak since toddlerhood. Curiosity about social relationships, international events, astronomy, social customs of faraway cultures, inner workings of automobiles occupy the expansive, extroverted eight-year-old mentality. There is no better time for implantation of complex ideas which in future years will be resisted because of their difficulty. General ideas about electricity, democratic rule, professional football formations, marital strife are readily assimilated, though not completely understood, by the eight-year-old. He courageously samples the most perplexing metaphysical riddles, accepting what appear to be feasible solutions; however, in their absence he concludes matter-of-factly that this particular riddle has no solution, at the same time appreciating that one may appear in future years. Eight is not emotionally overwhelmed by what he cannot fathom — he had enough of that when he was seven! The eight-year-old conjures up memories in the adult mind of the small town, good-natured young man of the 1940 movies who comes to the city expecting everyone to be as wholesome and agreeable as he is. Many parents find their relationship with their eight-year-old more congenial than it was in the past several years.

Increased maturity is reflected in physical changes. Body proportions are shifting away from the unisex shapelessness of earlier years and beginning to assume some adolescent features; arms are becoming more elongated and hands enlarged. Boys are especially fond of rough and tumble play, and are less prone toward fatigue than they were at seven. Definite trends in male superiority are becoming evident in activities which combine body coordination *and* strength. Girls are likely to be the best sprinters in a classroom of eight-year-olds but rarely could a girl "all-star" team handle its male equivalent in any of the traditional North American ball sports. Sex differences are more noticeable here than at any previous age; segregated gatherings are more frequent; the perverse habit of attracting the attention of an opposite sex member by shouting a derisive or insulting term is evident but still infantile when compared with the incredible extremes it achieves in eleven- and twelve-year-olds.

Collections obsess the eight-year-old. Rocks, stamps, posters, and records are favourites but the possibilities are by no means restricted to them. Precocious children havy been known to collect miniature replicas of prehistoric reptiles (a common fascination with dinosaurs exists at this age), space vehicles, and other items which require a good deal of historical knowledge as well as keenness of insight. Many a tranquil household evening has been shattered by the discovery that a younger sibling has invaded the sacred ground reserved for the collection which Eight so highly cherishes. A flurry of rage may be followed by genuine tears of remorse when an eight-year-old discovers his favourite model airplane has been broken or a treasured action photo of a Stanley Cup hero has been torn. Eight is not emotional about members of the opposite sex, but he is when it comes to his collections and special projects. They symbolize his new-found ability to organize, conceptualize, and categorize and in no way should be shown disrespect — they are close to the child's emotional centre.

Although eight-year-olds have a definite interest in sexual behaviour, it is qualitatively different from the interest shown by the adolescent going through puberty. The interest of the eight-year-old is based more upon his boundless curiosity than upon his impulse for sexual experience *per se*. Boys of this age will hang around as long as permitted while older boys talk about their insights into the wonders of sexual play. Eight will inspect pictures of nudes with interest but not enthusiasm, with curiosity but not desire, with a sense of daring but not guilt. The description is almost reversed during early adolescence. Some eight-year-olds have experimented with the genitals of either same or opposite sex friends, but the motivation for such behaviour should not be understood as sexual, at least not in the way sexual behaviour is experienced by adolescent or adults. Curiosity, exploration, adventurousness seem more viable explanations for the sexual play of eight-year-olds. Despite this we should keep in mind that sexual intercourse is possible at this age; there are recorded cases of eight-year-olds bearing children.

In summary, the eight-year-old shows a renewed interest in the physical environment and the principles upon which it operates; for the first time he is of the impression that the workings of the physical world are understandable. An increasing "evaluativeness" preoccupies his mental life; the eight-year-old evaluates not only himself but also the competence and expertise of others. He may indignantly announce that Miss Jones has no right to be a third grade teacher or that the local head coach should be dismissed because of his flagrant ineptitude. Eight has considerably more self-confidence than when he was seven, and is less awed by mysteries; he believes that most questions are answerable even if he may not have the answers. He is not sinking in the intellectual quagmire that made life so difficult for the seven-year-old. His self-concept is becoming progressively more differentiated. Instead of thinking of himself as exceptional in everything (as he did at four and five) he unashamedly admits that he is quite good in running and arithmetic but rather weak in spelling and tolerating females. Eight, becoming moderately poised in social settings, can be expected to cope with the requirement of custom and etiquette when introduced to adults. The fact that this is often done begrudgingly indicates that self-restraint is also at a lifetime high. Although he is argumentative, the arguments of eight-year-olds are not founded upon egocentric impulse alone; he is aware of coherence and continuity in logic and readily detects their opposite when an opponent attempts to establish a point on spurious grounds. Eight is usually good-natured in his arguments because he has not as yet reached the age when he is emotionally attached to the conclusions he logically derives. Arguments are playful exchanges and, for the first time in his young life, the child may suddenly have a strong flash of insight into the other person's point of view — egocentrism is losing its domination of the child's mind.

The Nine-year-old

The nine-year-old gives us ample occasion for pause and reflection. He is not easy to understand because his age precariously straddles two different worlds: that of the child and that of the pre-adolescent. He feels completely comfortable in neither, being too immature for the social complexity of the pre-adolescent and too elderly for the innocent goings-on of six or seven-year-olds. Despite this delicate balance, his emotional life is comparatively free of serious conflict; he is not characterized by excessive tensional outlet, rebellion, or inner turmoil. Nine is too engrossed in analysis and investigation of the outside world to dwell excessively on subjective turmoil. In this respect he distinguishes himself from the five and seven-year-olds. Essentially, Nine is an improved version of Eight, who refines his strengths and outgrows his weaknesses.

Most nine-year-olds are characterized by an intellectual attitude of *realism,* a social attitude of *reasonableness,* and a psychological attitude of *self-motivation.* Their earlier, less perceptive understanding of causality is replaced with genuine insight into the nature of cause and effect; Nine is intrigued with the explanatory prowess of science as he was with magic in the preschool years. An expanded awareness of the importance of others contributes to his overall reasonableness. No longer does he categorically reject an idea merely because it contradicts his own; nor does he refuse to listen to an argument simply because he dislikes the person from whom it emanates. The nine-year-old is more self-motivated than he was at eight. He is less reliant on praise and approval from adults, but still treasures it. His increasingly stable sense of evaluativeness allows more advanced self-evaluation and self-analysis. Parents cannot escape the realization that their child is gradually phasing out of childhood. The undeniable social, intellectual, and psychological trademarks of pre-adolescence are budding.

Eight-year-olds enjoy collecting. The expansive spirit of Nine leans toward classifying, categorizing, and planning. He acquires information so rapidly that he is forced to devise classification systems and inventory sheets almost in self-protection. Nine is addicted to minutiae and one of his favourite pleasures is to inform parents or teacher of a news item sponged from the television or newspaper. Sports heroes are classified into top ten hitters and point-makers; hobbies are categorized into special shelves and alcoves; Saturday excursions are planned in advance in clandestine basement meetings; Nine does not assault the world at random; he calculates, anticipates, and prepares. As parents and teachers are fully aware, however, the fruits of his calculations rarely are as magnificent as hoped for. Nine accepts his limitations, still being chained to the stoic resignation characteristic of most children. Nine is a year for psychic expansion.

The emotional life of the nine-year-old is deepening. He achieves a considerable depth of appreciation of the subjective workings of himself and others. He makes finer emotional discriminations than he did as a seven or eight-year-old. New emotions are rocking his life; though not as devastating as those encountered during adolescence, they are, on occasion, powerfully felt. The child at this age may respond tearfully to a touching movie scene, indignantly upon hearing of a wrong doing, empathetically upon learning of a family disaster. Nine is not a victim of his emotions, nor is he dominated by them as he was as a pre-schooler, but he is exposed to a new world of deeper emotion closer in its breadth and openness to that of the adult. Parents are brought to the realization that the transformation from child to young adult is well underway. However, Nine is still much more child than young adult.

Nine likes to be trusted, to be given advanced responsibility, to sample special freedoms. As a rule he does not disappoint because he takes special pride in justifying the confidence of adults. It fortifies his own sense of maturity. Nine-year-olds are capable of assuming considerable household responsibility when occasion demands. In instances of family illness, for example, nine-year-olds have taken over management of the household for days at a time. In low-income families, children of this age are not uncommonly delegated responsibility for feeding, dressing, and getting younger siblings off to school each morning. Nine is a good protector. He (or she) will stand up to anyone who abuses a younger sibling, defames the family name, or mouths unkind innuendoes. Nine often learns abruptly the consequences of standing up to opposition. It is the age for bloody noses, scratched faces, and injured pride; all three mend quickly in order to ready for another day.

Each sex becomes fascinated with the differences of the other but, in the mysterious workings of this period of sexual latency, the fascination moves the sexes apart rather than together. Some textbooks convey the naive (nonsensical is a better term) impression that boys of this age are not interested in girls. This statement presumably is based upon the fact that sex groupings are frequently segregated at this age and verbal hostilities are bantered back and forth. Despite this, there should be no misunderstanding of the facts: boys at this age are interested in girls, girl friends, girlishness; girls are even more interested in boys, boy friends, and boyishness. The interest, however, is tempered by an acute absence of social skills; boys find it easier to cope with girls by being rowdy, elusive, and rambunctious; girls find it easier to cope with boys by being coy, evasive, and alternately available and demure. The attraction between the sexes is not chemical, rarely leads to sexual play, and knows few rules of courtship. But, unmistakably, the attraction is present. Boys have a genuine interest in girls; however, they have even stronger interest in athletics. Girls have a genuine interest in boys, but share with them the realization that it is not the *dominating* interest of their age group. Segregated sex groupings allow both male and female to work out some of the nuances of male-female relatedness in the abstract. For the most part this is a shrewd move, if the awkward interaction patterns of pre-adolescence are any index of their ability to cope with opposite sex members.

Girls are much closer to puberty than boys at this age. Menstruation will begin in a year or two for many girls, fostering concern and preoccupation with body change and sexual maturity. For the most part, the facts of life for both boys and girls are still rather abstract. Nine assimilates ideas of sexual intercourse and reproduction well, but frequently overlooks the emotional or subjective dimension of human sexuality. He should be informed that human sexual behaviour is more than purely mechanical without being forced to dwell excessively upon the moral implications of promiscuous sexuality. The intellectual openness of Nine makes "scare" tactics unnecessary. Ethical beliefs about sexual behaviour can be discussed with the nine-year-old in a fairly straightforward manner. Rarely does he question what parents tell him in these matters. The onus is therefore on parents to say what they really want to say.

Nine is a willing learner. He is open to instruction and benefits from it. He is able to put up with a teacher he does not like if the teacher really can teach. He no longer believes teachers are perfect. His evaluativeness reflects detachment as well as judgment, "I don't like old man Fisher, but he's not a bad teacher"; or "Mrs. Trembley sure was in a bad mood today". The realization that adults are subject to mood swings and temper outbursts sinks in. The six-year-old cannot separate himself from the mood of the teacher but Nine does so adeptly. Nine is a flamboyant talker. He has a good deal to talk about. His horizons expand daily; equally important, he is *thrilled* by the expansion. Information is to be shared. Fact-sharing and gossip flourish at this age. Nine-year-olds often greet one another with a fact rather than a salutation.

Nine-year-olds in general tend to have a good deal of self-confidence. They get along well with parents for two reasons: (1) they appreciate the responsibilities of mother and father; and (2) nine-year-olds are not strongly attracted to behaviour which parents are opposed to. The chaos of parent-child relationships during the teen years is in large part due to the reversal of these two factors.

Conscience is taking hold. Distinct feelings of right and wrong emerge which may or may not completely reflect what has been taught at home or school. A cortex capable of remembering the orbits of the planets is likewise capable of making his own ethical judgments. Tremendous differences in guilt feelings prevail at this age. Some nine-year-olds are genuinely psychopathic in that nothing bothers their conscience. To tell a lie without batting an eye is common as is stealing without a pang of guilt. Though going through an Age of Enlightenment intellectually, some nine-year-olds are still in the Age of Darkness morally.

Prejudice and racism are easily learned or unlearned at this age. The viewpoint most cogently presented tends to win out, assuming all other factors equal. Nine is the age for *un*learning as well as learning. Much information acquired from peers needs to be re-analysed, sometimes even replaced with more correct information. At this age, good teachers must be good listeners in order to more fully understand the child's perspective. Frequently, the most significant learning of this age is the unlearning of prejudices, the realigning of uneven reasoning, the stabilizing of a weak conviction, the resurrecting of a lost ideal.

Nine has his limitations. He knows what he dislikes and will go to great lengths to avoid those things which are unpleasant for him. He demonstrates an uncanny knack for providing parents only with the information which he wants them to have. For the first time he may calculate days in advance a misdeed such as skipping school or swiping a friend's baseball bat. His increasing group allegiance impels him toward negative behaviour he would never consider on his own. His desire to be accepted, though not as overpowering as it will be in a few years, is beginning to exert more than subtle influence. When angered to the point of fist-fighting, a nine-year-old may fly into such rage that if he were more proficient with his fists he could easily maim or injure an opponent. Nine sometimes demonstrates a callous disregard for the feelings of others, especially if he has the backing of an older person.

He will brandish derisive names reserved for particular ethnic or religious groups such as Kike, Nip, Spick, Whitey, Nigger, Kraut, Cat-licker, Greaser, Mex if he hears them at home; he will ridicule a polio victim or retarded child, even taunt elderly citizens whose walking style betrays an infirmity. It is best to remind ourselves that Nine is neither angel nor devil, but essentially a reflection of the dominant forces in his life. Though he is a composite of his history, he is not bound to it. Ample time remains for positive or negative growth. The nine-year-old reflects his culture as well as his family life; he absorbs their weaknesses as well as their strengths, their virtues and vices. The effects of upbringing is becoming more obvious each year.

The Ten-year-old

For many children the year which produces the least difficulty, whether it be psychological or social, internal or external, is the tenth year. On the whole, Ten is rather well-adjusted to himself, his family, and his limited community. His equilibrium can be attributed to four conditions of ten-year-oldness: (1) Social demands are coped with fairly easily because they are not strenuous and because the child's increasing social facility makes him especially gifted (when compared with his proficiency at eight or nine) at coping with more interpersonal situations. (2) Biological impulses are in check. Most ten-year-olds, especially boys, are several years away from the endocrinological changes which transform the child into an adolescent and at the same time create mood changes and expanded awareness of self and body. Ten has outgrown the temper tantrums and impulsiveness of earlier years. His body causes such little difficulty that he tends to take it for granted, giving scant thought to it except when it needs minor repairs or recuperation from overactivity. (3) Ten has the advantage of being looked up to by younger children, thus reinforcing his sense of growth and maturity; at the same time he is coming into greater acceptance by parents and other adults who are pleased with his movement away from the immaturities of the seven, eight, and nine-year-old. (4) Ten believes in the future and is eager to venture into it. He has idols and heroes whom he aspires to mimic and pursue; he has personal ambitions for his adult life which he expects to actualize. He is eager, willing, and thinks he is able — all the ingredients for confident optimism. Most ten-year-olds are spared the impulsiveness of Six, the pensive introversion of Seven, the shallow flamboyance of Eight, and the complexity of Eleven. Of the childhood years, Ten most resembles Nine, which is also a year of comparative harmony and self-realization.

Ten is becoming recognizably pre-adolescent in individuality and maturity. He has his own characteristic methods for coping with problems which crop up; he thinks with caution; he employs strategies which have worked successfully in the past; his pool of experience is deepening; his self-confidence asserts itself even against formidable opposition. Ten has greater physical presence than ever before. Some girls display impressive flashes of social poise and finesse; the pelvis and breasts are beginning to round, Nature's indicators of emerging feminine contours. Many ten-year-old boys are athletic, mesomorphic, wiry, and rowdy. Fathers are discovering that playful fights require an extra reserve of energy; many mothers can no longer spank their sons without their consent. The signs have never been so unmistakably clear: the child each day becomes less a child and more a pre-adolescent. Ten is the calm before the storm.

Ten is easy to reason with because his attitudes are flexible rather than rigid and his mind is open rather than closed. He likes to hear alternative ideas and arguments though, for the most part, he still is highly partial toward his own. Ten is more skilled at criticizing the nature of his *own* thought than at any other time in his life cycle. He now grasps the idea that he arrived at conclusion A because of the sequence of information to which he was exposed. He occasionally admits that given a different sequence of information he well may have come to a different conclusion. Parents and teachers exhale a collective sigh of relief upon this significant intellectual breakthrough in the child's life, for it is the key which opens the door to a more honest as well as more rational insight into the origins of personal thought.

Ten cannot avoid making evaluative judgments, but he can keep the results of his judgments to himself. He distinguishes between public and private knowledge and has completely outgrown the preschool child's belief that private thoughts can be read by others. The flourishing clubs and secret organizations in the society of the ten-year-old attest to their fondness for secrets and other varieties of private information which by definition are not shared with parents. Privacy bolsters their sense of self-possession.

Sex differences are more pronounced at this age than heretofore. Far more boys than girls are interested in sports and sports idols; girls are consistently more inclined to acquiescence and feel more comfortable with it. Differences are not restricted to the physical:

> The psychology of a 10-year-old girl is significantly distinguishable from that of a 10-year-old boy of equivalent breeding and experience. The girl has more poise, more folk wisdom, and more interest in matters pertaining to marriage and family. This

213

> difference appears to be fundamental. . . . Girls are more aware
> of interpersonal relationships than boys are. They are more
> aware of their own persons, their clothes, and appearance. They
> may spend prolonged periods preening a coiffure. At the same
> time, they are more discerning of their individual relationships
> with others. (Gesell, 1946, p. 213 & 216)

Ten becomes aware of the gang, the clique, the in-crowd. He is not yet under their spell as he likely will be at eleven, twelve, and thirteen, but his behaviour definitely is influenced by them. Not since toddlerhood has the child come as close to mob psychology. The gang (this is not a derisive term, merely connotative of a group) is able to foster positive as well as negative behaviour. Although most gangs have a leader of sorts, the general rule is that very few ten-year-olds have the internal fortitude, the inclination, or the personal skills to go against the consensus of the gang. Parent and teacher justifiably worry about the appropriateness of friend selection at this age. A gang of boys led by a mischievous, perhaps even emotionally disturbed boy, is capable of serious vandalism. Even though his personal code may contradict this group code, the sense of group solidarity fostered by the gang is difficult for most ten-year-olds to resist.

Despite the possibility of negative gang behaviour, the ten-year-old is a model of good conduct. His personal and social harmony are much more conspicuous trademarks in his daily life than are their opposites. Ten is self-acceptant and self-confident.

> In general then, the ten-year-old is self accepting. He likes his
> body and his looks, he likes what he can do in the way of sports
> — which is considerable — and what he can do academically. His
> own self-acceptance is heightened by the acceptance accorded
> him by peers, by family, and by the school. There is a sort of
> mutual admiration society between the ten-year-old and his
> social world, which supports and reinforces his positive self-
> image, his self-confidence, and his self-acceptance. (Elkind,
> 1971, p. 83)

The Social World of Middle Childhood

It is somewhat misleading to speak about the social world of middle childhood because it implicitly suggests rules, regulations, consistency, and continuity. Though these exist in the child's social world, their existence is of considerably different character than that of their adult equivalent. The social world of middle childhood is exceptionally fluid and flexible; it twists and bends to suit the ever-changing needs and impulses of its constituents. Not uncommonly, the internal operations of a gang of eight-year-olds completely change merely because the king-pin has temporarily departed for dinner. More commonly than is believed by adults who assume that children are completely loyal to one another, a gang member may show up for a meeting only to discover that he was expelled during an impromptu meeting which he missed. Again, to the surprise of adults who assume that children are always idealistic, the same youngster may win back the good graces of the pack by buying them each a milkshake, or by threatening to kick the bejabers out of them if they do not reconsider their action. The social world of middle childhood society is a milieu of codes, rules, impulses, devices, and experiments. The primary function of all children's gatherings is to establish a social group whereby each individual is able to receive *acceptance*, achieve *competence*, and cultivate the *skills* required of *interpersonal relationships*. This is the age when children first attempt to get along with one another without adult supervision; it is their first adventure in self-government. The preschool child relies almost exclusively on adult authority to resolve conflicts — now he must negotiate them himself. The preschooler turns to adults when confronted with problems he cannot solve — now he must provide his own solutions. In the society of children, one hurriedly learns to take care of oneself, to learn rules and abide by them, and to become familiar with power politics as well as the responsibilities of continuing comradeship. Though William Golding is a bit more dramatic than necessary in his portrayal of childhood barbarism, *The Lord of the Flies* is by no means a distorted representation of the extremes which childhood behaviour can take.

One basic task of childhood is to establish a sense of identity which is not based upon *adult* evaluation. This is the age for peer identity. The child each year is moving farther from his household moorings. As he weans himself from the emotional security of the home, he learns new labels, identities, and ideas about himself; he learns that he is fat or skinny or strong; that he is ugly or attractive or nondescript; that he is a Black, Yellow, or White; that he is dependable, untrustworthy, or maybe a little of each depending on the situation; that he is bright, stupid, verbally swift; that his clothes are adequate, desirable, or undesirable; that his parents are looked down upon, respected, or unknown; that he is a provider, a sponger, or perhaps a touch of both. All these things the child learns about himself from his peers. The child, however, is not completely at the mercy of peer group evaluation; he does not always accept their opinions or judgments. Johnny no longer is thought to be a liar if he outshouts or outlasts someone who says he is; Mary is no longer taunted as a crybaby if her older brothers step in and outlaw that particular description of her;

Willie may start his own gang or boycott a group of former friends who hurt his pride by doubting his competence or masculinity. Though the group is not all-powerful, it exerts control over the child. The impulse to membership is such a dominant childhood force that the child will put up with almost anything rather than abandon group affiliation. The child is hungry for identity and, as a rule, he prefers a negative identity ("fatso," "wimpy," "lazy," "cheater," "scarface") to nonidentity. Children have identity crises of their own, even though they are less spectacular than those which occur during adolescence.

The child lives in several different cultures which do not share the same values. The school, the home, the society at large, and the peer group each have unique rules and regulations; a good deal of overlap exists among these cultures, but also a good deal of contradiction. (It is sometimes difficult to keep in mind that a few years ago, as a pre-schooler, the child's world rarely extended beyond the home and never beyond the authority of the parents.) One result of exposure to the outside world is that the child begins to think of himself in ways similar to those thought of him by others. He latches on to societal labels that make a firm impress on his suggestible mind. He learns that others identify him in terms of what he does rather than what he thinks (setting the stage for hypocrisy as well as model behaviour). He learns that others do not automatically think kindly of him; he learns the importance of proving himself. He has almost completely outgrown the social egocentrism of the preschool years. The child now tries to adjust to others rather than to demand egotistically that they adjust to him.

Parents recognize that their child is flowering, that horizons are expanding, that new customs are replacing the old. The child is less open with parents than formerly; he no longer assumes they are omniscient; he keeps (treasures) secrets; he is living a small but distinctly important life away from that of the household.

Group play during middle childhood is not random. One of its conspicuous features is that groups become separated by age as well as by sex: ten-year-olds do not mix with seven-year-olds (except in special circumstances where it is inevitable or advantageous), and males do not generally mix with females.

> The group play of children from 7 to 11 years differs in important ways from that of children 5 to 6 years of age. In the younger period, a boy may play — or fight — with either boys or girls. Their games may be feminine (e.g., playing house) or masculine (playing ball or building). Beginning at age 7 or 8, however, children begin to associate primarily with same-sex peers. The boys now chase and tease girls, rather than play with them. The boy seeks out other boys and is likely to be embar-

rassed if he is found alone with a group of girls. From age 9 through 11, there is usually considerable anxiety over associations with girls or revealing any interest in them. (Mussen, 1963, p. 576)

The child does not move toward peer groupings in order to gain greater *freedom* from home; he does so in order to: (a) partially establish a unique identity which does not depend on his household, (b) share time with other children who have similar social-psychological problems, and (c) acquire greater social competence. Freedom is not a major consideration for most children, rather, it becomes important only when its absence imposes some kind of undesirable situation. Most children eagerly relinquish future freedom in exchange for something they desire. Thus, they will agree to play in the backyard for the rest of the day in exchange for a hamburger at the local drive-in. They will agree never to swear in front of girls if somehow (don't ask me how in this day and age) they become convinced that it is unmannerly to speak crudely in the presence of tender feminine ears. Gangs and clubs uniformly invent rules to modulate the behaviour of the members, usually replacing freedom with duty. The following is an example of a set of rules established by a group of nine and ten-year-old girls, presumably for the purpose of enhancing their image as model citizens.

1. Do not tell a white lie unless necessary.
2. Do not hurt anyone in any way.
3. Do not hit anyone except Ronny.
4. Do not tell a black lie.
5. Do not use words worse than "brat".
6. Do not curse at all.
7. Do not make faces except at Ronny.
8. Do not be selfish.
9. Do not make a hog or a pig of yourself.
10. Do not tattle except on Ronny.
11. Do not steal except from Ronny.
12. Do not destroy other people's property, except Ronny's.
13. Do not be a sneak.
14. Do not be grumpy except to Ronny.
15. Do not answer back except to Ronny.

(Stone, 1968, p. 384)

Children have a special fascination for other children of their same age. It is as though they share parallel insights and world views nurtured by their common age and classification. They immediately understand and sympathize with personal problems which adults rarely perceive much less empathize with; they readily accommodate to one another's maturational limitations and handicaps without complaint or deference; they see in one another many differences, to be sure, but the magnetism of sameness pulls them together with predictable precision. Many family outings are bearable only when the ten-year-old daughter brings along her best friend to provide the kind of companionship which escapes adults. The blissful camaraderies of youth haunts the adult psyche, silently encouraging the reminiscence and nostalgia of spent youth. Childhood is rocky, but it is also intense, and the intensity of togetherness experienced by childhood companions is felt more deeply during the pre-adult years only by adolescent lovers bound together in erotic passion.

Why are some children more popular than others? Research suggests several trends in this puzzling matter of childhood social hierarchies. Young children who excel at culturally-valued skills tend to be more widely acclaimed by their peers than those children who do not. Therefore, athletic prowess is almost universally admired by children, continuing for many through the college years and into adulthood. Children skilled at coping with the numerous social-psychological dilemmas of particular ages are also looked up to. To be able to cope with parents, teachers, bullies, boring adult gatherings, or stern administrators is to be admired in the social world of childhood. Most forms of *competence* lead to peer popularity, especially when the group has a vested interest in one type of competence such as baseball, street fighting, Frisbee throwing, swimming, doll play, or whatever. In a review of the literature, Mussen (1963, p. 579) presents several interesting insights into the nature of childhood popularity. (1) Studies of school-age children often indicate that popular children are good-looking (by peer group standards), friendly, and good sports. (2) Among first grade girls popularity is closely associated with "acting like a lady"; however, the importance of "acting like a lady" declines in importance as girls grow older until by the fifth grade it has little to do with popularity or prestige. (3) First grade boys consider game skills, daring, and being "real boys" essential to social prestige. Interestingly, these same traits measure rather well the popularity index of males during the fifth grade as well. With regard to skills and abilities there is little doubt that the most talented, creative, and intelligent are more widely accepted than slow learners, retarded, and marginally competent children. Significant relationships have also been found between peer status and reading achievement, although the reasons for this relationship are conjectural.

Negative aspects of popularity (traits which encourage unpopularity) include anxiety, uncertainty, indifference, aggressiveness, hostility, and negatively-valued physical attributes such as obesity or limb handicap. These are not absolute indicators of unpopularity, but tend to be strongly associated with it.

The need to belong. All children share a fundamental need to belong, to involve themselves in the lives of other humans; this need is one of the dominant social forces of childhood existence. In the course of human growth the need for belonging takes different forms and manifests itself in diverse behaviour. During childhood several striking trends emerge which we would do well to look into.

During the first months of life the need for belonging cannot be distinguished from the need to be held, coddled, caressed, and comforted. The infant, only a few weeks removed from the sheltered tranquility of the womb, is accustomed to perpetual body contact. Undeniably, he *needs* the contact of his mother. As the first birthday approaches, the child's need for belonging becomes differentiated from his need for contact comfort. He now needs a sense of membership, relatedness, and togetherness. He needs to feel that he is a significant part of a small group of mother, father, brother, and sister. He needs family. His need for contact is still real, but no longer the same as the need to belong. Throughout life, however, contact comfort remains one of the primary means by which belonging is partially gratified. During *toddlerhood,* belonging needs are satisfied primarily by the immediate family. The *preschool years,* however, mark the beginning of monumental changes: the child's need for parental approval is generalized to other authority figures. No longer are mother and father the only source of adult approval. No longer is their approval or acceptance the exclusive concern of the child. While attending preschool, the child expands his narrow belonging needs. His sense of belonging is influenced by how well he is accepted by teacher and peer group. At this age he does not identify strongly with his preschool group, but his need for belonging can be shattered if he is disliked or rejected by his peers. The negative pains of rejection are more intense for the preschooler than are the positive pleasures of acceptance. To protect himself from the hurt of nonacceptance each child learns to belong, to fit in with others. After preschool the child becomes progressively less reliant upon mother and father though, without doubt, they are still the primary focus of his belonging needs. In addition to requiring *parental* acceptance, seven, eight, and nine-year-olds prize highly *peer* acceptance and *adult* acceptance. The belonging needs are mushrooming outward; circumference, like that of the growing oak tree, is expanding annually.

The need to belong assumes two basic forms during the first ten years of life: social belonging and psychological belonging. The need for *social* belonging is satisfied by group membership and participation, requiring involvement and participation with others. Among pre-schoolers social belonging may manifest itself in neighbourhood sandbox play; among eight-year-olds it may take the form of cub scouts or secret clubs. Simply being in the presence of others satisfies the need for social belonging. The need for *psychological* belonging is more subtle because it requires not only a social context but also that group members *accept* the person and hold him in some kind of *special* regard. Psychological belonging implies that the individual has an internal sense (feeling) of well-being and intimacy with the group which engulfs him. It is experienced more deeply than social belonging, which corresponds more with herd instinct. Ideally, the child is able to satisfy both the social and psychological dimensions of his belonging need. Realistically, the need for social belonging is much more easily achieved. The child possessed of low self-esteem, whose sense of trust and security are weak, has minimal prospects for thinking of himself as being held in esteem by peers. The child whose inner feelings are not positive has difficulty believing that he is viewed positively or held in high esteem by others. The child with an assured sense of confidence, reared to think proudly of himself, faces better prospects that social belonging will facilitate psychological belonging.

In summary, the child has a need for social as well as psychological belonging. Although both can be satisfied by group membership, the need for social belonging is gratified more easily. The crucial factor is the child's personal sense of self-worth and confidence. As we have established in previous chapters, the child's sense of self-worth is, in large part, a result of how his parents interacted with him during the first three years of life.

During childhood the need for belonging is not random. Certain people are more central to the child's belonging needs than others (sometimes they are referred to as *significant others*). The significant others of childhood are somewhat predictable. During the first three years, parents are the most significant humans in the life of the child. From three to six, parents remain significant but inroads are made by other adults (who hold positions of authority over the child) and by playmates or classmates. From six to eight years, parents remain the most significant figures, but less so than at earlier years; other adults, such as teachers, begin to lose importance acquired in preschool years, and peers continue their climb in importance. During the ninth and tenth years, parents still are at the top of the hierarchy but never have they been so closely challenged by their children's peers, while other adults fade even farther behind. Thus, during the first ten years of life, the child individuates himself from exclusive psychological dependence on parents. He opens his psychological self to other adults, but even more so to children of his own age.

As other psychological needs change, so also does the need for belonging. The child whose need for independence and autonomy is high may abandon the restrictive requirements of group belonging in order to satisfy other more pressing needs. The child with a strong need for security and approval may find considerable difficulty bucking the demands of any social group to which he belongs (this most commonly occurs between the eighth and tenth years, but it also shows prominence during the pre-adolescent and early adolescent years, roughly between ages eleven to fifteen). During childhood, the need to belong is always powerful — only the people and groups upon whom the need is focused change.

The need for belonging creates some unpleasant social realities for the child. Belonging, for some children, is more fully satisfied when they are able to exclude others from their group. By rejecting others their own sense of acceptance is assured; by excluding others their own sense of membership is bolstered; by establishing arbitrary rules they convince other children of the worthwhileness of their clique. Children do not mimic these techniques from parents; they invent them on their own. During childhood, exclusion serves as a psychological device to help satisfy the need for belonging. Group membership cannot be understood without examining its counterpart: group exclusion. The need to exclude is a by-product of the need to belong. Among some children this leads to the debasement and ridicule of others to confirm beyond doubt that they have been excluded from such and such a group. Without benefit of wise adult guidance, the child's need for group belonging often results in destructive, almost sadistic, patterns of social interaction. The child cannot be expected to spontaneously adopt rules of fair play and respect for the rights of others. These are not traits of his nature and, for the most part, need to be implanted by example and teaching. Some children are well into their teens before they recuperate from rejection or ridicule heaped upon them by peers during the middle childhood years. In fairness, however, it must be noted that the converse occurs: some children are well into their teens before they outgrow the unrealistic sense of importance accorded them by childhood peers.

The latency years: synthetic sexuality. The years of middle and late childhood have been described as the *latency period* to indicate that this is the time of the child's life when his sexual interests remain dormant (latent). During the pre-adolescent years, a shift of interest takes place (according to psychologists who assume that interest in members of the opposite sex is minimal during the middle childhood years). The interest between the sexes in pre-adolescence, however, is social rather than biological. With the onset of adolescence, sexual maturity ushers in a genuine *biological* attraction between the sexes. Some psychologists, especially Freudians, assume that the biological changes which take place during puberty *account for* the attraction between males and females at this age; that if puberty did not take place until, say, twenty years of age, the social world of the adolescent would be no more heterosexual than is the world of the pre-adolescent. In other words, biological changes *within* the person bring about social and sexual interest in the opposite sex. No doubt there is a ring of truth to this understanding of heterosexual development. During adolescence, males and females interact in ways they have not before experienced. Sexual drive is intense, as is the need for sexual expression and intimacy; this sexual intensity is founded upon the hormonal and endocrinological changes which take place during puberty. In this regard, male-female relationships during adolescence have an undeniable biological basis. However, to infer that children who have not reached puberty do not have an interest in the opposite sex is based more upon weak theory than upon actual observation of children.

During late childhood strong interest is manifested in opposite sex members. Before the preschool years, virtually no distinction is made among children in the matter of sex; during the preschool years (three to six) this changes marginally, but little differentiation exists about the importance of being male or female. In the vicinity of the sixth and seventh years, greater awareness of sex differences is evident. By the eighth, ninth, and tenth years, the child is acutely aware of sex differences. Girls may insult one another with names (such as "Tomboy") which call into question the completeness of one's sexual identity. Among males, the nickname "sissy" is a definite slur which often will incite combat. The distinction which must be made if we are to properly understand the nature of male-female interaction during the late childhood years is that it is based upon socio-sexual rather than bio-sexual realities. Early in life, probably during the preschool years, children in our society begin to understand (though not in an objective or precise way) that adult sexual patterns are different from childhood social patterns. This realization accentuates awareness of the unique nature of male-female romance. During the preschool years, girls talk about their boy friends with modest shyness, or with a sense of specialness. They are aware that there is a difference between male-male and male-female, or female-female and male-female attraction. If the word gets out that Charles takes a liking to Cynthia, it may temporarily disrupt the atmosphere of a second grade classroom. Ten-year-old girls talk among themselves about their latest boyfriend with romantic overtones which in no way can be lived up to. There can be no doubt that children between eight and ten have a remarkable interest in members of the opposite sex. Psychologists, as well as teachers, are deceived by children's tendency to segregate into same-sex groups: this is done to avoid the catastrophe which comes from a heterosexual social blunder rather than from lack of interest in the opposite sex. Adult social gatherings sometimes take on a similar voluntary bifurcation of the sexes, with the men in one room discussing business, athletics, or whatever while the women gossip about the insipidity of male companionship. No one suggests an absence of male-female interest in this gathering. It is segregated merely for social reasons. Same-sex gatherings are, as a rule, more psychologically safe than heterosexual gatherings. The penalty for social miscue is always greater in mixed groups, whether the group be composed of ten-year-olds or forty-year-olds.

Several difficult questions present themselves when we discuss male-female attraction during the late childhood years. One intriguing matter pertains to the nature of contact comfort during these years. Boys, as a rule, do not hang onto or drape themselves around female friends as they do with their male companions. Rarely does one observe ten-year-old sweethearts strolling casually through a park with an arm around the shoulder of the other; yet this gesture of affection is frequently observed among boys of this age who are good friends. It is sometimes impossible to get a ten-year-old boy to hold the hand of a girl or to give her a kiss. Yet how could there be such aversion if the boy were completely neutral or disinterested in the girl? Ten-year-old boys will kiss grandmother or younger sister if social protocol demands it, yet to kiss a girl of the same age is an adventurous act. As everyone knows, adventure comes only when there is an element of risk or danger.

The conclusion which most forcefully presents itself is that late childhood is not a period of disinterest in members of the opposite sex. Quite the contrary, these are years of heightened interest if contrasted to the relative unisexuality of the preschool years, but they cannot match the interest shown in the opposite sex after puberty.

Where then does opposite sex interest come from? To greatly oversimplify, it comes from the child's recognition that male-female relationships are the fundamental basis for adult society and that intrinsic to them is not only psychological intimacy but sexual intimacy as well. Though this insight does not dart through the child's mind in a conscious or rational manner, this realization cannot be avoided in our society. Parents are not surprised when children learn to convert athletes into heroes, when they show respect or admiration for services performed by medical doctors, or when they aspire to be like their teacher. Adults register surprise, however, when their children imitate television romanticism, or attach special connotation to courtship ritual, or associate kissing and caressing with adult sexuality. The child learns vicariously about sex, but his personal observation and experience confirm even further what he has assumed. Ours is a sexual society and the child recognizes it as such; being an imitator (but also an experimenter) he looks into the matter himself. The results are available to anyone who will look closely into the social world of child groupings.

The changing role of the parent during middle childhood. Parents learn a good deal about themselves as well as their children during the years of middle childhood. The most shocking realization for parents is that the child is in the gradual process of separating himself from the intimate bond of oneness established with them during the first year of life. The child has been giving signs of individuation for some time, but they are now unmistakable. Given a free choice, the child will commonly choose peer companionship over parental companionship (this reaches its peak in pre-adolescence when being seen with parents is almost cause for embarrassment). He confides some personal matters more openly with his best friend than with mother or father. Now and again he even intentionally (with forethought) deceives parents if there is a "sound" reason for doing so. The child never outgrows his emotional *attachment* to his parents but he does outgrow his *dependence* on them. This is a natural and inevitable part of healthy growth — the child's movement away from parental authority.

Parents encounter a certain difficulty accepting the facts of child growth, insisting that their ten-year-old should be little more than an enlarged version of their once dependent toddler. The pains of child growth are not restricted to children; nor are the pains of parenthood restricted to watching the child become his own man — there are plenty of problems when the child is merely being a child.

At different ages, the child acquires different skills and sensitivities from his parents. During the first year of life, it is imperative that parents be affectionate but also that they systematically tend to the biological basics of existence such as food and cleanliness. During the preschool years, parents should encourage expansion, exploration, and adventure so that new realities to which the child is exposed may be more fully assimilated into his maturing self. During the early school years, parents assist in reducing the stress of academic learning as well as provide reassurance for coping with social challenge.

Parents always serve as an information bank for children but, during the years between seven and ten, some interesting complications develop. Before this age (seven to ten) the child accepts information and knowledge in a matter-of-fact, almost detached way; he is not self-conscious or emotionally involved with knowledge — it simply is. As the child develops new conceptions of himself, he recognizes that facts have *social* implications. He learns that knowledge is not neutral, that it drastically influences day-to-day life. A three-year-old can say, "I am pretty", but with only slightly more pride than if she said, "Sister is pretty". When a nine-year-old says (and earnestly means) "I am pretty", it does not have the impartial ring as during yesteryear. It resonates with awareness and self-consciousness; it abounds with implications and complications; it is alive, not merely detached or impartial. She *feels* the fact. It is vibrant rather than calm. In other words, information has subjective qualities during middle childhood. A tearful eight-year-old may searchingly ask, "Am I really dumb, mommy?", "Do I really walk funny?". No longer are social facts impersonal. No longer is egocentrism dominant enough to block unpleasant thoughts or ideas from awareness. The child now must cope with the world objectively as well as subjectively. Because he rarely can do this without assistance, he turns to parents (and peers) for help. Just as he needed reassurance about the nature of the physical world as a preschooler, he now needs reassurance about the nature of the social world. Parental encouragement is required. If the parent is a good provider, the child will come back time and again. If the parent is reluctant or rebuking, the child will turn to others for assistance in this crucial developmental matter.

The child does not treat his parents equally, just as parents do not treat their children equally. There is an age factor which influences child-parent interaction. During the preschool years mother is the prime target of most of her child's questions and needs. During middle childhood this modifies. Girls frequently find one parent more confiding and easier to talk with than the other; this is based in part upon parental skill and in part upon habits developed during earlier years. Boys almost universally find it more natural to roughhouse with father because of his more congenial disposition for this kind of play as well as his constitutional capacity for it. (As mentioned earlier, it is not uncommon for a ten-year-old boy to be almost as physically strong in some games or exercises as his mother.) During the years of middle childhood, father is likely to have more say in family discipline than mother, especially if the household condones physical punishment such as spanking or strapping. Even in homes where punishment is not physical, father often represents firmness of authority which strikes a responsive chord in the child. Around nine and ten, some girls phase through a fascination with father which borders on the romantic but, of course, is only child-parent affection. At the same age, boys are known to become quite *un*fascinated with mother. They resent her insistence upon hygiene and cleanliness, considering it somewhat ridiculous to wash off elbow dirt which will simply reappear tomorrow. They also consider her concern for manners a trifle archaic, and absolutely cannot comprehend why a younger sibling should be tolerated rather than exiled to a remote corner of the house. Despite these altercations with mother, the household survives. Things are now calm when compared with the domestic strife which invades the household during the adolescent years. However, like toddlerhood, adolescence is a developmental disaster which the majority of people grow through without irreparable damage.*

Best friends. During middle childhood there is a narrowing as well as widening of social acquaintance. The widening is reflected in the child's increased outgoingness, lowering of barriers, and expansion of interests. The narrowing is reflected in his tendency to become more discriminating in the selection of friends and playmates. He no longer tags around randomly, commonly preferring privacy to the companionship of a peer who somehow does not stack up the the fluctuating criteria of acceptance. There is a tendency toward choosing a best friend with whom most free time is shared; sometimes best friends spend more time with one another than with all other friends combined. Especially in the latter half of middle childhood (eight to ten), pairs of comrades flourish. These pairings demonstrate striking durability, sometimes lasting into and even through adolescence. Selecting a best friend betrays the child's need for a confidant, an intimate companion with whom to share the adventurous growth through childhood. Exchanges of ideas, outlooks, and impressions are central to these relationships, but not the only reason for them. Usually best friends are of the same sex, but this rule has numerous exceptions, especially today when parents are not overly impressed with artificial concepts of childhood masculinity or femininity and do not impose them on their children.

Close friends are highly valued at this age because so much of the

---

* For an analysis of developmental crises during adolescence, see: J. J. Mitchell, *Adolescence: Some Critical Issues* (Toronto: Holt, Rinehart and Winston, 1971).

rest of the world is distant, separate, and impersonal. The togetherness every child accommodates to during infancy weakens during the school years — the child compensates by forming an intense involvement with a companion. There are other more practical reasons for best friends. Middle childhood is the age for inquisitiveness about all human relationships which are more expertly explored in tandem than in isolation. Whether exploring the dark confines of a secret cave or probing the shadowy mysteries of inner personality, the child does better when he has someone to share in the exploration. For the most part, social needs of this age are more completely met when one has a best friend. Just as the child's ideas are usually in advance of his ability to verbalize them, so his social impulses tend to precede his understanding of them. The impulse to seek out a best friend is body wisdom in action. It should be encouraged.

Hercules in Chains: Growth During the Middle Childhood Years

The middle childhood years is only one developmental period in the life cycle. At this age the child is as he is not only because of what he has been through but also because of what he will shortly become. Although he has undergone radical growth spurts in his short life (the first year of life is the year of the most rapid *rate* of growth in the entire post-birth life cycle; the preschool years also are characterized by remarkable growth), the most monumental growth spurt (puberty) lies beyond the childhood years. In preparation for the adolescent spurt, growth during the years of middle childhood is stable and slow. The calm of middle childhood is nature's way of stabilizing and pooling strength for the arduous task of adolescent growth.

A brief look at some trends of the human growth cycle will serve to accentuate the uniqueness of children in the six-through-ten age group. At birth, about 25 percent of the infant's weight is muscle, about 16 percent is made up of the vital organs, and 15 percent is composed of the central nervous system. At maturity, in contrast, muscle accounts for 43 percent, vital organs 11 percent, and the central nervous system only 3 percent (Breckenridge, 1965, p. 201). Middle childhood is one of the transitional stages during which this dramatic redistribution of body weight is taking place. During the pre-adolescent years, body fat tends to decrease on legs and arms but increase in the waist and chest; for boys, fat tends to decrease in the hips, whereas for girls, it increases. During adolescence, significant weight is added to muscle tissue, but this would not be possible without the loss of fatty tissue during middle childhood.

227

Significant changes also take place in body proportions during the growth cycle. The proportional growth of the head steadily diminishes; the legs become relatively longer until about midadolescence (at birth they constitute three-eighths total body length, in adolescence — one-half). The head, which accounts for one-fourth of the newborn's body length, is only one-tenth of the mature adult's body length. The chubby, rotund baby straightens out during toddlerhood, lengthens out in the preschool years, and fills out in the late childhood years. The shoulders of the baby, which sometimes are no wider than the widest part of the head, broaden during the childhood years, but expand dramatically during adolescence. The fatty, soft arms and legs of the one-year-old become hard and sinewy before the first grade.

The *rate* at which growth proceeds during the middle childhood years has considerable influence on the child's self-concept and body image. Late-maturing children experience a disadvantage in most peer group interactions which require physical skills; to compensate for this, they frequently assume the role of servant or follower in order to win acceptance of their more physically developed peers. Early-maturing children receive some benefits as a result of their physical advancement, but precocity favours males more than females. Girls who suddenly find themselves four to five inches taller than peers (including boys) may feel awkward or self-conscious to the point that they self-impose social exile. Another variable is added to the matter because fast-growing children reach sexual maturity earlier than others. The preoccupation of children of this age with body-image is reflected in their tendency to derive nicknames from body traits. "Skinny", "Stretch", "Fats", "Hook", "Big M", "Mousey", "Moose", "Wimpy", "Poxy", each convey physical description as well as a greeting in the social world of middle childhood. By age ten, most children have a social awareness of their body which they never before have experienced. With these developmental considerations in mind, let us look into some of the physical growth trends during the middle childhood years.

General trends in physical growth during middle childhood. Between six and ten physical growth is fairly stable and continuous. Though some children undergo accelerated development during a rather short time period, for the most part, growth during these years is regular and consistent. The dramatic growth spurt of puberty has no equal during the middle childhood years. The average North American six-year-old stands about 46 inches tall and weighs about 50 pounds. Height increases at the rate of approximately 6 percent per year during middle childhood, while weight increases about 10 percent per year. During the tenth year girls begin to weigh more and stand taller than boys of the same age even though they were slightly shorter and lighter at the ages of eight and nine. The trend toward female superiority in size and weight continues until about age thirteen or fourteen after which boys, as a group, mature into greater height and weight.

The gangly, gawky look of middle childhood comes about because of continued lengthening of the skeleton and the loss of fatty tissue. Eight and nine-year-old's often display a lean, hungry look which is outgrown when their body weight catches up with skeletal length. Nature's attempt to add weight partially accounts for the voracious appetite of this age as well as the need for protein and carbohydrates. A streamlined body profile, though common, is not a universal characteristic of middle childhood. Some boys differ from the regular trend by going through a period of plumpness between early childhood (six to eight) and early adolescence (twelve to fourteen). Even more commonly, girls of this age acquire a good deal of fatty tissue, contributing to a general roly-poly profile. Girls frequently outgrow their pudginess before midadolescence only to witness its reappearance during the middle or late twenties. Boys, on the other hand, who have never compiled much fatty tissue during adolescence, find themselves adding a spare tire around the midsection during the twenties. Although this addition does not create undue stress on the body, it has been known to create body-image problems for young men who heretofore thought of themselves as the prototype of universal masculinity. Eight-year-old girls with closely cropped hair (or boys of the same age with long, flowing hair) are difficult to distinguish from members of the opposite sex. Female breasts at this age are not yet *visually* noticeable as such; male shoulders are no broader than those of many girls; the hourglass profile is hard to find in a gathering of girls at this age. The appearances by which we visually distinguish male from female are strikingly absent during middle childhood, especially the first half. During the preadolescent years, however, boys and girls are rarely indistinguishable from one another. Boys add a great deal more muscle tissue to their limbs and chest whereas girls acquire relatively more fatty tissue. Boys expand through the chest cavity and broaden in the shoulders; the female breasts enlarge and assume more adult-like contours while at the same time the pelvic girdle expands and rounds. Female lines are now becoming distinctly feminine; male profiles are likewise approaching classic masculine features.

The middle childhood years are spent readying the body for the massive growth spurt of early adolescence. The foremost growth is social and cognitive rather than anatomical. However, just as during the first year of life when the child does not speak or walk, the underlying developmental processes are slowly preparing for the spectacular growth burst just around the corner. The child is as well spared the physiological stress which accompanies rapid growth because his energies are fully absorbed negotiating the numerous social nuances required of interpersonal living. The relative emotional tranquility of these years (midchildhood) is not accidentally related to its slow, stable growth rate. Accelerated growth creates strain on the child's total action system which includes not only his physiology and anatomy but also his psychology. Rapid physical growth is tough on the child because it forces him to expend energy on physical development which otherwise would be channeled into coping with social and psychological problems. It is a quirk of fate that our society has evolved in such a way that the individual must encounter the staggering growth spurt of puberty while at the same time going through major crises in sexual and personal identity. This is without doubt the most taxing of the developmental periods. Of the developmental stages only toddlerhood compares in growth difficulty, but at least the toddler is spared the frustration of aroused sexuality which is denied sanctioned release. When adults reflect upon difficulties they experienced as children, rarely are the years of middle childhood prominent in their thoughts. It is a good time of life.

The classroom provides an ideal laboratory for observing physical and motor differences during the middle childhood years. A classroom full of first graders is oceanic; everything and everyone seems to move and sway constantly. As Elkind put it, "looking in on a first-grade class with the constant motion, jiggling, shoving, pushing and talking can give the observer a distinct experience of seasickness" (1971, p. 65). The six-year-old gathering is an ant hill of action which becomes momentarily interrupted only when its members are sidetracked by an interest such as television, storytime, or colouring, or when they grow tired and need to rebuild energy reserves. A second grade classroom is less frenzied, action is more purposive and less random. Seven-year-olds are not passive by any stretch of the imagination but, when compared with what they were a year before, they demonstrate more self-control and physical discipline. Seven can sit at his desk for a length of time without giving the impression that another minute of sitting will result in insanity. Eight-year-olds add a modest degree of what adults consider a civilized pace to the classroom. The general appearance of the classroom is neater and tidier than during either the first or second grade. There is considerably less helter-skelter activity, less jumping in and out of desks, less scurrying about. There is more concentration of attention, restraint of limb movement, and general composure. Fourth and fifth graders show even greater motor maturity. Impulsive action continues to decrease, while purposive, direct action continues to increase. Students may remain seated up to one hour if engrossed in their work. Nine and ten-year-olds exude a business-like atmosphere; movement is parsimonious and economical. The notoriously poor posture for which children of this age are noted is hard to account for anatomically; for the most part, it is outgrown by midadolescence. Ten-year-olds have fairly stable motor characteristics; many possess characteristic physical trademarks such as a bouncy walk, drooping shoulders, hyperactivity, or lethargy which last through adolescence and into early adulthood.

Childhood body build is strongly correlated with behaviour. Boys with an athletic physique (*mesomorphic* body type) tend to be more active, assertive, and robust than boys with a rounded, loose, chubby body build (*endomorphic* body type). Breckenridge asserts that the "typical" mesomorph boy is assertive, expressive, fearless, and energetic and uses these traits in physical encounter with other children. On the other hand, the "typical" *ectomorph* (slender, delicate body build) tends toward conformity, caution, and emotional restraint (1965, p. 203). We can assume that general body build influences behaviour for physiological as well as social reasons. Games which require physical mobility, agility, or roughness are more easily mastered by children of mesomorphic body types. Their proficiency in athletics leads them toward further interest in it. Children gravitate toward activities for which they have competence. Endomorphic children, who lack excess muscular energy, find indoor activities more in line with their constitutional makeup and, consequently, tend to acquire more sedentary habits and interests.

This period of life is thought by many psychologists to be the most placid and predictable of the entire growth cycle. Although the terms "placid" and "predictable" have the tendency to lure one into a false sense of security, the middle childhood years are physically less dramatic and traumatic than most. Glandular development is in the same general balance at the end of the period as it was in the beginning. Disease is less prevalent than at any other period in the growth cycle. Skeletal advancement is consistent but not spectacular. Girls at age eleven are about one year more physiologically mature than boys, and some girls have begun their pubescent growth spurt. The outstanding physical developments of this age are: (a) increased manual dexterity, (b) increased strength, (c) increased resistance to fatigue, and (d) increased overall body coordination. These refinements in muscular and motor coordination allow greater freedom of play and work as well as endurance. Games last longer and fatigue comes later. As with all developmental ages, the child has an organic impulse to thoroughly exercise his newly-emerging skills, therefore, the middle childhood years are filled with compulsive exercise (Blair, 1951, p. 139).

Mental Development During Middle Childhood

All of the childhood years are characterized by the search for information. The toddler explores and investigates throughout the day, acquiring, assimilating, and accommodating new information into his mental framework. The preschooler is likewise insatiably hungry for learning about his world. During the middle childhood years no reduction occurs in the child's zesty search for knowledge. It directs his mental energy, creating daily behaviour similar to that of a miniature Sherlock Holmes, investigating, uncovering, and digging up information that somehow will piece together the great environmental puzzle. The eight or nine-year-old is a much better investigator, however, than either the toddler or the preschooler. He has more sophisticated tools which he employs more deftly; his past experience is utilized commendably in tackling new problems; his social skills permit greater interpersonal mobility which, in turn, results in increased experience. We shall look more closely at the mental skills of the child during these years shortly. First, a word about his intellectual attitude.

The years of middle childhood are the first in which the child realizes that information which does not fit into his immediate understanding of the world has a viable purpose, and likely fits into a network independent of his limited world. He now understands, for example, that French words are part of a separate language structure; he recognizes that fractions are part of the larger discipline of arithmetic and as such have purpose beyond immediate understanding. Between six and ten the child toils in the grip of egocentrism, but the grip is lessening. Facts need not directly relate to personal experience in order to be fascinating. The skills of experts interest him and he strives to emulate them; he asks endless questions which may or may not have relevance to his personal life. He wants to know how grasshoppers eat, how seals go to the bathroom, and whether Chinese parents love their children. The world is a vast question mark which he attempts to convert to an exclamation mark.

The world opens up so explosively that the child is in a continual state of discovery. He is daily amazed by new revelations and insights. Newness intrigues him, sometimes to the point of domination. He is obsessed with the inner workings of machines as well as the outer manifestations of people. History (especially the study of Neanderthal man) holds a special fascination for him; biology (especially the study of insects) impresses him; etiquette (especially proper behaviour in social settings) is likewise impressive, but more so for girls than boys. Children at this age become convinced that all questions have *some kind* of rational explanation, which contrasts with the agnostic outlook of the preschooler. The child is hungry for knowledge. He searches it out, pouncing on its every presence. Exceptions to this rule occur *only* when the process of learning about the world has been painful, frustrating, and dehumanizing for the child. When this is the case, when learning is stultifying rather than gratifying, the child denies his biological impulse for learning in order to avoid further anxiety and ego injury.*

Maturational factors which influence mental abilities. As has been stressed throughout this book, it is difficult to arbitrarily classify changes which occur during childhood (or any other part of the life cycle) as resulting from *either* environmental *or* maturational factors. Environment and maturation always work together in human growth. However, there are times when environment exerts only minor impact because the person is not maturationally ready to benefit from experience. Several examples have been cited previously to clarify this important point: infants do not benefit from attempts to walk if the attempts take place before they are maturationally ready; toddlers do not learn to speak before they are maturationally ready, no matter how much teaching or coaching they are given. Infant and toddlers benefit considerably from practice *after* they have reached maturational readiness, however. In this section we shall look into some of the maturational factors which enhance mental development during middle childhood. Rather than artificially dichotomize, we shall suggest that "maturational factors" are those which are more dependent upon *biological age* than upon *personal experience.*

Memory. During middle childhood, memory increases in power and precision. The child becomes capable of remembering greater quantities of information and is able to retrieve this information with greater accuracy and consistency than during any previous developmental stage. Increased powers of memory exert noticeable effects of the child's cognitive abilities: he is able to retain considerable information from past experience; he recalls how things went before; he copes with

---

* We would be remiss in our duty if we did not point out that many contemporary educational critics claim that our educational system, as it presently exists, dampens, sometimes even destroys, the child's natural eagerness to learn. These critics claim that primary schools, with their de-emphasis on the individual and overemphasis on the group, force the child to stifle his sense of importance as well as his lusty curiosity about the entire world. The pros and cons of this criticism are not discussed in this book, but the reader would do well to investigate the writings of P. Goodman, I. Illich, P. Jackson, and C. Silberman on this topic.

new situations by drawing upon accumulated information stored in his memory bank. His ability to think about several lines of thought simultaneously is dependent upon maturity of memory not present in the preschool years.

Between six and ten the child becomes more adept at *short-term* as well as *long-term* memory. Memory is less scattered than during the preschool years when the child was as likely to remember nonrelevant trivia as important information. Since memory becomes more coordinated in midchildhood, there is less of the hit and miss recall which characterizes preschoolers. The average five-year-old is able to recall only about four numbers read to him at one-second intervals; the ten-year-old, however, can recall six or seven consecutive numbers. Some ten-year-olds commit to memory a dozen or more separate telephone numbers, the batting averages of the top ten batters in each division of the major leagues, the name of every classmate, and innumerable chemistry formulae. The *inconsistency* of childhood mental skill plagues them, however; they may fail to remember the name of last year's teacher or the third of three items on a shopping list.

Individual differences in memory are apparent during middle childhood not only among children but also within the same child. A child may demonstrate rather impressive number memory but only average or weak concept memory; some children have gifted *visual memory* (remembering what they have seen) but poor *audio memory* (remembering what they have heard). For most children, however, memory skills are comparatively uniform and there is little basis to *assume* inconsistency in memory function unless it is demonstrated by the child.

When the child is required to remember more than he is capable of remembering he tends to forget much information which he would otherwise have retained. For example, if an eight-year-old is given the following numbers at one-second intervals: 7-8-4-6-9, he will likely be able to recall them in the sequence they were given (of course, some children of this age would not be able to repeat them correctly). However, if the same child who repeated these numbers correctly were given the following sequence of numbers: 7-8-4-6-9-3-5 (the same sequence with the addition of two digits), there is a strong chance he would not be able to repeat correctly even the first three numbers of the sequence. This points out an important principle of memory: when taxed beyond its limits, memory works less effectively than when working slightly below its limits. When required to remember more than he is able to handle, the child will retain less information than if he were given a less demanding task. Memory can be improved with practice, but it must be gradual, increasing in slight increments. It is interesting to note that numbers given at one-second intervals produce similar results with adults, the only difference being that a greater number of digits is required to overload the adult memory.

Vocabulary. With advancing age the child matures in his capacity to use and understand abstract vocabulary. Increased sophistication of vocabulary is dependent upon experience as well as maturation. Children exposed to verbally fluent adults learn to assimilate complex words into their vocabulary more easily than children whose verbal world is less enriched. However, *exposure* to words is only one part of the global process of *understanding* words. Abstract words require cognitive maturity before they are used meaningfully or productively. A child (or a parrot for that matter) can be taught to recite highly abstract words, however, in the absence of cognitive maturity, their usage of these words betrays limited understanding of what the words really mean.

The child's ability to verbally formulate hypotheses or to respond to questions is directly related to the richness and quality of his vocabulary. As vocabulary increases the child is able to benefit from verbal teachings which otherwise would pass him by. He learns antonyms and synonyms; he is able to decode complex messages; he learns to express himself with words which are suited to the listener. This last example merits special comment because it marks the child's entry into nonegocentric speech. During the toddler and preschool years children speak only from their own frame of reference; it becomes the responsibility of the listener to piece together misused words or incomplete ideas. During middle childhood, *the child learns to use words which fit the listener's frame of reference.* He learns to speak loudly and clearly to elderly citizens; to speak carefully and simply to younger children; to speak briskly and academically to teachers. He does not begin sentences with pronouns without informing the listener to whom the pronouns refer.

Perhaps the most important role of vocabulary in mental development is to facilitate incorporation of subtle and complex concepts into the child's understanding of the world. Each year the world becomes progressively more verbal. Words are the medium; ideas the message. Without the former, the latter falters.

Abstraction. The range of thought within the preschooler's realm of comprehension is more limited than during the middle childhood years. The preschooler has difficulty understanding *concrete* facts for which he has no experience; he has even more difficulty with abstract concepts which express a quality apart from any object. Ideas such as honesty, purity, and ethnic are, for the most part, beyond his developmental level. The five or six-year-old may be able to cite specific examples of these terms, perhaps even use them properly in a sentence; however, his limited powers of abstraction are obvious when he attempts to relate the meaning of the abstraction to the lives of others.

During middle childhood abstraction skills increase markedly. A seven-year-old may be able to answer the question, "In what way are wood and coal alike?", pointing out that they come from the ground and are used for heat. He may also be able to answer satisfactorily, "In what way are a baseball and an orange alike?", indicating that each is round. Very few seven-year-olds (or eight-year-olds for that matter) are able to provide an adequate answer to, "In what way are snakes, cows, and sparrows alike?". This question requires a higher level of abstraction; its proper solution is dependent upon mental maturity as well as educational experience. The last question is commonly answered by ten and eleven-year-olds.

As one might expect, children have difficulty with abstractions which go against their egocentric nature. Abstractions which support the rights and integrity of others are rarely understood during childhood, but they can be taught at a superficial level. Abstractions concerning God, eternal truth, spiritual permanence are almost never incorporated with much confidence until middle or late adolescence.

The ability to think in the abstract is seriously influenced by education and practice; however, their effects are registered within the limits of the child's developmental maturity.

As powers of abstraction increase the child is better able to understand *relational* terms and ideas. He begins to perceive that the strength of one man, for example, is relative to the strength of another man; that one man is strong when compared with one person but perhaps weak when compared with another. The preschooler usually does not make relative comparisons such as this; his discovery that father is not the strongest person in the world is a genuine insight because he has erroneously equated strongest in the house with strongest in the world. One developmental requirement of middle childhood is to place in perspective ideas and attitudes which during the preschool years were understood as absolute. However, the ability to classify in a relational context, that is, to relate the relative qualities of one object to another, is dependent upon mental maturity as well as sound teaching.

Selective perception. The ability to concentrate on one small aspect of the environment, to the exclusion of other environmental stimuli, is referred to as *selective perception.* Toddlers, as well as the preschoolers, possess the ability to concentrate on one particular environmental object, however, they do so with considerably less freedom and intention than the middle-years child. Selective perception requires that the child block out of conscious awareness stimuli which distract from the focus of concentration. In other words, to *not* pay attention to certain aspects of the environment. As the child ages, his power of selective perception increases. The six-year-old has difficulty attending to school-work if any kind of social disruption occurs within the classroom. He reflexively turns about to investigate what has taken place; he cannot fail to respond to this new stimuli. Rarely before the fourth or fifth grade is the child able to concentrate on reading in the midst of social distraction, because his powers of selective perception are still imma-ture.

The main advantage of selective perception is that it allows complete investment of mental energy in one narrow part of the environment. The child benefits in that he can attend more fully to what he is attempting to master; he suffers in that he misses out on what is going on elsewhere. Without selective perception the child has difficulty mastering skills which require attention and concentration. One of the most common characteristics of low academic achievers is their inability to concentrate on schoolwork for lengths of time; the converse is true of high achievers.

During the preschool years, academic learning takes place most congenially when the act of learning is so interesting and stimulating that it absorbs the attention of the child. If the learning task does not hold the child's interest, he has only limited ability to discipline and focus his concentration. The preschooler cannot be expected to enforce his own mental discipline; he cannot be expected to concentrate in the midst of distraction unless the distraction is not distracting to him in the first place. The middle-years child differs from the preschooler in that he is able to focus his mental energy to a sharper degree. Selective perception requires mental discipline; therefore, children frequently complain tht it is beyond their abilities. The adult would do well to consider their pleas because, in many respects, demands upon the child are excessive in this matter; however, the adult would also do justice by considering that children between the ages of six and ten have the notorious habit of claiming that everything which they are not in the mood for is beyond their developmental level.

Acquired skills which influence mental abilities. The mental abilities of childhood are not solely the result of maturation. Mental abilities must be cultivated, practised, and refined. The following *acquired skills* are among the more important determinants of childhood mental abilities. *Learning to learn.* Children learn to learn. They *acquire* skills of investigation and analysis. Unlike the insect, man does not have genetically determined investigatory habits. Man has only the organic impulse to investigate, not the specific modes to carry it out. By midchildhood several striking examples illustrate progress in the matter of learning to learn. The child asks better, more relevant, and more specific questions; he guides adults so that they provide *specific* information. Before the tenth birthday the child develops remarkable skills in avoiding questions which yield little or nonimportant information. This contrasts with his preschool tendency to ask questions which only partially reflect what he *really* wants to know about. The child acquires a *mental set* for coping with hypothetical or theoretical questions. He learns to postulate what would happen if A combined with B; if the obvious conclusion differs from what he hoped for, he will sample another combination, perhaps A plus C. The nine-year-old can see the relationship between theoretical possibilities and practical realities — an insight which comes only from experience.

The child also learns *strategies* of problem solving. He acquires an important outlook which eluded him during the preschool years: different kinds of problems are best solved by different kinds of approaches. He learns subtle social skills which allow him to persuade a younger child in a manner different from that employed on an older child; he learns physical skills which allow him to apply muscle when it is needed or finesse when it is called for; he learns mental skills which allow him to calculate numbers as well as to compose sonnets. The child is learning to wisely assemble what he already knows in order to master something about which he knows less. Knowledge is truly becoming a tool but, like all tools, it must be constructed; it does not come into existence on its own.

Differentiation of thought. Mental energy can assume different degrees of concentration; it can be diffuse (called undirected or free-floating), or it can be specific (directed or channeled). *Undirected* thought refers to daydreaming, free associations, dreams, free-flowing thought, and other forms of spontaneous mental activity. This form of thought is very important and the intent here is not to slight it. Undirected thought is the basis for most creative thinking. *Directed* thought refers to mental energy specifically concentrated toward problem solving. It is, by definition, narrow, focused, and applied. During the first four or five years of life mental energy tends to be diffuse and free-floating. The child's stream of consciousness is expansive rather than narrow; it responds to all parts of the environment rather than merely one part; concentration is brief and scattered rather than lengthy and specific. As the child matures he learns to focus his range of thought when the situation so demands. He learns to restrict free-floating mental energy, channeling it into more specific areas. One of the fundamental differences between the five-year-old and the ten-year-old is the ability of the latter to enforce directed thought at his own command and to sustain it for a length of time.

The ability to channel thought requires more than self-discipline: it requires mental maturity as well as *practice*. Practice is especially important because thought, like bodily functions, requires practice before it is able to respond to personal command. The child should be exposed to learning situations where directed thought is expected (and reinforced) in order for this ability to develop optimally. One of the major insights which has emerged from the study of class differences with regard to academic achievements is that middle-class families reward directed thought which facilitates academic skills much more than do lower socio-economic families. As a result middle-class children have considerable advantage in the classroom when they reach school age. As the child ages he is exposed to tasks which require directed thought; his ability to adjust to these demands will, in large measure, determine his ability to cope with life problems.

Reorganization of experience. One of the primary skills acquired during the middle childhood years is the ability to apply past experience to future possibilities. Perhaps it is unfair to suggest that this skill is *acquired* during middle childhood for, as we have observed, this skill characterizes both the preschooler and the toddler. However, the middle-years child reorganizes past experience with such expertise that it is elevated to a science when contrasted with its use during earlier years. The eight-year-old, quite obviously, has more mental equipment for dealing with past experiences than does a younger child. His powers of memory and abstraction are keener; his vocabulary is more advanced; his social graces are dramatically mature. Consequently, his ability to benefit from experience is commendable. He learns to avoid the same mistake twice, to direct thought where it yields most profitable returns, to align strength against weakness, to consider the frame of reference of others. The child reconstructs his past and, by doing so, productively channels mental energy so that it can cope maximally with the future. Any learning experience which requires the child to use his past experience in order to solve a present problem facilitates this important skill.

Deficiencies of thought during middle childhood. Despite remarkable growth during the past several years, many flaws and weaknesses persist in the thought patterns of children between six and ten. Their thought remains *egocentric* as witnessed by their stubborn refusal to notice their periodic thought inconsistencies. A good deal of *emotionality* permeates cognition during these years, which is to be expected when we remember that this is also true for adults; however, emotionalism has a much stronger grasp upon the eight-year-old than upon the eighteen-year-old. Children of eight are remarkably adept at inventing facts and figures to confirm a personal belief or to prove the point of an argument. To listen in on a debate between two nine-year-olds is to hear one series of facts after another, backed up by authoritative quotes and references. However, it is difficult to separate real from imagined facts, and true from fabricated quotes. Among nine-year-olds, stamina is often the deciding factor in arguments. Logic and consistency win out in the classroom, but rarely any place else during the middle years of childhood. Understanding of causality is spiraling upward, but frequently the child is so obsessed with finding an answer to every question that he readily succumbs to faulty or ridiculous explanations. During middle childhood *superstitious beliefs* are epidemic and earnest. Nine-year-olds may understand at an elementary level certain molecular structures, but at the same time may be afraid to open an umbrella inside their house because of the tragedy which befalls people who do such bizarre things. When asked to account for how the tragedy would come about, that is, what forces would cause it, the lack of a reply does not dampen their conviction in the truth of the superstition.

During middle childhood youngsters carry an abundance of *misinformation* most of which has been gathered from peers. A bright eight-year-old may cling sincerely to the belief that Indians are able to live for months without eating, that at one time horses ruled the world, or other equally absurd ideas *if* this information has been provided by an earnest and apparently logical friend. Ten-year-olds have an almost universal inclination to believe that vacant houses are inhabited by eccentric old men who haunt about after midnight. Curiosity generally triumphs over apprehension, however, (as it does throughout childhood), and eventually a collective of ten-year-olds will investigate the matter first-hand, usually bringing back disappointing, but consoling information.

Logic is still crude and awkward even though it is considerably more advanced than during the preschool years. Children stumble upon just about every kind of logical inconsistency imaginable. Aristotle must have winced in agony at their total misuse of syllogism. Children of this age understand that if A equals B, C can be inferred, but frequently they try too hard, forcing C into existence even when X, Y, or Z is more appropriate. Finally, the middle-years child has the tendency to use his intellect to protect his emotions and personal feelings. He *scapegoats* blame to others which is rightfully his; he constructs reasons to prove that a classmate is really an unworthwhile person; he gives logical reasons why he has no responsibility toward his younger sister. It is not until midadolescence that he fully understands that the powers of the mind cannot be callously used to deny the rights or integrity of others. Some emotionally immature people never acquire this distinction.

In summary, the mental capacities of the child are growing dramatically, but a great deal of additional growth is in store.

Samson and Delilah: The Emergence of Sex Differences

Developmental psychologists have long been concerned with behavioural differences between the sexes. There are, quite obviously, anatomical differences between the sexes, but it is generally assumed that these differences do not adequately account for the wide variety of behavioural differences which exist between the sexes. Sex differences are not constant from society to society. In some cultures females are responsible for virtually all manual labour, for leadership, and for carrying out acts of war. In our society these roles are, for the most part, reserved for men. In other societies women are not allowed to show themselves in public, they may not contradict their master-husband, and they are not allowed to participate in any communal decision-making. Some societies avoid these extremes and demonstrate a fairly equitable division of labour, responsibility, and rights. From this divergence how are we to make order? From this diversity of social organization how are we to infer the nature of male-female sex differences? Are human sex differences merely the result of cultural rules and laws, or do they have a biological foundation as is the case with other animals such as the chimpanzee or timber wolf?

Sex differences exist in our society and their presence is manifested during the early years of childhood. Some sex differences appear to be rooted in anatomical differences, but most are the result of social rules and cultural mores. Differences in dress are easily noticeable. The classic portrayal of the importance of dress was communicated by a young boy who when asked whether his new friend was a boy or girl was unable to reply because the friend was not wearing any clothes, therefore his sex could not be determined.

During middle childhood significant differences are observable between boys and girls. Although male-female behaviour is not mutually exclusive (males engage only in A while girls engage only in B), there is a strong trend for males to engage in certain kinds of behaviour more commonly than females and vice versa. For example, during middle childhood girls are more likely to settle arguments with verbal exchanges, whereas boys are likely to push or fight. Boys are considerably more prone toward preoccupation with athletics than are girls; on the other hand, girls have a more consistent preference for domestic activity and responsibility than boys of this age. Boys are more rowdy, boisterous, rambunctious, arrogant, cantankerous, assertive, combative, and athletic than girls in North American society. The question we must be most concerned with is: How do these sex differences come about? Are they the result of arbitrarily invented cultural norms? Are they the result of a mixture of cultural norms, some of which harmonize with innate sexual differences and some of which have no hereditary origin whatsoever? The matter of where sex differences come from is certainly the most important question to be confronted. We know that women bear children and nurse them because they are biologically equipped to do so. We do not overlook the importance of biological factors when observing that childbearing (not child-rearing) is an exclusively female responsibility. We do not suggest that women give birth to children only because it is socially prescribed that they do so. We recognize that it is so socially prescribed because of its biological necessity. Most differences between the sexes, however, are not this clear-cut in their biological genesis. For example, in North American culture it is a loose, but fairly uniform cultural norm that girls wear dresses when dressing formally, but men do not. This social rule is comparatively arbitrary when compared with cultural rules concerning the nursing of infants. There is no *biological* reason why this particular code of dress should be enforced. There is no viable reason why rules of dress cannot be changed and modified with time and taste. Indeed, if we note the various grooming and clothing trends over the past centuries we easily detect considerable variance in this matter. Thus far we have presented an example of cultural expectation based upon biological circumstances as well as upon social convention. The former, quite obviously, is more stable and enduring than the latter, because the species traits of man are more constant than are his social traits.

Can all behavioural differences between the sexes be honestly understood as deriving from *either* biological factors *or* social custom? Some psychologists think not, preferring instead to hypothesize that many social rules are designed to correspond with *biological or psychological inclinations of our species.* This viewpoint requires special attention not only because it provides a theoretical alternative to understanding the nature of sex differences, but also because it assumes that man does, in fact, possess biological and/or psychological inclinations. A *biological inclination* is merely the tendency or predisposition to behave in a certain way. Inclinations are not regulated by anatomy or instinct, but they are *influenced* by them. An example from the animal world may serve to help clarify the nature of biological inclination. Seals, at birth, do not know instinctively how to swim. If left unattended in rough water, they are likely as not to drown. However, seals are extremely *predisposed* to learn how to swim. Their biological and anatomical makeup is geared for water life and they take to swimming easily and rapidly. Thus, even though seals cannot instinctively swim, they are highly predisposed toward *learning to swim*. Humans have similar predispositions with regard to speech. The newborn infant does not have the ability to speak; nor does he possess an instinct which will assure that he will later learn to speak. However, if the child's biological equipment matures in the normal species pattern, he will be quite predisposed to *learn* to speak somewhere near his second birthday. Children do not learn to speak only because it is expected of them any more than seals learn to swim only because they are trained to do so. Children are expected to speak near their second birthday because adults have learned from experience that they are maturationally ready for speaking at about this age. Seals do not learn to swim expertly and efficiently because of the expectations of seal culture; they learn to swim as they do because of their genetic and biological predisposition to accommodate to the demands required of swimming.

Assuming that humans do possess inclinations or predispositions toward certain classes of behaviour, what does this tell us about sex differences? It tells us very little, but it does pose several interesting alternatives to the rather limited explanations psychology has thus far generated in the matter of the origins of sex differences. It creates an atmosphere from which we can think about differences between the sexes without having to rely upon an explanation which suggests that anatomical factors force men and women into certain roles, or that male-female roles are only arbitrary inventions which could be either reversed or abandoned without serious consequences.

It has been suggested by some psychologists that boys and girls act the way they do because they imitate their elders. This viewpoint claims that boys are rough and rowdy because they observe hockey players, cowboys, and soldiers. Girls, on the other hand, are more compliant and passive (both terms are misrepresentative because girls rarely are either compliant or passive, they merely disguise their motives more cogently than boys) because they observe adult females in a variety of compliant roles. The child's tendency to imitate is strong and it is possible that imitation does account for some differences in the behaviour of children. One is tempted, however, to ponder how it is that boys have the tendency to imitate adult males but only a weak tendency to imitate adult females. What is it that causes children to imitate same-sex figures? The question takes on even further significance when we note that most boys spend considerably more time with women than men, yet they model more consistently after males. The other side of the coin is also interesting. Why should (do) girls imitate the behaviour of women? Is there any particular reason why young girls should be more fond of female roles than those of men? How is it that girls who are raised by their father, in the absence of their mother, adopt patterns of behaviour similar to girls who have a mother at home to imitate? Likewise, how does one account for the observation that young boys raised without an adult male in the household do not distinguish themselves by patterns of behaviour different from young boys reared by a traditional family? It appears that children do not behave as they do merely because of what they observe in their own homes. Even when children do behave in a way similar to what they observe we still do not know with assurance that they are *merely imitating.* Possibly what they observe actually corresponds with their biological or psychological predispositions and is therefore easily copied. In our society male roles may involve the kinds of behaviour which boys naturally take to; likewise, female roles may involve patterns of behaviour congenial to young girls. A further limitation of the theory which states that children do as they see is its failure to take into account why adults behave as they do in the first place! Do adults follow their roles merely because their parents did? One must have a great deal of faith in man's ability to remain constant in the midst of change to assume that he acts as he does merely because he has observed someone else acting in a like manner.

Sex differences among North American children. During the first six years of life, differences between the sexes are not as noticeable as they are between the seventh and tenth years. As anatomical differences become more pronounced, so also do behavioural differences; this maxim holds true despite the fact that anatomical changes *account for only a few* of the basic sex differences among children. In our society there are few feminine roles which an eight-year-old girl can perform with greater expertise than a normal eight-year-old boy. However, by the age of eleven or twelve, certain roles generally understood as being feminine rather than masculine (sewing, cooking) are beyond the range of an average boy because he has not *acquired* the skills essential for these activities. As time marches on, sex differences acquire a *practise* function which serves to make difficult exchange of sex-based roles.

Certain roles require so much practice and skill that by midadolescence one sex may possess a conspicuous skill factor over the other. During childhood, before the practise factor applies, the sexes are fairly equal in their abilities if we take into consideration that girls are, on the average, about six months to one year more physically advanced than boys the same age.

Some sex differences are influenced by the physical superiority of boys, especially in skills requiring strength and stamina. By late childhood, boys have a definite advantage over females in skills requiring arm or leg strength, power and forcefulness, aggressiveness, rowdiness, or rough physical contact. In recent years, female athletic achievements have dispelled the myth that men are naturally superior athletes. Female gymnasts, swimmers, fencers, and runners can compete with men favourably, though for the most part men have slight superiority in these events. During middle childhood, males possess stronger upper body muscles than girls; this advantage is genetically-based and holds true as a generalization for adults as well.

The effects of cultural learning are noticeable by middle childhood. Boys learn that it is not manly to cry, to show weakness or cowardliness, or to continuously lose out in competitive engagements. They compensate for these negatively-valued behaviours by excelling in their opposite: showing sternness instead of tears, showing boldness instead of fearfulness, showing competitive excellence rather than weakness. Girls learn that it is not womanly to fist fight (many eight-year-old boys are greatly relieved about this turn of events as they know all too well about the physical wrath which an angered girl can dish out), to engage in games in which physical contact is abusive rather than gentle, to call into question the masculinity of boys. Because girls have psychological needs for belonging, just as do boys, they learn social maneuvers which encourage masculine response. The most *efficient* way to encourage boys is to assume weakness in an area where boys assume strength, therefore creating an "excuse" for the sexes coming together. Males, quite obviously, cultivate the same habit of assuming incompetence so they can persuade a female to bring her competence, as well as her presence, into closer proximity. Sex roles bring the sexes together as commonly as they keep them separate. Divisions of labour, sex-based or not, are generally designed to promote social cohesion rather than social fragmentation.

It is easy to agree on some of the behavioural differences between young boys and girls in our society. The pressing question, as we have mentioned before, is to determine *why* these differences come into existence. Social learning plays an important role; anatomical differences play an important role; biological inclinations and predispositions may or may not influence the nature of male-female differences.

It is necessary to keep in mind that few sex roles in a free society are *completely* restricted to one sex and, when they are, it is invariably due to biological determinants. Any behaviour which does not require *specific* biological equipment can, in most cases, be executed by either sex equally well if learning conditions are held constant. However, it is quite possible that certain kinds of behaviour are more in accordance with the inclinations and predispositions of males or females, therefore, one sex may be able to learn a given behaviour more *easily* and *naturally* than the other. This last line of reasoning may prove to be a productive way of analysing sex differences, although it, too, has its share of theoretical problems. Generally speaking, adults to whom the care of children is entrusted, will do justice by thinking of them as *children* rather than as *male* or *female*. The needs of childhood are clear and easily defined; the needs of male or female are not.

The Rights of Children

What are the rights of children? Do children have only those rights given them by parents or civil law? Must children earn their rights or are they bestowed automatically? Are different children entitled to different rights? Each of these questions is central to our understanding of child growth and development. Societies have differing interpretations of the rights of children. North American society has no enforceable specific codes about the rights of children other than legal rights. Some educators have stated that the rights of children extend into realms where currently there exists almost no legal definitions. In the "Charter of the Rights of the Child" drawn up at the 1950 convention of the International Federation of Teachers Association, the following statements were presented concerning the natural rights of children.

1. The child has the right to be considered as a child without any discrimination as to its birth (legal or illegal), its sex, its language, its nationality and color, its social conditions, its creed or its opinions.
2. The child has the right to be enabled to develop physically, intellectually, and morally in a normal, healthful way in an atmosphere of liberty and dignity.
3. The child has the right to have the benefits of economic and social security. Even before its birth its health must be protected in an appropriate way.

4. The child has the right to healthful food, clothing, and lodging, and also to recreation and to games.
5. The child has the right to have the possibility to grow up in a friendly atmosphere of affection and understanding which will further the harmonious development of its personality.
6. The child has a right to peace. If the responsible adults are not in a position to assure peace, the child and its mother should be the first ones to receive protection and help, as in any situation which jeopardizes the welfare of the child.
7. The child has the right to receive an education which will give it harmonious and complete development of its faculties so that it may become a useful member of society. It has therefore a right to receive gratuitous instruction at all levels of education, the only criterion being its capacities. Its education must give it at the same time cultural background, guidance, and training for a vocation.
8. The child has the right to be protected against any form of neglect, cruelty, and exploitation. It must not be admitted to any employment which will hinder its instruction, harm its health, or prevent its development.
9. The child who is suffering from a physical, mental, or social deficiency has the right to receive the special treatment, education, and care which its particular condition requires.
10. The child has the right to be protected against everything that might incite it to feelings of discrimination or hatred. It must be educated with the idea that it will attain its full unfolding and that it will certainly receive the maximum of satisfaction if it consecreates the best part of itself to the service of its fellow men in a spirit of brotherhood and universal peace.*

Some Developmental Needs of Middle Childhood

As the child ages he encounters new developmental requirements; middle childhood is no exception to this rule. During the years between the sixth and tenth birthdays the child encounters a host of growth obligations which he must negotiate to the best of his abilities. As is true throughout childhood, the adult must participate meaningfully with the child if he is to successfully meet the challenges required of

* Adopted at the annual convention of the International Federation of Teachers Associations at Amsterdam, Holland, August 1-5, 1950.

continued growth. Here we shall mention several of the larger categories of learning required of the child during the middle years of childhood.

Learning to establish an identity somewhat independent of the family. During the middle childhood years, especially between eight and ten, the child's definition of himself expands. He no longer thinks of himself solely in terms of family relationships, although they still are prominent in his thoughts. The middle-years child evolves a broader and more expanded self-concept; friends and playmates figure prominently in his daily life and he wants desperately to be thought well of by them. He wants to be recognized as a *bona fide* person. He does not wish to be known *only* as the child of his parents, preferring instead to be identified by his points of excellence, by his positive assets, by his self. Because the child is in the process of sampling new identities, he is in need of constant feedback and reassurance. His need is so strong that he gravitates almost automatically to anyone who will provide it.

For some children the surge of independence characteristic of this age marks the first split in parent-child bonds. For some parents it is a hurtful realization that the child is growing beyond the narrow confines of home. There is no reason why the parent should feel regret or remorse about the child's quest for identity; it is as natural as twelve-year molars, only it comes a bit sooner.

It is important that the child have a base of security to return to after he ventures out into his expanded social world; it rarely is as understanding as home and its weight sometimes becomes burdensome. Parents encourage individualization when they praise the child's attempts to establish a circle of friends. Even though the child works hard to establish identity away from his household, parents are still the most important persons in his psychological life. Expansion of social acquaintances does not signal the loss of parental importance, it merely signifies the emergence of new people with whom to share life and growth.

Learning social and physical skills required of group life. The child cannot establish a positive identity within his peer group unless he is able to interact with them according to the unwritten but real rules of middle childhood society. These universally include: (a) the ability to "give and take" as the situation demands, to be able to compromise, negotiate, and exchange with other members of the group; (b) the ability to participate in the physical skills required of group members; (c) the ability to make decisions and abide by them, to be predictable and comparatively trustworthy; (d) the ability to keep to oneself the information which is meant to be private.

Social and physical skills are learned easily and naturally by most children, but every child has some difficulty along the way because of conflicting rules. Rules of the society of children do not always jibe with those of adult society. Children's rules also frequently contradict themselves because they stress subservience to the group as well as the rights of the individual — usually the former wins out. The ability to cope with the fluctuating demands and expectations of other children is the child's first major test of his interpersonal skills. If the conflict becomes too strenuous, he usually will return home, mull it over, re-group, then drift back to the world of peers.

Although adjusting to group life is a normal demand in our society, it can nevertheless be taxing for the individual. He often re-quires adult assistance as well as assurance. The parent who becomes too sheltering during this time of life may be instrumental in preventing the child from acquiring the essential skills required during this develop-mental level. Most developmental skills demand that the individual "pay a price". For the toddler the price of learning to walk is thousands of spills and falls; for the preschooler the price of learning about the rightful demands of others is hundreds of hours of fighting and squabbl-ing; for the middle-years child the price of learning group life is ridicule, periodic ostracism, and a good deal of modestly painful introspection.

Learning to satisfy psychological needs within a social context. All children have a number of psychological needs which they must satisfy if growth is to be continuous and complete. These include the need for affection, security, acceptance, self-respect, achievement, recognition, order, independence, contact-comfort, and self-actualization of inner potentialities. These needs are prominent during the middle childhood years, but during this time there is *a major shift in the means by which these needs are gratified.* In virtually every realm of psychological need the child moves toward increased focus on peer involvement and de-creased focus on family involvement. The need for affection, which up through the preschool years is almost exclusively gratified by parents, now shifts away from parents toward the peer group. The need for acceptance, perhaps more than any other, reflects this trend away from family, but the need for recognition, achievement, and self-actualiza-tion also are expressed in settings away from home. The family still exerts considerable influence on the child, but the child is acted upon by forces outside the family with greater impact than ever before. The extent to which the child can successfully adopt to new systems of psychological need gratification in large measure determines how suc-cessfully he will phase through the important developmental era of middle childhood. Because adjusting to new ways of satisfying psycho-logical needs is sometimes emotionally difficult, the middle childhood years are not without their share of hurt. However, most children of this age are sufficiently resilient to cope with ego injury and it usually does not result in long-range distress. It does, however, require adjustment and flexibility. The extent to which the child is incapable of flexing or adjusting is directly proportional to the difficulties he will incur during middle childhood.

Learning greater control of internal impulses. The *preschool* years are the most important during childhood for learning control of internal impulses. This is due to the fact that during toddlerhood such little control of internal impulses is required that a great deal must be learned in the short period of the preschool years. During *middle childhood* the individual refines and acquires even greater control over his internal impulses. His environment forces this upon him. At school and home he is expected to account for his temper outbursts, his fits of anger, his impulsiveness in general. He learns that to act impulsively invites consequences, some of which are not pleasant. Because of this, greater control of inner impulses takes place during the years of middle childhood. As greater control of impulses is acquired, greater predictability in behaviour occurs. Social custom, etiquette, and general politeness become part of the child's daily repertoire; impulsive outbursts become less characteristic.

One negative consquence of controlling impulses is the child's tendency to *redirect* hostility and anger to persons or objects who cannot reply. This phenomenon is sometimes referred to as *displacement* or *scapegoating.* By whatever term it is labeled, the dynamics are the same: the child restrains his inner impulses in situation A because of his fear of punishment, and releases these impulses in situation B when he is comparatively exempt from punishment. Thus we have the bully who specializes in releasing internal tension on weaker children.

Adults facilitate the child's need for impulse control by providing outlets where he can release tension without having to pay a price for doing so.

Learning appropriate sex-roles. In recent times there has been a reduction in the number of rigidly held beliefs about what constitutes appropriate male behaviour or appropriate female behaviour. As a result of society's more relaxed outlook toward male-female roles there is reduced emphasis upon the importance of sex-roles during the years of middle childhood. There are, however, numerous generalities which influence the child's sense of masculinity or femininity. Youngsters today are not likely to think a boy masculine merely because he can kick a football farther than anyone else in the class, although this may help his masculine image. Among boys of this age, masculinity is an *attitude* rather than a *series of roles or behaviours*. The attitude of masculinity is quite similar to that held by the dominant society, though slightly more exaggerated. For young boys masculinity generally implies: (1) standing up for one's rights (however loosely rights may be defined), (2) not being dominated except by consent (this is why boys are such good followers: there is no loss of self-pride when one "voluntarily" chooses to be subservient), (3) proficiency at masculine skills (however loosely these skills may be defined), and (4) excellence at *any* skill, except those specifically designated as feminine. For young girls, femininity is less precisely understood. Several factors contribute to its ambiguity: (1) our society does not publicly praise feminine roles as highly as masculine roles, therefore, there is less opportunity to model after particular behaviour patterns; (2) one of the more highly prized feminine roles is adaptability, therefore, consistent rigid patterns are less common than among males; (3) even during childhood, girls in our society are taught the importance of accommodating to masculine activities and roles. For each of these reasons, girls usually have less clearly defined ideas about what is feminine than do boys about what is masculine.

For the middle-years child one of the major developmental tasks is to *learn* how to best blend their own particular strengths and skills with general behaviour patterns in such a way as to avoid being labeled as unacceptable and to facilitate being perceived as worthwhile. For some children this involves little more than blindly imitating the standards established by others, and therefore, may or may not coincide with their true *inner* feelings. Some children, however, especially those with leadership skills, are able to persuade peers that *their* behaviour is acceptable regardless of its nature. In this respect childhood society is flexible rather than rigid. As is true with adult society, some individuals carry more weight and influence than others.

Children do not learn sex-roles merely because they are expected to do so, although this certainly is one factor. Children learn sex roles because they recognize that there are differences between masculinity and femininity and they learn that these differences are to be proud of rather than ashamed of. Therefore, children who possess expertise in what is considered "masculine" or "feminine" continue to engage in such behaviour, *rewarding others who follow with acceptance and recognition*. For the middle-years child, few things are more important than peer group acceptance and recognition. Thus, it is hard to expect the child to do other than adopt sex-roles as they are understood by his peers.

Learning cognitive maps. The child requires cognitive maps in order to understand his world and not get lost in it. The world views and outlooks which carried him through toddlerhood and the preschool years are now outgrown and thus obsolete. More sophisticated understanding of the world is required if the child is to cope adequately with the magnified demands which accompany maturity. The child must develop tools which allow him to more completely understand the mechanical workings of the universe, the inner secrets of the personality, the underpinnings of social interchange. Magical or incomplete explanations do not suffice as they did during the preschool years. The middle-years child needs to believe that mysteries can be solved, that questions can be answered. He cannot merely accept this on faith, however. He must learn about systematic methods of investigation; he must learn how to evaluate information which is fed to him; he must learn to be critical as well as assimilative. When a nine-year-old is unable to construct a meaningful explanation for an event, he is baffled and discouraged; if no viable explanation is offered, he resorts to either superstition or disinterest — both of which are disastrous to his future mental development. In short, the child during the middle-years must learn mental concepts which allow him to make sense out of the apparently inexplicable aspects of his environment. All children, of course, require explanations. During middle childhood, however, mental skills are sufficiently developed that not just any explanation will work: it must meet certain minimum standards imposed by the mental maturity of this age. If cognitive maps are cultivated during the middle years, the child will be ready for the advanced thinking required of mature adolescent thought. If not, the transition from child-thought to adolescent-thought will be hampered, perhaps permanently impaired.

Bibliography

Armstrong, I. L. and Browder, J. J. *The Nursing Care of Children.* Philadelphia: F. A. Davis Co., 1966.

Ausubel, David P. and Sullivan, Edmund V. *Theory and Problems of Child Development,* 2nd edit. New York: Grune and Stratton, 1970.

Baldwin, Alfred L. *Theories of Child Development.* New York: John Wiley & Sons, Inc., 1967.

Baldwin, A. L., Kalhorn, J., and Breese, F. "Patterns of Parent Behavior," *Psycholog. Mono.* 1945, p. 58.

Baller, Warren R. and Charles, Don C. *The Psychology of Human Growth and Development,* 2nd edit. New York: Holt, Rinehart and Winston, Inc., 1968.

Beck, Joan. *How to Raise a Brighter Child.* New York: Trident Press, 1967.

Bereiter, C. and Engelmann, S. *Teaching Disadvantaged Children in Preschool.* Englewood Cliffs, New Jersey: Prentice-Hall, Inc., 1966.

Bernard, H. W. *Human Development in Western Culture.* Boston: Allyn & Bacon, 1970.

Bernard, J. "Human Fetal Reactivity to Tonal Stimulation," *American Psychologist,* 7, 1946, 256.

Blair, Arthur Witt and Burton, William H. *Growth and Development of the Preadolescent.* New York: Appleton Century-Crofts, Inc., 1951.

Bloom, B. *Compensatory Education for Cultural Deprivation.* New York: Holt, Rinehart and Winston, Inc., 1965.

Bowlby, J. *Maternal Care and Mental Health.* Geneva: World Health Organization, 1952.

Bowlby, John. "Some Pathological Processes Engendered by Early Mother-Child Separation," *Infancy and Childhood.* Packanack, New Jersey: Foundation Press, Inc.

Breckenridge, M. E. and Murphy, M. N. *Growth and Development of the Young Child.* Philadelphia: W. B. Saunders Co., 1969.

Breckenridge, Marian E. and Vincent, E. Lee. *Child Development: Physical and Psychological Growth Through Adolescence.* Philadelphia: W. B. Saunders Co., 1965.

Bronson, G. "Critical Periods in Human Development," *British Journal Medical Psych.* 35, 1962, 127-133.

Brown, R. and Bellugi, U. "Three Processes in the Child's Acquisition of Syntax," *Harvard Educational Review.* 34, No. 2, Spring, 1964, 133-151.

Bruner, Jerome S. *Processes of Cognitive Growth: Infancy.* Barre, Mass.: Clark University Press, Barre Publishers, 1968.

Burke, B. "The Nutrition of the Preschool Child," in *The Healthy Child.* Edited by H. C. Stuart and D. G. Prugh. Cambridge, Mass.: Harvard University Press, 1960, pp. 169-176.

Caldwell, Betty. "What is the Optimal Learning Environment for Young Children?" in Ellis Evans, ed., *Children: Readings in Behavior and Development.* New York: Holt, Rinehart and Winston, Inc., 1968.

Chukovsky, K. *From Two to Five.* Berkeley: University of California Press, 1963.

Church, Joseph. *Language and the Discovery of Reality.* New York: Vintage Books, Random House, 1966.

Church, Joseph. *Three Babies.* New York: Vintage Books, Random House, 1966.

Cohen, Stewart, ed. *Child Development: A Study of Growth Processes.* Itasca, Illinois: F. E. Peacock Publishers, Inc., 1971.

Cole, Michael. "Russian Nursery Schools," in *Readings in Psychology Today.* Del Mar, California: CRM Books, 1972, pp. 214-219.

Coopersmith, Stanley. *The Antecedents of Self-Esteem.* San Francisco: W. H. Freeman and Company, 1967.

Corner, G. W. *Ourselves Unborn.* New Haven, Connecticut: Yale University Press, 1944.

Craig, W. S., Morgan, D. M., and Pattullo, M. *Care of the Newly Born Infant,* 4th edit. London: E. and S. Livingstone Ltd., 1969.

Cratty, B. J. *Perceptual and Motor Development in Infants and Children.* London: Macmillan and Company, 1970.

Cunningham, Ruth and Associates. *Understanding Group Behavior of Boys and Girls.* New York: Bureau of Publications, Teachers College, Columbia University, 1952.

Dennis, W. "On the Possibility of Advancing and Retarding the Motor Development of Infants," *Psychological Review.* 50, 1943, 203-218.

Dennis, W. and Dennis, M. G. "The Effect of Cradling Practices Upon the Onset of Walking in Hopi Children," *Journal of Genetic Psychology.* 56, 1940, 77-86.

Dodson, F. *How to Parent.* New York: Signet Books, 1970.

Elkind, David. "The Case for Academic Preschool: Fact or Fiction," from *Young Children.* XXV, 3, January, 1970.

Elkind, D. *A Sympathetic Understanding of the Child: Six to Sixteen.* Boston: Allyn & Bacon, 1971.

Endler, Norman S., Boutler, Lawrence R., and Osser, Harry, eds. *Contemporary Issues in Developmental Psychology.* New York: Holt,

Rinehart and Winston, Inc., 1968.

Engelmann, Siegfried and Engelmann, Therese. *Give Your Child a Superior Mind.* New York: Simon & Schuster, 1966.

English, Horace B. *Dynamics of Child Development.* New York: Holt, Rinehart and Winston, Inc., 1961.

Felsenthal, H. "The Developing Self: The Parental Role," in *The Child and His Image.* Edited by K. Yamamoto. Boston: Houghton Mifflin Co., 1972.

Flavell, John H., *et al. The Development of Role-Taking and Communication Skills in Children.* New York: John Wiley & Sons, Inc., 1968.

Flavell, John H. *The Developmental Psychology of Jean Piaget.* Princeton, New Jersey: D. Van Nostrand Co., Inc., 1963.

Fraiberg, Selma H. *The Magic Years.* New York: Charles Scribner's Sons, 1959.

Flanagan, G. L. *The First Nine Months of Life.* New York: Simon & Schuster, 1962.

Gardner, D. B. *Development in Early Childhood: The Preschool Years.* New York: Harper & Row, 1964.

Gardner, George E. *The Emerging Personality: Infancy Through Adolescence.* New York: Delacorte Press, 1970.

Garrison, K. C., Kingston, A. J., and Bernard, H. W. *The Psychology of Childhood.* New York: Charles Scribner's Sons, 1967.

Gesell, A. and Ilg, F. L. *The Child From Five to Ten.* New York: Harper and Brothers, 1946.

Gesell, Arnold and Amatruda, C. S. *The Embryology of Behavior.* New York: Harper and Brothers, 1945.

Gesell, Arnold, *et al. The First Five Years of Life.* New York: Harper and Brothers, 1940.

Gesell, Arnold and Ilg, Frances L. *Infant and Child in the Culture of Today.* New York: Harper and Brothers, 1943.

Gesell, Arnold, Halverson, Henry M., *et al. The First Five Years of Life: A Guide to the Study of the Preschool Child.* New York: Harper and Brothers, 1940.

Gesell, Arnold. *How a Baby Grows.* New York: Harper and Brothers, 1945.

Ginott, Haim G. *Between Parent and Child.* New York: Macmillan Co., 1965.

Goldfarb, William. "The Effects of Early Institutional Care on Adolescent Personality," *Journal Exper. Educ.* 12, 1943.

Gooch, Stan and Pringle, M. L. Kellmer. *Four Years On.* London: Longmans, Green and Co. Ltd., 1966.

Gordon, Ira J. *Human Development From Birth Through Adolescence.* New York: Harper & Row, 1969.

Gray, G. W. "Human Growth," in *Human Variations & Origins.* Edited by W. S. Laughlin. San Francisco: W. H. Freeman & Co., 1967, pp. 127-137.

Havighurst, R. J. *Human Development and Education.* New York: David McKay Co., Inc., 1953.

Hawkes, Glenn R. and Pease, Damaris. *Behavior and Development From 5 to 12.* New York: Harper and Brothers, 1962.

Hurlock, E. B. *Child Development.* New York: McGraw-Hill, 1964.

Jersild, Arthur T. *Child Psychology,* 6th edit. Englewood Cliffs, New Jersey: Prentice-Hall, Inc., 1968.

Kagan, Jerome and Moss, Howard A. *Birth to Maturity: A Study in Psychological Development.* New York: John Wiley & Sons, Inc., 1962.

Kagan, Jerome. "On Class Differences and Early Development," in *Education of the Infant and Young Child.* Edited by V. H. Denenberg. New York: Academic Press, 1970.

Kagan, J. "Up From Helplessness," from *Readings in Developmental Psychology Today.* Del Mar, California: CRM Books, 1970.

Kennedy, Wallace A. *Child Psychology.* Englewood Cliffs, New Jersey: Prentice-Hall, Inc., 1971.

Lane, Howard and Beauchamp, Mary. *Understanding Human Development.* Englewood Cliffs, New Jersey: Prentice-Hall, Inc., 1959.

Leeper, S. H. *Good Schools for Young Children.* New York: Macmillan Co., 1968.

Lenneberg, E. H. *Biological Foundations of Language.* New York: John Wiley & Sons Inc., 1967.

Levy, D. M. *Maternal Overprotection.* New York: Columbia University Press, 1943.

Lewis, M. M. *Language, Thought and Personality: In Infancy and Childhood.* New York: Basic Books, Inc., 1963.

MacFarlane, Jean W., Allen, Lucile, and Honzik, Marjorie P. *Developmental Study of the Behavior Problems of Normal Children, Between 21 Months and 14 Years.* Berkeley and Los Angeles: University of California Press, 1954.

Maurer, A. "What Children Fear," *Journal of Genetic Psychology.* 106, 1965, 265-277.

McCandless, Boyd R. *Children: Behavior and Development,* 2nd edit. New York: Holt, Rinehart and Winston, Inc., 1967.

Medinnus, Gene R. and Johnson, Ronald C. *Child and Adolescent Psychology.* New York: John Wiley & Sons, Inc., 1969.

Merry, F. K. and Merry, R. V. *The First Two Decades of Life,* 2nd edit.

New York: Harper & Row, 1958.

Montagu, Ashley. *On Being Human.* New York: Hawthorne Books, 1966.

Munsinger, Harry. *Fundamentals of Child Development.* New York: Holt, Rinehart and Winston, Inc., 1971.

Mussen, Paul H., Congor, John J., and Kagan, Jerome. *Child Development and Personality.* New York: Harper & Row, 1963.

Mussen, P. H. *Psychological Development of the Child.* Englewood Cliffs, New Jersey: Prentice-Hall, Inc., 1963.

Nice, N. M. "On the Size of Vocabularies," *American Speech.* 6-27, 2, 1-7.

Pines, M. *Revolution in Learning.* New York: Harper & Row, 1966.

Pollard, Marie B. and Geoghegan, Barbara. *The Growing Child in Contemporary Society.* Milwaukee: The Bruce Publishing Co., 1969.

Ribble, Margaret. *The Rights of Infants.* New York: Columbia University Press, 1943.

Shane, H. G. "The Renaissance of Early Childhood Education," in *As the Twig is Bent.* Boston: Houghton Mifflin Co., 1971.

Shirley, Mary M. *The First Two Years: A Study of Twenty-Five Babies* (Vol. I, Postural and Locomotor Development). Minneapolis: The University of Minnesota Press, 1931.

Shirley, Mary M. *The First Two Years: A Study of Twenty-Five Babies* (Vol. II, Intellectual Development). Minneapolis: The University of Minnesota Press, 1933.

Shirley, Mary M. *The First Two Years: A Study of Twenty-five Babies* (Vol. III, Personality Manifestations). Minneapolis: The University of Minnesota Press, 1933.

Sinclair, David. *Human Growth After Birth.* London: Oxford University Press, 1969.

Singer, Robert D. and Singer, Anne. *Psychological Development in Children.* Philadelphia: W. B. Saunders Co., 1969.

Skodak, M. and Skeels, H. M. "A final follow up study of one hundred adopted children," *J. of Genet. Psychol.* 74, 1949, 18-125.

Smith, M. E. "An investigation into the development of the sentences and the extent of vocabulary in young children," *Univ. Iowa Studies.* 3, No. 5, 1926, 92.

Smith, H. T. "Development of conscience in the preschool child," from *The Young Child.* Washington, D.C.: National Association for the Education of Young Children, 1967.

Spencer, T. D. "Sex-role Learning in Early Childhood," in *The Young Child.* Washington, D.C.: National Association for the Education of Young Children, 1967.

Spitz, Rene. *The First Year of Life.* New York: International Universities Press, Inc., 1965.

Spock, B. *Baby and Child Care.* New York: Pocket Books, Inc., 1957.

Stone, Joseph L. and Church, Joseph. *Childhood and Adolescence,* 2nd edit. New York: Random House, 1968.

Stott, Leland H. *Child Development: An Individual Longitudinal Approach.* New York: Holt, Rinehart and Winston, Inc., 1967.

Trasler, Gordon, *et al. The Formative Years.* British Broadcasting Corporation, 1968.

Vinacke, W. E. "Concept Formation in Children of School Ages," *Educ.* 74, 1954, 527-534.

Weiner, Irving B. and Elkind, David. *Child Development: A Core Approach.* New York: John Wiley & Sons, Inc., 1972.

White, Burton L. *Human Infants Experience and Psychological Development.* Englewood Cliffs, New Jersey: Prentice-Hall, Inc., 1971.

Wolff, Sula. *Children Under Stress.* London: Allen Lane The Penguin Press, 1969.

Woodward, M. A. *The Earliest Years, Growth and Development of Children Under Five.* Oxford: Pergamon Press, 1966.

Index